Breath and Bone

David & Indy,

Blessings!

Chris Wright

Langham

GLOBAL LIBRARY

Breath and Bone

Living Out the Mission of God in the World

Festschrift in Honour of
Christopher J. H. Wright
on the Occasion of His Seventieth Birthday

General Editors
Riad Kassis, Pieter Kwant, Paul Windsor

Langham
GLOBAL LIBRARY

Published 2017 by Langham Global Library
An imprint of Langham Creative Projects

Langham Partnership
PO Box 296, Carlisle, Cumbria CA3 9WZ, UK
www.langham.org

ISBNs:
978-1-78368-297-3 Print
978-1-78368-299-7 Mobi
978-1-78368-298-0 ePub
978-1-78368-300-0 PDF

British Library Cataloguing in Publication Data
A catalogue record for this book is available from the British Library

ISBN: 978-1-78368-297-3

Cover & Book Design: projectluz.com

CONTENTS

Foreword by Mark Hunt

International Executive Director
Langham Partnership

In September 2006, my wife and I had an outing with Chris and Liz Wright to Cambridge. The weather was magnificent, and we explored meaningful places dating from Chris's days there as a student. When he learned of the day trip, John Stott pronounced that once we had been to Cambridge, "our education would be complete." At one point during the day, I took a photograph of Chris standing next to a blue plaque that commemorated the discovery of the DNA double helix by Watson and Crick in 1953. On our return to London, I used Photoshop to modify the plaque to make it celebrate the discovery of the Old Testament triangular ethic by Christopher J. H. Wright in 1973. It was our private joke, but somehow it felt appropriate that Chris's work should be recognized, even if its significance was missed by the purveyors of blue plaques.

Six years later I discovered that our prank was prescient, though the focus now was on *The Mission of God* rather than *Living as the People of God*. In 2012 the Society of Biblical Literature held its annual conference in Chicago, and attending the session on missional hermeneutics disabused me of any thoughts that Chris's work may have gone unnoticed. Starting with the first paper, references to his thinking on this topic abounded. Clearly Chris's writing was held in high esteem by his academic peers, and I suspect a number of those present attended the session more to meet Chris and hear his response than to listen to the papers being read.

The Mission of God: Unlocking the Bible's Grand Narrative, without a doubt Chris's most critically acclaimed book, was the reason for his warm reception at the Chicago conference. In it he develops a hermeneutic for understanding the Bible that is built upon seeing the Bible as a statement of God's mission in the world. From this perspective, he explores how God's plan shapes what his people are called to be and do. This approach to Scripture provides a unifying theme in which God's agenda to redeem his world touches every aspect of our lives. We discover in fresh ways, perhaps for the first time, that Scripture has much to tell us about how God calls us to interact with political, economic, social, and spiritual realities.

Over the years I have taken particular pleasure in hearing Chris take a subject and trace its connection to and development in the overarching story of Scripture. Typically, we begin in Genesis, often with God's great promise to bless every nation through Abraham, and in five or ten minutes we emerge in Revelation with an entirely new perspective on the issue at hand. This is such a hallmark of Chris's preaching and speaking that his family and friends sometimes tease him about the appearance of Abraham in every sermon. The exercise of seeing the world in this way seems effortless for Chris, and often results in a new and moving understanding of both the subject at hand and the biblical text. A perfect example of this took place during the November 2015 International Council for Evangelical Theological Education Consultation in Antalya, Turkey. Chris spoke at the opening session on the topic of "effectiveness and impact in theological education from a biblical perspective." Hardly a promising topic to consider our call to participate in God's mission, but as Chris took his listeners on a journey from Genesis to the writings of Paul, they came away convinced that theological education outcomes are significant to God's mission.

Chris has written many books, some academic and others for a more popular audience. His work resonates with both audiences because his approach provides a means to affirm that the whole of Scripture speaks to the issues that confront and trouble us each day. We live in an era in which the world seems broken at many levels. At times governments on every continent seem more taken with their own wealth and power than with the good of the people. While an increasing number of people at the global level are rising above abject poverty, vast numbers continue to barely subsist. Human slavery is at its highest level in human history. The natural world faces growing ecological crises. Should Christians be addressing these issues, and does Scripture provide any direction as to how we should respond? Chris responds with an unequivocal yes, and his thinking and writing provide models for doing this.

For most of his life Chris has focused his energy on global theological education. For five years, he taught at Union Biblical Seminary in Pune, India. He served as dean and principal at All Nations Christian College, located in Hertfordshire. As the name implies, the purpose of this school is to train and equip individuals for cross-cultural mission. When John Stott approached Chris to become the international ministries director for Langham Partnership, it was a good and natural fit. In 2005 The Lausanne Movement asked Chris to chair their theological working group, a position John Stott held during the 1974 Lausanne Conference on World Evangelization. For the next several years

Chris led an international team through many working sessions that resulted in the publication of *The Cape Town Commitment: A Confession of Faith and a Call to Action.* This long history of interacting with friends from a diversity of cultures and backgrounds challenged and shaped Chris's thinking. While widely appreciated for the skills he brought to these discussions, Chris is quick to acknowledge the expertise and insights brought by his global colleagues.

To this point my focus has been on the contributions that Chris's writing has made to biblical theology. I would be remiss not to write a few words about him on a more personal level. Given his prolific output of books, it may be tempting to imagine him as an academic, spending his days closeted in his study. Such an image could not be further from the truth. Chris and his wife, Liz, have served together as a team in all his varied roles. Their home has been a centre of hospitality and joy for all who come into contact with them. Their four adult children and ten grandchildren are a source of pride and joy, and they are often found in the sitting room of Papa and Nanny.

To Chris's great embarrassment, John Stott would refer to him as "that rare combination of a scholar-athlete." But the truth is that he loves being outdoors and active. During his days in Cambridge he rowed for his college, and he still treasures any opportunity to be on the water with an oar in his hands. His love of rugby led him to become a referee, as well as a player, in his younger days. Students found that he was eager to join them in a game of football (of the global variety), and more recently, on at least one occasion, he joined in a game of football of the American sort. A successful finisher of the London Marathon in 2000, Chris still likes to start the day with a good run. The boyish and youthful energy he exudes belies his reaching the milestone of seventy years.

This volume is a celebration of Chris's life and his contribution to theology and biblical studies. It is appropriate that the writers contributing to it are representatives of the burgeoning number of theological and biblical scholars across the globe. These essays were written to honour Chris, and the geographic diversity of the authors is in itself the fruit of Chris's ministry over the years. Special thanks goes to Jennifer Cuthbertson of Langham Preaching for her work in mobilizing these authors, and also to Dahlia Frasier and Isobel Stevenson of Langham Literature for editing this work.

Psalm 92 states, "The righteous will flourish like a palm tree, they will grow like a cedar of Lebanon; planted in the house of the Lord, they will flourish in the courts of our God. They will still bear fruit in old age, they will stay fresh and green, proclaiming, 'The Lord is upright; he is my Rock, and there is no wickedness in him.'" At seventy Chris still seems to be far from old age. He continues to travel the globe and is working on a list of writing projects. My prayer for my friend and colleague is that he will continue to flourish, fresh and green, as the psalmist affirms, and that we may continue to benefit from fruit of his friendship, study, and writing for many years to come.

Foreword by Jonathan Lamb

Former Director of Langham Preaching,
Minister-at-large for Keswick Ministries and a Vice-President of IFES

The British comedian Spike Milligan was once taking a train journey, when someone asked him where he came from. *"From London,"* he said. So his fellow-traveller continued the question, *"Oh, which part?"* To which Spike Milligan replied, *"All of me."*

It's a good answer. We Christian believers must live the whole of life in faithful obedience to the God who has redeemed us. Everything about us should be shaped by God's purposes of grace. Through our understanding and application of God's Word, our worldview should be integrated and coherent, and our personal, family, work and church commitments should be entirely in sync. The essays which follow in this volume underline the many ways in which our friend Chris Wright has called the global church to think and act in such an integrated way. Several authors highlight the significant contribution Chris has made in his crafting of an integrated view of mission, and this is one prime example of how his commitments arise from a comprehensive vision of God's purposes for his world. This has had several significant components.

First, Chris is committed to the authority of Scripture, and to seeing it applied to all areas of life. This has strengthened evangelical scholarship, not only through his own significant theological writing but also through his personal engagement with evangelical scholars around the world and his support for the development of robust theological training institutions. His high view of Scripture and his determination to encourage faithful and relevant application is a significant contribution to the academy, and his commitment to seeing the Scriptures address all areas of society is reflected in many of the articles that have been written in his honour.

Second, Chris is committed to the well-being of the local church. He is one of those rare authors who can combine deep theological reflection with an accessible style, such that his commentaries and other writings have impacted the non-academic, and shaped the attitudes of church leaders in highly significant ways. This is supported by the fact that he is himself committed to the cause of biblical preaching, ready not only to address thousands but also to speak to a small congregation in a local church. He displays no sense of superiority or arrogant scholarship but writes and speaks with the meekness of Christ.

Third, Chris is committed to the global church. His contribution as a missiologist has been characterized by a wide interest in every corner of the world. His involvements in the Lausanne Movement, and especially his crafting of its most recent statements, have been significant expressions of global evangelical unity, and it is no surprise to see reference to this surface in the chapters which follow. But further, Chris is committed to understanding the needs of the global church. It is intriguing that today's debate about the exact parameters of mission seems far less polarized in those parts of the world where the church daily confronts poverty, corruption and injustice. Unlike in the Western context, these everyday realities in the Majority World cannot be ignored, and the themes of lament or justice or development in some of the following chapters are born out of the struggles of our fellow believers to address such challenges with biblical and personal integrity. Chris himself is not an academic who is removed or distant from the realities of a fractured world, having lived in India and having travelled widely across the Majority World. He has confronted these global challenges, and many of us have been grateful that he has not been afraid, in both his speaking and his writing, to acknowledge the mystery of suffering, as well as to articulate positive and hopeful ways forward in the cause of the mission of God in the broken world with which we must engage.

Chris's integrated view of life has also rightly extended to care for his family, and no expression of thanks should omit reference to the supportive ministry of Liz, his tirelessly energetic wife. Behind every great man there is a surprised woman, they say, and in Chris's case the Lord has provided a strong partnership in marriage and in family life. Chris's commitment to the whole of life has also influenced his proper concern for personal health, and his physical fitness is such that one can hardly believe he has reached the age of seventy. My own view on jogging arises from the wisdom of Proverbs 28, where the teacher reminds us that "only the wicked run when no one is chasing them," but unlike the athletic Dr Wright, I am no Old Testament interpreter.

The whole of life for Christ – this is the call that lies behind Chris's understanding of the Scriptures, his articulation of mission, his engagement with the church worldwide, and his personal priorities. It is this comprehensive commitment which makes his contribution so compelling and his ministry so effective. We thank God for all that he has allowed Chris to achieve, and pray for many more fruitful years to come.

1

A Life Devoted to the Mission of God

Ian J. Shaw

Ian J. Shaw *is provost of the Union School of Theology in Wales. He was previously the associate international director of the Langham Scholars programme and a lecturer in church history at International Christian College, Glasgow. He holds a PhD in church history from Manchester University and has written a number of books and articles on the history of evangelicalism and global Christianity.*

Christopher Joseph Herbert Wright was born in Belfast, Northern Ireland, on 9 October 1947. He was the youngest of four children and his older siblings, Sheila, Paul and Trevor, affectionately called him Herby Joe. Home was a house on Sicily Park, a suburban road in the southwest of Belfast.[1]

A year before Chris Wright was born his parents had returned to Northern Ireland after working for twenty years (1926–1946) as missionaries in Brazil with the Unevangelized Fields Mission (UFM). Their work had been among indigenous tribal people. With parents named Mary and Joseph perhaps God had something special planned for Chris! Certainly their passion for cross-cultural ministry was to have a significant impact on him. Mary was widely known as Maimie, and Joseph was always Joe.

Chris Wright enjoyed the privilege of a childhood filled with strong, loving, care and spiritual nurture. He later put it simply – "I grew up in a home where

---

1. Many thanks are due to the Wright family (Liz, Catharine, Timothy, Jonathan and Suzannah) for kindly supplying detailed information about Chris Wright's upbringing and early life – without Chris knowing it!

the Lord Jesus was loved and worshipped." These influences did not come only from his parents. When he was about six years old, his older brother Paul asked him if he knew whether his name was in the Lamb's Book of Life. Young Chris replied that he did not know, and his brother said he needed to be sure. Chris remembers asking Jesus to come into his heart and forgive his sins. He considers it an enormous blessing to have grown up through his childhood and teenage years knowing that he had Jesus as his Saviour.[2]

After his return to Belfast, Joe worked as missionary secretary for UFM, and was widely known in evangelical circles across the north of Ireland. His ministry continued right to the end of his life. The day before he died (at the age of 85) he visited the "old folks" in a nearby home for the elderly.

The family attended Berry Street Presbyterian Church. During Chris Wright's formative teenage years, the minister was Glynn Owen, a fine Bible expositor. Throughout his ten-year ministry, each Sunday morning and evening Owen preached 45-minute sermons that were biblical, expository and heart-warming. As a Welshman, Owen also had an emotional dimension to his preaching, and this, combined with clear and compelling biblical exposition, had a powerful effect. Through Owen, Chris learned the importance of biblical preaching for Christian faith and growth.

Owen's ministry in Belfast ended in October 1969 when he was called to Westminster Chapel, London, to succeed the famous preacher Dr Martyn Lloyd-Jones. A few years later he moved to Knox Presbyterian Church in Toronto, Canada. The Berry Street church was understandably reluctant to let Owen leave, because his ministry had been so well received. Chris and a number of other young people who had benefitted from Owen's ministry would eventually go into full-time Christian ministry. Berry Street was also where Chris met his future wife Liz. They both sang in the choir, and together led the Christian Endeavour group.

After attending Finaghy Primary School, Chris Wright moved on to Methodist College in Belfast (still known as "Methody"), one of the leading grammar schools in Northern Ireland. Despite its name, it was an interdenominational school founded in 1865 with a reputation for academic excellence and sporting achievement. Chris excelled in both these dimensions –

---

2. Details supplied in an audio interview Langham Hong Kong conducted with Chris Wright in early 2016, extracts of which are published as "Knowing Chris Wright, Part I," *Langham Foundation Newsletter*, Spring, 2016; and "Knowing Chris Wright, Part II," *Langham Foundation Newsletter*, Autumn 2016.

he won trophies for rowing at the Irish schools' championships, and eventually a place at Cambridge University.

At Cambridge, Chris Wright studied classics at St Catharine's College. His sporting success continued. He rowed in his college's first "eight," but missed out on a chance to row at the famous Henley Regatta when another crew member pulled out because of family illness, and it was too late to find a replacement. Moving to England to study brought challenges for the young man from Ulster, but his father's wise advice to "nail your colours to the mast" by being clear and open about his Christian faith from the outset helped him set his spiritual compass. He was also sustained by cakes sent over from Northern Ireland by Liz, patiently waiting for him to return!

After completing his degree, he returned to Belfast to teach classics for two years at Grosvenor High School in Belfast. Liz also worked as a schoolteacher. Chris and Liz were married in 1970. The sense of call to further study and eventually to full-time ministry was growing, and in 1971 he and Liz moved to Cambridge. Here he started a PhD, researching the ethics of land, family, economics, debt and slavery in the Old Testament. The 1970s were a time of considerable economic turmoil, with high levels of unemployment, inflation and industrial unrest in the West, coupled with soaring oil prices. Evangelical Christians were increasingly debating such issues, and seeking ways to respond as Christian believers. This concern found notable expression at the 1974 Lausanne Congress on World Evangelization, in which John Stott played a prominent role. The resulting Lausanne Covenant stressed how evangelism and social action should be intimately related to one another, as they had been throughout the history of the church.[3]

Chris Wright's thinking was developing along similar lines. He was convinced that the gospel is not just a matter of inner piety and the eternal security of the soul, but is for the whole of life. Christians needed to be aware of not just spiritual realities but also social realities such as poverty and injustice. Therefore, issues of economics, law, politics, and business needed to be the subject of serious biblical reflection. His research supervisor at Cambridge was Ronald Ernest Clements, a noted British Old Testament scholar, who was at the time a fellow of Fitzwilliam College and lecturer (later professor) in Old Testament Literature and Theology at the University of Cambridge. Another

---

3. For the Lausanne debates see J. D. Douglas, *Let the Earth Hear His Voice* (London: Worldwide Publishers, 1974). For John Stott's personal thinking on such issues see J. R.W. Stott, *Issues Facing Christians Today* (Basingstoke: Marshall, Morgan and Scott, 1984), 3.

who encouraged him in his studies was Professor C. F. D. Moule, a renowned New Testament scholar.

Chris and Liz lived in a small house in Cambridge. With the arrival of their first daughter, Catharine, there was limited room for a desk and books. So his study space during his doctoral studies became Tyndale House in Selwyn Gardens, a research and study centre for evangelical scholars. From 1976 to 1978 Chris Wright served as secretary of the Tyndale Fellowship Committee. Then in 1978 he took over the co-ordination of Tyndale Fellowship's Theology Project in which a number of study groups worked to make connections between biblical studies and theology and to address the key issues of the day within a biblical framework. By 1978 there were Old and New Testament study groups, and a historical theology group. A Christian ethics study group was started in 1979, which Chris Wright chaired until 1982.[4] In 1989, he became the international secretary of the Tyndale Fellowship, and he delivered the Tyndale Lecture in Christian Ethics in 1991.[5] His role with Tyndale House and with the Tyndale Fellowship allowed Chris Wright to interact with a group of rising evangelical scholars who were to play a significant role in theological education in Britain over the next two decades. They included Howard Marshall, Joyce Baldwin, Tony Thistleton, Donald Guthrie, Tony Lane and Dick France.

In Cambridge Chris and Liz attended St Phillips Church, the nearest church to where they lived. Here they were both confirmed into the Anglican Church, and the vicar Donald Salway encouraged Chris to take on leadership roles. Also in the St Phillips congregation at the time was Vinay Samuel, an Indian postgraduate student at Cambridge who was being supported in his studies by the Langham Trust, which had been established by John Stott.[6]

Towards the end of his PhD studies, Chris Wright also started training for the Anglican ministry at Ridley Hall in Cambridge. He was ordained a deacon of the Church of England at Rochester Cathedral in 1977. With his doctorate completed, he worked for nearly five years as a curate in the parish of St Peter and St Paul in Tonbridge, Kent. Here the vicar, Charles Searle-Barnes, was committed to training future Christian leaders and maintained a large team

---

4. Noble, *Tyndale House*, 147–149; 174–175.

5. C. J. H. Wright, "The Ethical Authority of the Old Testament: A Methodological Study," *Tyndale Bulletin* 43, no. 1 (1992) and 43, no. 2 (1992).

6. On the Langham Trust see I. J. Shaw, "John Stott and the Langham Scholars Ministry," in *Reflecting on and Equipping for Christian Mission*, ed. Stephen Bevans et al. (Oxford: Regnum, 2015), 308–326.

of curates. Chris Wright's ongoing involvement with the Tyndale House study groups ensured he was able to develop as a pastor-scholar during those years.

In 1978 he met John Stott for the first time when Chris was invited to give a Bible exposition at a conference on evangelical social ethics. As a result of his role at the Lausanne Congress, Stott was now acknowledged as a global evangelical leader. He began to follow Chris Wright's work with interest, and regularly corresponded with him. With Stott's encouragement, Chris began to consider opportunities for theological teaching in the Majority World. He applied to the Bible Churchmen's Missionary Society (now Crosslinks), and was accepted as a mission partner. When an opportunity to teach Old Testament at Union Biblical Seminary (UBS), an evangelical theological college in Pune, India, was offered, he began the long process of seeking a visa for himself, Liz and their four children – Catharine born in Belfast in 1971, Timothy and Jonathan born in Cambridge in 1972 and 1973, and Suzannah born in Harlow in 1982.

There followed months of significant prayer and heart-searching, with a growing sense of frustration at the visa-issuing authorities over their tardiness. There were occasions when Chris and Liz questioned whether they had mistaken God's guidance in leaving parish ministry and preparing to go to India. It was also a time of considerable financial hardship. Having left the curacy in 1982 in anticipation of the move to India, they were forced to live for a while with friends. The visa delay lasted eighteen months. Help came in the form of a short-term teaching post at All Nations' Christian College at Ware in Hertfordshire, with an open door to return in the future if the need arose.

Finally, in 1983 the visa was granted, and the Wrights embarked on a new adventure. The next five years were devoted to teaching Old Testament at UBS where there were about 250 students. On the faculty were leading Indian scholars such as Ashish Crishpal and Brian Wintle. Some of the students Chris taught went on to become key leaders and thinkers in the Indian evangelical scene.

There were inevitable challenges in living in India with a young family far from home. For one thing, UBS was very much a building site when they arrived. There was no regular piped water yet and for a while their water was delivered in goat skins. Chicken did not come chilled and shrink-wrapped, but very much alive and needing to be despatched before being prepared. Yet the family remember their time in India with affection. Their home was open and many students came by in the evenings to enjoy a more relaxing environment than the common room. Chris and Liz Wright have a natural instinct for hospitality, from which many have benefitted over the years.

John Stott visited them in India, and encouraged Chris to accept invitations to speak in other parts of the Majority World. This led to trips to Africa and Hong Kong. Some were for meetings related to the Evangelical Fellowship in the Anglican Church (EFAC), which had been constituted in 1961 in order to provide a network for evangelicals throughout the global Anglican Communion who often found themselves extremely isolated.[7]

The decision to leave India after five years came in July 1988. It was driven by the educational needs of the older children, who were ready for A-level studies and needed a period of secondary schooling in the UK to qualify for university grants. The door to return to All Nations Christian College remained open, and Chris Wright was to spend the next thirteen years working there, first as academic dean and then for eight years after 1993 as principal. All Nations, an evangelical theological college with a specific focus on training for cross-cultural mission, had at the time around 150 students. Its faculty included well-known scholars such as David Harley (the principal when Chris Wright arrived), Martin Goldsmith, Dave Burnett, and Richard Harvey.

By the time Chris Wright had reached his early 50s, the possibility of staying at All Nations to retirement was a very real one. He had developed a wide speaking and writing ministry, and one of his commitments was serving on the board of trustees of the Evangelical Literature Trust (ELT), which had been founded by John Stott in 1971. Its ministry was sending evangelical literature to pastors, students and theological colleges in the Majority World. Funding came in part through the royalties from John Stott's own writings, which by 1996 had totalled over half a million pounds sterling.[8]

The ELT brought Chris Wright into regular contact with Stott. As he reflected on what the next step for him in ministry might be, he wrote to Stott, seeking his advice. He wanted to remain active in theological teaching and writing, but in a more international capacity. He also wanted to do this while rooted in a local church. John Stott was at that time almost 80, and he too had been reflecting on the future for the ministries he had developed. During his time as rector of All Souls Church, Langham Place, London, from 1950 to 1975, he had enjoyed a remarkably successful ministry. Stott's model of expository biblical preaching and a well-organized evangelical parish ministry

---

7. On EFAC, see T. Dudley-Smith, *John Stott: The Later Years, A Global Ministry* (Downers Grove: InterVarsity Press, 2001), 51–56.

8. Dudley-Smith, *Global Ministry*, 357.

attracted a very large congregation. He spoke at conferences and conventions around the world and was a prolific and widely read author writing over fifty books and many more articles.[9]

In 1969, John Stott had founded the Langham Trust, which helped to support his future international ministry (much of which was conducted in the Majority World) after he stepped down from full-time leadership at All Souls. In 1971, the Langham Trust also began supporting gifted evangelical leaders from the Majority World to enable them to undertake doctoral studies in theological disciplines. They were equipped to return to their home countries to lecture in evangelical colleges and seminaries and serve as strategic leaders.[10] Friends in the USA had also founded the Langham Foundation in 1974, and other Langham bodies were founded in Canada and Australia, which raised funds to further this work.

At Stott's instigation, the question of the continuance, or not, of the Langham Trust, the Evangelical Literature Trust, and the other Langham bodies after the death of their founder, began to be discussed in 1999. Stott wanted the programmes to continue only "so long as they are perceived to be necessary and are still wanted by Third World Christian leaders."[11] There was no question of institutionalizing these ministries, or of continuing them just to perpetuate his memory.[12] He consulted a range of leaders from the international evangelical community, who urged that the work be continued, and that he should appoint an international director to succeed him.[13] Yet, Stott seemed an almost impossible act to follow.

These discussions were taking place just at the time when Chris Wright was seeking advice from John Stott about his future ministry. The outcome was that in 2001 Langham Partnership International was founded, bringing together the Langham Trust (which became Langham Scholars), the Evangelical Literature Trust and the Langham Writers Fund (which became Langham Literature) in one organization, together with the Langham bodies in the United States, Australia and Canada (those in Hong Kong and New Zealand joined later).

---

9. T. Dudley-Smith, *John Stott: The Making of a Leader, Vol. 1* (Downers Grove: InterVarsity Press, 1999), 89, 93–94; and Dudley-Smith, *Global Ministry*, 291.

10. All Souls Newsletter, June 1970, cited in Dudley-Smith, *Global Ministry*, 141.

11. Dudley-Smith, *Global Ministry*, 389, 421.

12. John Stott, John Stott Ministries (USA) and the Langham Trust (UK). "An Easter 1999 Memorandum from John Stott about the Future: Five Third World Ministries," May 1999.

13. Dudley-Smith, *Global Ministry*, 422–423.

All agreed to work together with a common statement of faith and vision.[14] A crucial initial decision made by Langham Partnership International was to appoint Chris Wright as international ministries director.[15]

John Stott continued to play a role in the ministry of Langham Partnership, undertaking preaching and speaking tours, and providing support and encouragement to its work. He was regularly consulted about the ministry, but executive responsibility now lay with Chris Wright. Chris was a natural choice: his ministry mirroring much of what Langham's founder had done as a Bible expositor, writer, and theological educator with wide international experience. The task of developing the vision statements, statement of faith and core values statements for Langham Partnership was placed in his hands in December 2001.[16] The protocol developed was approved at a meeting of the Langham Partnership International Council in April 2002.[17] So, although he had the support and help of John Stott, David Cansdale (chair of Langham UK), and David Spence (chair of Langham USA – then called John Stott Ministries), the creation of Langham Partnership International with its ethos and vision owes a significant debt to Chris Wright. The Langham vision was to see "Majority World churches being equipped for mission and growing to maturity through the ministry of Christian leaders and pastors who sincerely believe, diligently study, faithfully expound and relevantly apply the Word of God."[18] Its operational ethos was clear:

> Langham programmes will above all else promote the honour and glory of the Lord Jesus Christ and the truths of historical, Biblical Christianity as preserved and presented in God's Word. The Langham Partnership wishes to serve the church at large, and therefore Langham programmes will be multi-denominational in approach, while evangelical in content.[19]

In his "Easter Memorandum" written in 1999, John Stott had stressed the importance of the preaching seminars he had been running.[20] Chris Wright

---

14. Report to Langham Scholarship Committee by John Stott and David Cansdale, 20 September 2001.

15. Langham Scholarship Committee Minutes, 27 February 2001.

16. Langham Partnership International Council (LPIC) Meeting Minutes, 7 December 2001, Radnor, Pennsylvania.

17. LPIC Minutes, 20–21 April 2002.

18. Langham Partnership International (LPI) Protocol, 23 February 2004, Section 2.

19. LPI Protocol, 8, 2, 1–2.

20. John Stott, "Easter Memorandum," 1999, John Stott papers.

joined John Stott on a visit to Latin America in 2001, sharing in the delivery of these seminars. This led to the decision in 2002 to form Langham Preaching, the third Langham programme. Its aim was to equip pastors and lay leaders from the Majority World with biblical preaching skills. Jonathan Lamb, who had previously worked with the International Fellowship of Evangelical Students, was appointed International Director of Langham Preaching.

An important aspect of Chris Wright's role with Langham was his commitment that he should remain rooted in a local church. This led to his appointment to the staff team of All Soul's Church, Langham Place, by its rector Richard Bewes. The Wrights moved into the parish of All Souls, and Chris began preaching regularly in the services. John Stott continued to live in a small flat in Bridford Mews, behind the All Souls rectory in Weymouth Street, and Chris Wright met with him regularly.

For the next eleven years, Chris Wright held the role of International Director of Langham, combining regular international speaking and preaching ministry with writing and executive leadership responsibilities. His international travel became very extensive, and close connections were formed with the International Council of Evangelical Theological Education (ICETE) to which Langham made an annual contribution.[21] In 2008, with the growth in the size and complexity of Langham and its ministries, it was recognized that the executive administrative demands on Chris Wright's time were increasing, and so Mark Hunt was appointed international operations director. In this way, more of Chris's time would be freed for writing and international speaking.[22]

Under Chris Wright's leadership, Langham flourished. By 2016 there were preaching movements in sixty countries. Over 410 Langham Scholars had received funding to complete doctoral studies in order to return to the Majority World to teach and train the next generation of pastors and teachers. Langham Literature was supporting more than 600 evangelical colleges and seminaries with annual library and book grants, and it was facilitating the creation, digitization and distribution of influential evangelical books and publications written by Majority World scholars for their own contexts. These included one-volume commentaries such as the Africa, South Asia and Slavic Bible commentaries.

The growing influence of Chris Wright in global evangelical theology was evident when in 2004 he was invited to chair the Lausanne Theology

21. LPIC Minutes, 26 Sept 2003.
22. LPIC Minutes, 28 Sept 2008.

Working Group. This led to the writing of the Cape Town Commitment, a comprehensive statement of evangelicalism for the twenty-first century. The distinctive character of the commitment was noted in its foreword: "Many doctrinal statements affirm what the Church believes. We wished to go further and link belief with praxis."[23] These twin missional emphases have been characteristic of Chris Wright throughout his ministry.

International travel became a regular feature of Chris Wright's diary. This included a significant ministry visit to China in 2006, along with John Stott.[24] 2010 saw him playing an important role with Ian Shaw (also of Langham) at the ICETE-convened meeting in Beirut, at which the *Beirut Benchmarks* for doctoral programmes in theological education were developed. Their creation answered a significant call Chris had himself issued at the ICETE Conference in Chiang Mai in 2006.

In 2012 the Langham Partnership International Council, recognizing the global nature of Chris Wright's work, decided that he should focus on the presentation and promotion of Langham's three programmes through preaching, teaching and writing. His role was renamed international ministries director, and Mark Hunt was appointed to the role of executive director, taking on the executive and strategic leadership of Langham Partnership International.[25] This revision of his role allowed Chris to devote some 35 percent of his time to writing and 40 percent to international teaching and preaching.[26]

Chris Wright has so far published more than thirty-five books and booklets, as well as many articles in journals and magazines. His first major book, *Living as the People of God: the Relevance of Old Testament Ethics*, was published by IVP in 1983.[27] It was started while he was working as a curate in Tonbridge and was completed in the months he spent waiting for his India visa and teaching at All Nations. It was designed as a comprehensive theological, social and economic approach to Old Testament ethics, an area in which comparatively few scholars were working in those days. It was republished in revised and

---

23. Doug Birdsall and Lindsay Brown, Foreword to *The Cape Town Commitment: A Confession of Faith and a Call to Action*, Didasko Files, Lausanne Movement, 2011.

24. Langham Partnership Scholarship Committee Minutes, 9 March 2006.

25. LPIC Minutes, 1–4 November 2012.

26. LPIC Minutes, 20 Oct–1 Nov 2015.

27. C. J. H. Wright, *Living as the People of God: The Relevance of Old Testament Ethics* (Leicester: IVP, 1983). Also published as *An Eye for an Eye: The Place of Old Testament Ethics Today* (Downers Grove: InterVarsity Press, 1983).

expanded form in 2004 as *Old Testament Ethics for the People of God*. One reviewer described it as

> desperately needed both in two-thirds and first-world cultures . . . Wright explicitly rejects one of the most common dualisms of modernity, that of dividing theology and ethics into two non-overlapping magisteria . . . This holistic approach is necessary to combat both modernity, which explicitly divides the two, and postmodernity, which falsely claims to bring both together.[28]

John Barton, of Oxford University, while not fully in sympathy with the book's theological stance, reflected very positively on its scholarly awareness and fairness to others:

> the assessments are judicious, and – like everything in the book – scrupulously fair, even when it is clear that Wright does not agree with the scholar in question. This, indeed, is one of the most attractive aspects of the book. It is written from a definite perspective, but with an open-minded willingness really to understand the positions of others.[29]

His magnum opus, *The Mission of God: Unlocking the Bible's Grand Narrative*, was published by IVP in 2006. This is a definitive statement that the entire Bible is generated by, and is all about, God's mission. Therefore, to understand the Bible, we need a missional hermeneutic in tune with this great theme. This provides a solid and expansive basis for holistic mission. The book was widely acclaimed, and in 2007 won the *Christianity Today* Missions/ Global Affairs Book Award. One writer commented, "This book should be a required text for theologians and exegetes, pastors and students, missionaries and Christians in general."[30]

Some scholars outside the evangelical tradition have questioned this approach to biblical hermeneutics rooted in biblical theology. One such was Stephen Fowl of Loyola College, yet he still welcomed the *Mission of* God for its "discrete examples of exegetical brilliance and edification . . . one of the

---

28. Mark R. Kreitzer, Reformed Theological Seminary, "Review of *Old Testament Ethics for the People of God* by Christopher J. H. Wright," *Review & Preview* at www.globalmissiology. org, April 2008.

29. John Barton, "Review of *Old Testament Ethics for the People of God*, by Christopher J. H. Wright," *Studies in Christian Ethics* 20, no. 1: 150–152.

30. Quoted on rear cover of C. J. H. Wright, *The Mission of God* (Downers Grove: InterVarsity Press, 2006).

best examples of this genre currently available."[31] Daniel Carroll stressed the importance of the biblical basis given: "this is a book that needed to be written. Over the years, one of my constant frustrations has been the little attention given to the Old Testament in books that purport to provide a biblical basis for Christian mission or missions." He ranked it alongside David Bosch's landmark study *Transforming Mission* in significance.[32] However, other evangelicals had reservations about the holistic approach taken in the book. A review in *Christianity Today* commented, "Wright's huge, all-embracing umbrella of God's mission could renew fears that evangelism and church planting will be lost. If he seems to indicate that everything is mission, the risk is that nothing is mission in the end."[33]

The companion volume, the *Mission of God's People* sought to relate the *missio Dei*, to the task of churches and their members. The emphasis remained holistic – "We need a holistic gospel because the world is in a holistic mess." However, there was no question of advocating a deeds-of-compassion-are-enough approach to mission. Ministries to human need were never adequate by themselves; evangelistic proclamation is always essential: "The mission of God's people is to bring *good* news to a world where *bad* news is depressingly endemic."[34] Chris Wright extended ministry into the public arena, fulfilling the cultural mandate, thereby giving dignity to the ministry of lay people there. Stephen Strauss urged: "Everyone engaging in full-time ministry should read either *The Mission of God* or *The Mission of God's People*."[35]

Theology and mission were to be inseparable – "No theology without missional impact; no mission without theological foundations."[36] As one reviewer from the Majority World commented, "this book exemplifies Wright's ability to bring biblical theology to the masses in a compelling way . . . Few

---

31. Stephen E. Fowl, Loyola College, Baltimore, "Review of *The Mission of God* by Christopher Wright," *Theological Studies* 69, no. 1 (2008): 221–222.

32. M. D. Carroll, "Review of *The Mission of God* by Christopher Wright," *Bulletin for Biblical Research*, 1 January 2008. David Bosch's book was published by Orbis in 1991.

33. Jim Reapsome, Baptist pastor, "Review of *The Mission of God* by Christopher Wright," *Christianity Today* 51, no. 6 (2007): 73.

34. C. J. H. Wright, *The Mission of God's People* (Grand Rapids: Zondervan, 2010), 110, 179.

35. S. Strauss, "Review of *The Mission of God's People* by Christopher Wright," *Bibliotheca Sacra*, July–September 2012.

36. Wright, *Mission of God's People*, 20.

readers will fail to be moved by Wright's integrative and inspiring vision for what a biblical theology of the church should be."[37]

The primary subject matter of Chris Wright's writing has been Scripture, especially the Old Testament. He has produced a number of commentaries, often on the more difficult parts of Scripture, including Deuteronomy, Jeremiah, Lamentations, and Ezekiel. In his review of *Old Testament Ethics for the People of God* John Barton, summarized Chris Wright's high view of Scripture, together with his scholarly care in expressing this:

> The critical assumptions are conservative: the patriarchal stories are treated as history, and the book of Daniel is read as coming from the Babylonian Exile. The doctrine of biblical inspiration is a high one . . . It is clear throughout that there *is* a divine author alongside the human one. That said, however, Wright allows the "human authors" and the communities behind them a weight not so usual with such conservative scholars.[38]

Following the example of John Stott, Chris Wright's commentaries demonstrate the ability to bring together the horizons of the text and of the contemporary world. One Catholic reviewer of the commentary on Deuteronomy, while unhappy with the early dating given to the text, still expressed admiration for his missiological applications, noting how "many fine comments on contemporary applications of the text . . . show not only the relevance of Deuteronomic thinking but also Wright's keen homiletic instincts."[39] This ability to make Deuteronomy relevant to the contemporary world was also appreciated by other writers:

> Oh, that rare breed: a commentary which combines investigative biblical scholarship with engaging cultural relevance to today's world. Intellect and faith go hand in hand . . . Students, clergy, or university Christian workers who seek a better biblical understanding for answering the challenge which post-modernism poses to our age, this commentary is for you.[40]

---

37. J. Hwang, "Review of *The Mission of God's People* by Christopher Wright," *Themelios* 37, no. 1 (2012): 176–177.

38. J. Barton, "Review of *Old Testament Ethics for the People of God.*"

39. W. S. Morrow, "Review of *Deuteronomy* by Christopher Wright," *The Catholic Biblical Quarterly* 60, no. 3 (1998): 550–551.

40. D. H. Jackson, "Review of *Deuteronomy* by Christopher Wright," *Themelios* 23, no. 3 (1998): 65–66.

Another agreed – "This is Wright's *forte*, for his main interest is in applying the Old Testament to the area of mission and ethics."[41]

The quality of the writing itself has attracted positive comment. One reviewer of the Ezekiel commentary summed this up: "Wright's prose, in the highest traditions of the British, is pleasant to read for its cadence, color, and clarity. Expositors looking for commentaries that will improve their understanding and their presentation of the text need to read this volume."[42] Similar observations were made about his book *Sweeter than Honey*, which deals with preaching from the Old Testament.[43] It was awarded the *Christianity Today* award of merit, and one of the judging panel commented,

> Wright's excellent book combines a robust biblical framework with practical communication steps in an easy-to-read style . . . Even more refreshing is the emphasis on exalting Jesus in ways that are true to the text and relevant to our culture.[44]

Given his holistic understanding of mission, creation care has been an important emphasis for Chris Wright. This has seen the creation of gardens in many places where he has worked. He transformed a former building site at UBS, Pune, into a tranquil spot filled with flowers including purple bougainvillea. Bird watching has also been a favoured pastime, pursued in the Algarve in Portugal, a favourite family holiday destination, and also at the Hookses on the Pembrokeshire coast, the retreat where both John Stott and Chris Wright have written many books. There the writing desk looks out to sea over Dale Bay, and the neighbouring headland is a haven for rare choughs.

For all Chris's success and accolades as an author, and the remarkable growth and development of Langham Partnership, the bedrock of his life (alongside his Christian faith) has been his family. By 2017 the four children of Liz and Chris had produced ten grandchildren, to whom he is affectionately known as Papa.

A major change for Chris Wright and for Langham came with the death of John Stott in 2011 at the age of ninety. This came after a period of declining health, with his latter years spent in a nursing home in Sussex where Chris and

---

41. H. Lalleman, "Review of *Deuteronomy* by Christopher Wright," *European Journal of Theology* 24, no. 2 (2015): 196–197.

42. W. D. Barrick, *The Master's Seminary Journal* 17, no. 2 (2006): 255–256.

43. Published in the USA as *How to Preach and Teach the Old Testament for All Its Worth*.

44. Comments of Zack Eswine, Director of Homiletics, Covenant Seminary, member of the *Christianity Today* judging panel on Christopher J. H. Wright's *How to Preach and Teach the Old Testament for All Its Worth* (Grand Rapids: Zondervan, 2016).

Liz Wright visited regularly. It was somehow fitting that on the day of his death, Chris Wright was giving the Bible expositions at the Keswick Convention, where both men have often spoken so effectively.

As he cleared out John Stott's papers after his death, Chris Wright found a short piece of unpublished writing which encapsulated his life's work:

> My vision, as I look out over the world, is to see every pulpit in every church occupied by a conscientious, Bible-believing, Bible-studying, Bible-expounding pastor. I see with my mind's eye multitudes of people in every country world-wide converging on their church every Sunday, hungry for more of God's Word. I also see every pastor mounting his pulpit with the Word of God in his mind (for he has studied it), in his heart (for he has prayed over it), and on his lips (for he is intent on communicating it).[45]

The drive to fulfil this vision inspired John Stott and the foundation of Langham, and was passed on to Chris Wright. He has continued to work faithfully towards fulfilling it through years of preaching, writing and teaching, often commenting "it is a privilege to be paid to do what I love." He has helped to shape key leaders in churches, Christian ministries and theological education, building a living legacy for future generations to continue to engage in the *missio Dei*.

References

Barrick, W. D. *The Master's Seminary Journal* 17, no. 2 (2006): 255–256.

Barton, John. "Review of *Old Testament Ethics for the People of God* by Christopher J. H. Wright." *Studies in Christian Ethics* 20, no. 1: 150–152.

Birdsall, Doug, and Lindsay Brown. Foreword to *The Cape Town Commitment: A Confession of Faith and a Call to Action*. Didasko Files, Lausanne Movement, 2011.

Carroll, M. D. "Review of *The Mission of God* by Christopher Wright." *Bulletin for Biblical Research*, 1 January 2008.

Douglas, J. D. *Let the Earth Hear His Voice*. London: Worldwide Publishers, 1974.

Dudley-Smith, T. *John Stott: The Later Years, A Global Ministry*. Downers Grove: InterVarsity Press, 2001.

———. *John Stott: The Making of a Leader, Vol. 1*. Downers Grove: InterVarsity Press, 1999.

---

45. From John Stott's unpublished papers.

Fowl, Stephen E. "Review of *The Mission of God* by Christopher Wright." *Theological Studies* 69, no. 1 (2008): 221–222.

Hwang, J. "Review of *The Mission of God's People* by Christopher Wright." *Themelios* 37, no. 1 (2012): 176–177.

Jackson, D. H. "Review of *Deuteronomy* by Christopher Wright." *Themelios* 23, no. 3 (1998): 65–66.

Kreitzer, Mark R. "Review of *Old Testament Ethics for the People of God* by Christopher J. H. Wright." *Review & Preview* at www.globalmissiology.org, April 2008.

Lalleman, H. "Review of *Deuteronomy* by Christopher Wright." *European Journal of Theology* 24, no. 2 (2015): 196–197.

Morrow, W. S. "Review of *Deuteronomy* by Christopher Wright." *The Catholic Biblical Quarterly* 60, no. 3 (1998): 550–551.

Noble, T. A. *Tyndale House and Fellowship, the First Sixty Years.* Leicester: IVP, 2006.

Reapsome, Jim. "Review of *The Mission of God* by Christopher Wright." *Christianity Today* 51, no. 6 (2007): 73.

Shaw, I. J. "John Stott and the Langham Scholars Ministry." In *Reflecting on and Equipping for Christian Mission,* edited by Stephen Bevans et al. Oxford: Regnum, 2015.

Stott, J. R. W. *Issues Facing Christians Today.* Basingstoke: Marshall, Morgan & Scott, 1984.

Strauss, S. "Review of *The Mission of God's People* by Christopher Wright." *Bibliotheca Sacra,* July–September 2012.

Wright, C. J. H. "The Ethical Authority of the Old Testament: A Methodological Study." *Tyndale Bulletin* 43, no. 1 (1992) and 43, no. 2 (1992).

———. *Living as the People of God: The Relevance of Old Testament Ethics.* Leicester: IVP, 1983.

———. *The Mission of God's People.* Grand Rapids: Zondervan, 2010.

2

A Seed Bears Fruit in Latin America

Igor Améstegui

Igor Améstegui *is associate director for Latin America - Langham Preaching. He holds a degree in psychology and has been a staff worker and later secretary general of the Comunidad Cristiana Universitaria (a movement affiliated to IFES). He has also worked as a clinical psychologist and university teacher. He and his wife took courses in biblical studies and cross-cultural missions at All Nations Christian College.*

> *[The kingdom of God] is like a mustard seed, which is the smallest of all seeds on earth. Yet when planted, it grows and becomes the largest of all garden plants.*
>
> *– Mark 4:31, 32*

The church in Latin America is growing rapidly. So we can imagine how many sermons are being preached every week throughout the continent. From small garages and rooms adapted for Sunday services to massive temples in larger cities, everywhere in Latin America there are weekly meetings involving preaching. But the question is: What is being preached, and how? I am afraid that for many years we could not say that the Word was being preached as Paul encouraged his young disciple Timothy to do (2 Tim 4:2).

Many of the sermons that are preached are unplanned, testimonial and thematic at best. And preaching from the Old Testament is rare, and generally allegorical and legalistic. How long will the Latin American church continue in this way? Many people are praying fervently for deeper growth through a meaningful and contextual study of the Word of God.

The Beginning

In September 1999 my wife Charito and I arrived at All Nations Christian College, where Chris Wright was then the principal. After more than nine years of service with the Comunidad Cristiana Universitaria, a student movement affiliated with IFES, I had been given a sabbatical year to pursue my studies. Charito was heading an organization called *Mosoj Yan*, which focused on serving girls living on the streets, and she also needed a year of renewal. Our daughters and son joined us in this adventure. Sara was ten, Daniela eight, and Esteban three.

So we met Chris while he was principal of All Nations. Just when we were about to finish, he stepped down from that position to work alongside John Stott. My wife and I enjoyed Chris's lectures and quickly understood why students were eager to sign up for them. We liked his passion for the Old Testament, the clarity of his teaching, and the fact that his English was easy to understand (for us this was very important since we were both in our first year of studying in English). We took some courses in which Chris taught on the prophet Isaiah. His biblical knowledge and the enthusiasm with which he communicated the truths of the text were admirable. One of the books which we studied was his own book, *Knowing Jesus through the Old Testament*. It gave us a new perspective on Jesus's Jewish identity and how important it is to know its roots in the Old Testament.

In August 2000 we returned to Bolivia to continue serving the Lord in our city. In mid-2004 I saw an advertisement for a course in hermeneutics and biblical exposition to be taught by Chris Wright. I was one of the first to register, for I was aware of the need for exegetical preaching in the pulpits of the Bolivian church. I had long been passionate about expository preaching, to which I had been exposed in my years in the student movement where we had great role models and a clear emphasis on the centrality and authority of the Holy Scriptures. I later learned that the course that Chris taught from 18–22 October 2004 corresponded to Level 1 of the Langham Preaching programme and that it marked the beginning of Langham's ministry in Bolivia. (It was not the start of Langham's work in Latin America as John Stott and Chris Wright had done preaching training in Buenos Aires, Argentina and Lima, Peru in 2001.)

The joy I felt in receiving this training is comparable to the joy of the Israelites in Nehemiah 8 when they understood the Word of God. Chris gave us the basics of expository preaching, emphasizing three essential characteristics: faithfulness to the biblical text, relevance to the context, and clarity in communication. He taught us how to use these three elements to evaluate a biblical sermon.

He used the following illustration to explain the meaning of fidelity to the biblical text: Imagine you are preaching on the book of Isaiah and the prophet himself is in the church, listening to your sermon. If you are communicating an idea that is totally different from the intention of the original author, what would Isaiah's facial expression be? But it you are expressing his core ideas in accessible and modern language, can you imagine the look on Isaiah's face? Chris's demonstration of Isaiah's facial expressions was so vivid that we would laugh out loud – but the lesson stayed with us.

Another aspect that stood out to me about that first module was the explanation about the two worlds in which a preacher moves (the biblical world and the world we live in) and the necessity to build bridges between them. What made this course practical and unforgettable was that in the afternoons we would work in small groups to prepare our first draft of a message and would share with others our attempts to find the central idea of the text and the skeleton of a message. During the mornings Chris gave a series of Bible expositions on the Old Testament. These expositions, besides being excellent spiritual nourishment, exemplified the principles of exegesis, hermeneutics and homiletics that Chris was teaching us.

Fernando Fernandez, the pastor of our church, and a very close friend from our days at university, also attended the first module and together we immediately applied what we had learned to our preaching in our local church in Cochabamba.

In an informal conversation, possibly during a meal, Chris told us about the preaching group at All Souls who would get together for breakfast once a week to evaluate the previous Sunday's sermon and to listen to an initial draft of the sermon for the next Sunday. He told us he would share his own sermons and get feedback from the team. We thought this was a good idea and we decided to implement it at our church, Dios en Cristo. For many years now, we have been getting together every Wednesday night to evaluate the last sermon and listen to the upcoming one. Last year, we decided to invite the worship leader for the upcoming Sunday to participate in our meetings so that the worship would have the same theme and spirit as the sermon. For the last six months we have been going through the book of Revelation and, inspired by the biblical text, we have had extraordinary opportunities to worship the one who is seated on the throne and the Lamb.

In November 2006, two years after the first preaching module, Chris returned to Cochabamba for the Level 2 seminar on preaching the Old Testament. Our pastor, Fernando Fernandez, my wife Charito, and I were the first to register for the course. One of the emphases of this module is learning to preach the Word while respecting the different literary genres in which it was written. So Chris gave us a panoramic view of the different voices in the Old Testament and emphasized preaching from the books of the Law. I recognized that we seldom preached from these books, and when we did so, it was done in a very legalistic way. This was due, I believe, to a misunderstanding that had set up a false opposition between law in the Old Testament and grace in the New Testament. Chris showed us that when Paul says in 2 Timothy 3:15–16 that all Scripture is inspired by God, he was basically referring to the Old Testament and that this included the Torah. He taught us that the law is also founded in grace (so we do not need to divide law and grace); that the law is motivated by the mission of God for Israel; that the law is based on the character of God; and that the law of Israel should be a model to all the nations. All of this was new to us and a true challenge to preach from the law and find its relevance for today.

One morning Chris talked about the need to plan our preaching over longer periods, like three years. He used the example of a mother who wants to make sure her family eats a balanced diet. He then encouraged us to plan series of sermons from both the Old and New Testaments, including different literary genres to give our congregations a fuller knowledge of God's Word (Acts 20:27). This is another lesson that we applied in our church. Before this module, we would plan series that lasted three or four months, but we did not plan for longer series that would give our congregation a panoramic view of the Bible and an opportunity to taste the different genres of Scripture. We have now finished preaching from the whole Bible over a period of four years.

This Level 2 training in Cochabamba in November 2006 was to have great significance for me. One evening, Chris talked to me about the possibility of working with Langham as the Latin American facilitator. Requests for preaching programmes were coming in from different parts of the continent, and Langham needed someone who could give full-time attention to this. I was very excited, and we started a process that concluded in June 2007 when I met with Jonathan Lamb in Oxford. Since then I have been coordinating the ministry of Langham in Latin America. God has been so faithful and generous to the ministry in this region. We are now serving in the following countries: Chile, Argentina, Bolivia, Peru, Ecuador, Colombia, Panama, Costa Rica, Honduras and Cuba.

I would like to share how this ministry grew from the small seed planted by Chris to a tree that welcomes many pastors and leaders from across the continent.

Training and Prayer

Jorge Atiencia's ministry with the Escuelitas de Formación de Expositores Bíblicos [Bible Expositors' Training School] has been a very influential aspect of the Langham Preaching ministry in Latin America. He started this ministry in Colombia in 2000. Jorge and Dr John Stott shared the same passion for expository preaching and they both desired to train pastors and lay preachers in this region.

I met Jorge when I worked with the Comunidad Cristiana Universitaria [Christian University Community]. Jorge was responsible for training across Latin America. His role required him to come to Bolivia to train students and workers with the movement. We also met and shared in different gatherings and events across the continent.

In 2006, I was invited to participate in one of the gatherings for the Escuelitas in Colombia that Jorge had started in 2000. Something that impacted me profoundly was the discipline of "praying the Word." The first morning, just before the Bible exposition, we had a time of prayer around a Bible text. It was not the typical prayer, asking God to bless the preacher. It was a time that combined reading the Bible, silence, meditation and short prayers in response to what the text was saying. I was amazed by this approach of reading Scripture and praying. Later, I discovered that many call this discipline "reading prayer."

From the beginning we included praying the Word in our Latin American seminars. I remember that on the first day of our first seminar in Santiago, Chile, I shared a lunch table with four or five of the participants. One of the pastors said spontaneously: "If for some reason, the event should end right now, and I have to go back home, I would say that it had been worth it. What we did this morning has already made coming for this four-day seminar worthwhile." I asked him with surprise, "What do you mean?" "I'm talking about praying the Word," he replied. I was very excited, because he added that he was going to introduce it at home and in his church.

I think the enthusiastic response to praying the Word in Latin America is due to the fact that it highlights our dependence on God when we preach. Praying the Word demonstrates that preaching is eminently a spiritual task. Many times, we hear the participants in our seminars make comments such as this: *"I thought that this expository preaching was something academic, cognitive. I thought it was something for scholars, divorced from spirituality. But, when you taught us that observation of the passage starts with praying the Word, my perspective was totally changed. I see now how profoundly spiritual Bible exposition is."*

But, what is praying the Word? It consists of five steps. First, we read the Bible passage to listen to God. We have the strong conviction that God keeps talking today through his written Word, so when we read it, we do it with the attitude of someone who is listening to God speak.

Second, we are silent to meditate. Silence is an essential element in reflecting on Scripture.

Third, we use our imaginations to identify ourselves with the text. The idea is to incarnate the text, to put on the Bible characters' sandals, so to speak.

Fourth, we pray, responding to what God has said to us through the text. These may be prayers of confession, of supplication or whatever the reflection on the text evokes.

Finally, we live the Word to glorify God. The real challenge is to put into practice what the text is telling us.

Small Groups

A second contribution from the ministry in Colombia to Langham Preaching has been the emphasis on the small groups that we call *"escuelitas"* (preaching clubs). "Escuelita" is the diminutive form of the word "school." In Latin America it is common to use the diminutive to express care and affection. We are aware that no annual event, regardless of whether it lasts three, four or five days, is going to change the way preaching is done in our churches. It is the monthly meetings in small groups (escuelitas) that give stability and depth to the preaching ministry.

What does a meeting of an escuelita look like? The coordinator welcomes all the members of the group. Then, they pray the Word using the same text that is going to be preached. A member of the group preaches on the text for ten minutes; this is their opportunity to practise what they learned in the preaching seminar. After the exposition, the coordinator introduces a time of evaluation with the questions: What did we hear from God? What are the changes that God wants me to make? And so we evaluate the three pillars: faithfulness to the text, relevance to our world, and clarity in the communication. Then there is a break and snacks. The last part of the meeting is dedicated to studying one of the books provided by Langham and assigning responsibilities for the next meeting: who leads praying the Word, who preaches, etc.

Coordinating an escuelita has been one of the most gratifying and formative experiences for me. I have been part of many escuelitas, but walking along side one of them for more than five years has been an incredible experience. Many of the members have started their own escuelitas and we are experiencing geometric multiplication. The national coordinator in Bolivia was trained in this escuelita. He speaks Quechua and Aymara, and runs the programme in these two native languages.

Experience has taught us that it is better to train the preaching club coordinators before the Level 1 seminar takes place, instead of forming the preaching clubs at the seminar. This is working well and is now standard practice. At the seminar the coordinators are helped to understand their role, especially their role in coordinating the monthly meetings in the three-year process. The big advantage of this system is that every participant is being mentored and encouraged throughout the whole process. Because of this, the dropout rate has been reduced significantly. The depth and growth provided by the monthly meetings encourage people to stay in the programme more enthusiastically and to anticipate the next seminar. In general, this model has worked very well, although better in some countries than others. We already have many generations of people around the continent who have completed the three-year programme using this model.

Teamwork and Mentoring

One of God's greatest gifts in our ministry has been the formation of a regional team for Latin America. The growth and impact of the ministry in the continent has been possible thanks to the creative and sacrificial support of Jorge Atiencia from Ecuador, Dionisio Orjuela from Colombia, and Alex Chiang from Peru. All four of us were part of the IFES movements in our countries. Our friendship, our passion for biblical preaching, and our deep commitment to our Latin American reality make us a true team. Jorge is our mentor and adviser. Alex, besides being a great preacher, is an expert in adult education. Dionisio is a tireless worker who coordinates the ministry for

Colombia and Central America. We try to get together two or three times a year. In our meetings, we pray, evaluate, plan and share our challenges in our personal, family and ministry lives. We laugh a lot together, as good Latinos.

When we realized that our work involves educating adults, we set out, as a Latin American team, to research how adults learn. One of the first things we discovered was that the Brazilian educator Paulo Freire was well known globally as an expert in this field. So we asked Alex Chiang to research more about applying Freire's work to our ministry. One of the questions that Alex asked at the beginning of his investigation was, If Freire were alive today, what would he say about Langham Preaching work? His answer was: You need to emphasize dialogue with the participants, make a previous assessment that takes into account their needs and expectations, and make the learning process more interactive. It was necessary to change our paradigms, which is a difficult and painful process. We realized that as preachers we use the monologue approach, which is quite different from the facilitator's role, which encourages the involvement and participation of the learners. Jennifer Cuthbertson's input as the international coordinator for training facilitators was key for us. She helped us to realize the need to change from a teacher-centred model to a learner-centred one so as to enhance the learning process.

The implementation of the new paradigm allowed us to develop a three-year training programme for the facilitators. We experienced Paulo Freire's relevance in this process. We use the education paradigms mentioned before. We practise a more interactive and participative approach in planning the three different levels of the preaching programme. We work with thirty-five facilitators from nine different countries who are ready to keep developing our programme in a contextual way.

Reviewing the years of ministry in Latin America, I can identify three stages. First, we depended on English-speaking facilitators. Then we invited seminary professors as facilitators. Finally, we trained a new generation of facilitators, who had been through the Langham Preaching programme, and are now training others.

One of our dreams as a regional team was to have a programme for "good and faithful" preachers who stood out among the different movements around the continent. Inspired by the parable of the talents, we saw the need to offer one-on-one mentorship to a group of ten preachers from seven different countries. We called this group the "seedbed." Our first gathering was on November 2015. Each member of the regional team agreed to mentor 2 or 3 people from the "seedbed" group. We even travelled to their cities and listened to them preaching in their local churches. In November 2016, we had our second gathering, with a focus on narrative preaching. Each of them did an exposition from a passage in Mark's Gospel and received feedback from the groups and regional team. We have found that investing in this kind of mentorship bears much fruit.

Conclusion: A Continuing Influence

There can be no doubt Chris Wright has had a significant influence, especially in laying the foundation of the basic principles on which the ministry is based. His influence was first felt through his teaching in seminaries in Argentina, Peru, Bolivia and Ecuador. Now we have a number of Latin American facilitators who are leading the movement in ten countries of the region. Chris's influence continues now mostly through his writings, and specially through his latest book *Sweeter the Honey: Preaching the Old Testament*, which has been translated into Spanish. This extraordinary book responds to two important questions: Why preach the Old Testament? How can we preach from the Old Testament? The way Chris focuses on how to include the person of Jesus in the preaching of the Old Testament is really innovative and balanced. Many of the initial lessons that he taught between 2004 and 2008 on how to preach the narratives, the law, the prophets and poetry of the Old Testament are tackled really well and he includes examples from the different genres.

In July 2016 we had a Level 3 preaching seminar for thirty-five preachers, each of whom received a copy of Chris's book. I have been told that the facilitators from Central America have also used it in their last training seminar held in Panama in August 2016. There is no doubt that this book will become our most used manual for our Level 3 seminars which focus on preaching the Old Testament.

I started this article by describing the rapid growth in numbers in the evangelical church in Latin America, and said that it was growing without depth and without managing to have any impact on society. I have the firm conviction that the Word of God is powerful to transform lives, churches, communities and society as a whole. When the Word of God is preached faithfully, clearly and in a relevant way, there will be lasting changes in Latin America.

John Stott's dream that Langham Partnership would support indigenous growth is now happening and the support of Chris Wright in this endeavour is undeniable. The Lord Jesus said, God's kingdom is like a grain of mustard seed. Chris's first seminar in October 2004 in Cochabamba may have appeared small and insignificant, but by God's grace we now have a strong preaching movement not only in Bolivia, but throughout the continent. Obviously, there is still a lot of work to do, but the impact of those who have taken the training and their preaching is the yeast that leavens our societies.

3

The Challenges of Biblical Preaching and the Response of Langham in Pakistan

Qaiser Julius

Qaiser Julius *has been director of Open Theological Seminary, Lahore, Pakistan since 2003. He received a PhD in Practical Theology from the Australian College of Theology in Sydney. He had previously completed an MA in Theological Studies at Trinity College, Bristol, UK, and an MDiv at Gujranwala Theological Seminary, Pakistan. He is general secretary of the Theological Educators Forum in Pakistan and country coordinator for the Langham Preaching Programme. His studies and writing have focused on the Christian response to persecution, particularly in the context of Pakistan.*

This article pays tribute to Dr Chris Wright for his role in starting the Langham Preaching programme in Pakistan. This programme focuses on one of the major challenges we face in Pakistan, namely the lack of training in biblical preaching. Langham has provided a quality training programme for preachers in order to foster the culture of biblical preaching within the country. This article tells the story of Langham Preaching in Pakistan and how this became an indigenous movement that is spreading rapidly throughout the country.

The Challenges of Biblical Preaching

Preachers in Pakistan are not trained in text-based preaching. Random preaching is part and parcel of the majority of preachers' pulpit ministry. Preachers rarely follow any plan for systematic, text-based preaching. This leaves the congregants uninformed about which passage will be preached on the next Sunday. It has also been observed that the majority of preachers almost never preach from the Old Testament, perhaps because they think it is no longer relevant or find it difficult to preach from. Instead, they only preach on a few of their favourite New Testament passages. One of the drawbacks of this selective preaching is that people do not have an opportunity to hear the whole of God's Word. Another is that preachers who lack skills in expository preaching often stray far from the text.

Yet God's Word is extremely important for the life and maturity of the church. It offers a lamp for our feet and a light on our path (Ps 119:105). As John Stott says, "It is the Word of God that keeps the church alive, directs and sanctifies it, reforms it and renews it. Christ rules and feeds his church through the Word of God."[1] J. I. Packer put it this way, "The church must live by God's Word as its necessary food and steer by that Word as its guiding star."[2]

Without expository preaching, churches will not be fed with God's Word as they should be, especially where churches have no Bible study programmes and the Sunday sermon is the only opportunity for teaching the Bible. How will people hear God's Word in churches in which "too often, the Bible does not set the agenda; it is simply the background music."[3]

Who is responsible for this state of affairs? Is it the preachers, or the theological colleges, or the congregations who never complain that their thirst for God's Word remains unquenched?

My purpose here is not to blame anyone. I merely wish to highlight some of the factors that may be hindering the development of a culture of biblical preaching in Pakistan.

- Many of the pastors who minister in the growing number of independent, non-denominational churches have no training in preaching at all. So it is unfair to expect text-based systematic preaching from them.

---

1. John Stott and Greg Scharf, *The Challenge of Preaching* (Carlisle: Langham Preaching Resources, 2013), 21.

2. J. I. Packer, *Engaging the Written Word of God* (Peabody: Hendrickson, 2012), 246.

3. Jonathan Lamb, *Preaching Matters* (Nottingham: IVP, 2014), 22.

- Once they leave seminary, pastors have few opportunities for ongoing training through refresher workshops or preaching conferences where they could be exposed to good biblical preaching. Additionally, after completing seminary training, some preachers do not feel the need to be further equipped.
- There is no good material in Urdu on expository preaching and hermeneutics to enable preachers to learn this skill from books. The Christian publishing house, MIK, has had one or two books translated into Urdu, but that material is not sufficient. There are good books in English, but most preachers cannot benefit from them because of the language barrier. Economic factors are also relevant, as pastors cannot afford to buy books or pay for training programmes.

All these factors contribute to a church culture in which there is a lack of good biblical preaching. As one pastor has said, "preachers cannot be blamed for not doing expository preaching as they have not been trained with this tool."

The Role of Langham Preaching Training

In 2004 Dr Pervaiz Sultan invited Dr Chris Wright to come to Pakistan and teach a workshop on expository preaching in the city of Multan. The method of preaching taught by Dr Wright was new to the majority of the participants and was eye-opening for them. Dr Wright's way of teaching was impressive, and his model sermons were outstanding examples of good expository preaching. I myself was at that workshop, and I still remember the impact they had on the participants. I and many of the others made a commitment to try to preach God's Word in this way.

It is appropriate here to share my own testimony. Dr Wright's training had such an impact on my preaching that since then I have tried as much as possible to preach every sermon in an expository way. Dr Wright's ability as trainer and preacher was so powerful that many of us who participated in that first workshop went on to become part of the Langham Preaching training group which now trains many others in Pakistan.

The Langham Preaching programme in Pakistan has gone on to make a significant contribution by training lay and ordained preachers. So far Langham has trained more than 1150 preachers from a range of denominations across the country. It is amazing to see how Langham Preaching is filling the gap in training in Pakistan.

Langham was eager to see training programmes offered in local languages. So it strategically identified potential local trainers and trained them by giving them the opportunity to lead workshops alongside experienced international trainers. These local trainers came from three regions: Karachi in the south, Rawalpindi/Islamabad in the north, and Lahore in the central part of the country. This strategy proved so successful that all three regions took independent initiatives to conduct Langham Preaching workshops with their local resources. Three theological colleges also played a key role, namely St. Thomas Theological College in Karachi, Zarephath Bible Seminary in Rawalpindi, and the Open Theological Seminary in Lahore.

With the passage of time, Langham Preaching has become a movement that is firmly established in Pakistan with local leadership, partly due to the Langham strategy of avoiding any impression that Langham Preaching is a foreign organization with unlimited funds. All Level 1 programmes are now run by locals with local resources. We receive assistance from our international partners to run Level 2 and Level 3 programmes, and to enable our work in some of the poorer areas.

Methodology of Langham Preaching

Preachers in Pakistan who have been exposed to the Langham training in expository preaching are glad to have acquired a simple and easy technique that they can use in sermon preparation, especially considering that they have very few resources of books to draw on. They find themselves equipped to study the Bible text on their own by reading it over and over again to mine its riches. They testify that this method equips them to prepare sermons without having access to resources like Bible commentaries, Bible dictionaries and the like.

One of the strengths of Langham Preaching is that the training is done in a manner that is simple and easy to understand. This has made the programme very popular in Pakistan. One participant who attended the programme in December 2016 commented: "I used to complain a lot about not having many helpful books, but this training by Langham in expository preaching has enabled me to do good preaching with my Bible alone."

Participants in the Langham Preaching workshops often get excited when they start to find truths from the biblical text for themselves. Their confidence level increases to such an extent that they feel that they can now dig treasures from God's Word on their own, simply by paying attention to the text. It is emphasized in the Langham Preaching workshops that "observation is your great asset! All you need is your eyes and your brain, and a few good questions."[4]

The Langham Preaching programme of training is exceptionally well structured, proceeding step by step to help preachers prepare sermons that are faithful, clear and relevant. Level 1 lays a good foundation by teaching basic principles of exegesis and explaining how we move from text to sermon. Level 2 teaches participants how to handle the various genres of the New Testament, while Level 3 teaches the genres of the Old Testament. As previously mentioned, preachers in Pakistan seldom preach from the Old Testament, perhaps because they think it is no longer relevant. Level 3 training shows preachers the importance of the Old Testament. In this regard, Chris Wright's book *Sweeter than Honey* is a wonderful addition to Langham resources and explains why Christians need to know the Old Testament as well as the New. These reasons are as follows: (1) The Old Testament comes to us from God; (2) The Old Testament lays the foundation for our faith; (3) The Old Testament was the Bible of Jesus.[5] The three levels of the Langham Preaching curriculum build a good understanding so that preachers can distinguish the different genres of biblical literature and take this into account in dealing with the text.

Preaching Fellowships

Those who have participated in Langham training are encouraged to form preachers' fellowships in their local areas to hone their skills in expository preaching. These fellowship groups are called preaching clubs in other parts of the world, but in Pakistan we do not use the word "club" because it has negative connotations here; instead we use the word "fellowship."

The primary function of these groups is to provide an opportunity for preachers to receive feedback on their sermons. In our part of the world, preachers do not like sharing the outlines and content of their sermons, and they hate receiving feedback on them. Feedback is perceived as negative criticism. However, Langham Preaching training brought about a big change for the better and helps participants to be ready to receive healthy feedback that refines their preaching and is ultimately good for the preacher.

---

4. Christopher Wright, "Understanding the Bible as the Words of Human Authors," in *Understanding and Using the Bible,* eds. Christopher Wright and Jonathan Lamb (London: SPCK, 2009), 28.

5. Christopher Wright, *Sweeter than Honey* (Carlisle: Langham Preaching Resources, 2015), 1–10.

Langham Preaching approaches this issue in its training sessions. There is always an opportunity for the participants to critique the model sermon preached by one of the trainers. This encourages the participants to be willing to receive productive feedback themselves. After attending the training, pastors meet once a month in the preaching fellowships and continue this process of receiving and giving feedback on each other's sermons. They are guided in their assessment of each other's work by this advice from John Stott: "This assessment should consider the way we speak, our gestures, manner and mannerisms, as well as the content of the sermon, our use of Scripture, the clarity with which we present our dominant thought and aim, structure, words, illustrations, our introduction and conclusion."[6]

Langham graduates continually inform us that these Langham fellowships have helped them to improve their sermons by positive feedback using the criteria of faithfulness, clarity and relevance.

Outcome of Langham Preaching Training

The feedback we have received from preachers trained by Langham Preaching and from some of their congregations testifies to the impact of the Langham Preaching training programme in Pakistan.

One pastor said,

> Langham Preaching is unique and deep training through which I have learned a new tool to work on the text of the Bible and this tool has made my preaching so effective.

Another pastor states,

> With the help of Langham training, I am now more confident in preaching and I find my congregants listening to me more attentively, and as a result my church is growing spiritually. Now I can see the dynamics of God's Word when it is preached with faithfulness, clarity and relevance. I really thank God for Langham for equipping me with such a wonderful preaching tool.

The lead pastor of a church in Lahore that trained their preaching team through Langham had this to say,

> We thank the Langham Preaching programme for providing training to our preachers. It was hard to get good preachers but

---

6. Stott and Scharf, *Challenge of Preaching*, 73.

now we use our own people. They do quality biblical preaching by using the principles they learned in the Langham training programmes. It has helped us to develop sermon series as well. Our congregation is so pleased because they hear good biblical preaching, which is indeed a blessing for them.

The Langham Preaching programme has been active in Pakistan since 2004, but for a long time security concerns made it impossible for us to conduct training in Quetta in Baluchistan (one of the four states of Pakistan), despite many requests from pastors there. But in November 2016 we were finally able to hold a Level 1 programme in the city of Quetta. Police authorities were not giving permission for any kind of gathering other than Sunday services, but the local pastors were so keen to have this training program that they approached the government and obtained special permission for the Langham event. A heavy contingent of police were deployed outside the church where the training was held. All the participants were extremely grateful to Langham and made a commitment to preach God's Word in an expository way. I still receive telephone calls from the participants at Quetta in which they share their sermon outlines. It is clear that they are eager to put into practice what they have learned.

It is very encouraging to see the outcome of Langham Preaching's training. These examples indicate the change that is coming in Pakistan with regard to the development of a culture of biblical preaching.

Ten Year Celebration of Langham Preaching in Pakistan

In September 2015, we celebrated ten years of Langham Preaching in Pakistan. Events were organized in three major cities where Langham Preaching has a good foothold. Dr Chris Wright graced all three occasions with his presence as the guest of honour and preached the Word of God. In Lahore, we held the programme in one of the hotels where non-Muslim hotel staff heard the testimonies of the Langham graduates and the preaching of Dr Wright. The manager of the hotel was very impressed by the preaching of the Word of God. He listened to the whole of Dr Wright's sermon and told us that he had been blessed by it. On this historic occasion the services of the Langham facilitators were acknowledged with awards of appreciation. We also initiated the John Stott Preaching Award to encourage young preachers in expository preaching.

Conclusion

All that has been said makes it clear that Langham Preaching has put down deep roots in Pakistan and given new direction to preaching in Pakistan. We thank the Lord that Langham graduates are now doing text-based preaching because they are convinced that transformation comes through the Word of God.

We also thank the Lord that the Langham Preaching training is making a difference by developing a culture of biblical preaching. Local facilitation teams are committed to the vision of taking the Langham expository preaching training to all corners of the country so that the Bible can be preached faithfully in every pulpit in Pakistan.

4

Liberating Theology?: The Mission of God in Engagement with Public Life and Its Implications for Evangelical Theological Education in Zimbabwe

Collium Banda

Collium Banda *is a Langham Scholar who studied at the Theological College of Zimbabwe, the University of South Africa (Unisa) and at Stellenbosch University in South Africa, where he completed a doctoral thesis in 2016 entitled "Empowering Hope? Jürgen Moltmann's Eschatological Challenge to Ecclesiological Responses in the Zimbabwean Context of Poverty." He has held a church pastorate and military chaplaincy in Zimbabwe and lectures on systematic theology and theological ethics at the Theological College of Zimbabwe. His research interests include Christian doctrines in the African public space, African traditional religions, African indigenous knowledge systems and Christianity in African contexts of poverty.*[1]

---

1. The author gratefully acknowledges Bishop Jake Shenk, Pastor Patson Netha and Pastor Timothy Tavaziva for being willing to be interviewed. Mrs Kuda Santungwana, Dr Raymond Motsi and Dr Bob Heaton assisted with details about the EFZ, while Dr Mike Burgess, Dr Victor Nakah, Mr Inock Siziba and Ms Busi Zwana were valuable editorial and conversation partners.

This paper evaluates the public role of evangelicalism in Zimbabwe as represented by the national body, the Evangelical Fellowship of Zimbabwe (EFZ), in the light of Christopher J. H. Wright's notion of the mission of God as a comprehensive mission. It deals with the extent to which Zimbabwean evangelicals' engagement with the national public space reflects an understanding of the comprehensive mission of God, and with the regard for theological education among Zimbabwean evangelicals in light of the need for liberating and empowering theological resources in the sociopolitical and economic crises in the country. The manner in which the EFZ has engaged moments of crisis and the actions it has taken spring from its underlying perceptions of mission.

Time and space do not allow for a detailed historical analysis of the EFZ and the socioeconomic and political crises in Zimbabwe's history. Therefore, attention will focus only on major trends within the EFZ. It should however, be noted that in their daily operations individual churches and denominations often follow different paths from those taken by the bodies to which they are affiliated.[2] It is anticipated that reflection on Wright's notion of the comprehensive mission of God will ultimately stimulate Zimbabwean evangelicals to consider prioritizing theological education that empowers and liberates them to engage their crisis-stricken context meaningfully.

The Missional God and His Comprehensive Mission

Christopher Wright is convinced that YHWH is a missional God who undertakes comprehensive redemptive and restorative work in this broken world. Furthermore, Wright conceptualizes the mission of God from a perspective that sees implications that extend beyond the covenant community of the faith. Reading and interpreting the Bible from a missional hermeneutic, Wright concludes that in the Bible we encounter a missional God.[3] *Missional* is defined as "denoting something that is related to or characterized by mission, or has the qualities, attributes or dynamics of mission."[4] The missional nature

---

2. For instance, S. Dorman points out that while the Anglican Church was supportive of Smith's UDI government, the Zimbabwe Council of Churches, the ecumenical body to which it was affiliated, provided aid to the liberation struggle through its humanitarian wing Christian Care. See S. R. Dorman, "'Rocking the Boat?': Church – NGOs and Democratization in Zimbabwe," *African Affairs* 101, no. 402 (2002): 75–92.

3. C. J. H. Wright, *The Mission of God: Unlocking the Bible's Grand Narrative* (Nottingham: IVP, 2006), 33–69.

4. Ibid., 24.

of God is present in "the self-giving movement of . . . God toward his creation and us, human beings in God's own image, but wayward and wanton."[5] Drawing from Charles R. Tabber, Wright concludes that the missional nature of God comprises his committed refusal to forsake and give up on his rebellious people and his determination "to redeem and restore fallen creation to his original design for it."[6] Thus God is missional in his redemptive, restorative, self-revealing and self-giving nature by which he reaches out to fallen humanity held captive by the dark and oppressive powers of sin. The cornerstone of the missiological character of God lies in his committed pity for hopeless, wayward captives. It was this that prompted him to take the initiative to redeem the lost and restore the broken relationship between him and his people, as exemplified in the exodus and in Jesus Christ.

Consequently, for Wright the Bible is missional in character[7] because the gist of its witness is "the story of God's mission through God's people in their engagement with God's world for the sake of the whole of God's creation."[8] This statement reveals Wright's view of the breadth of the missiological character of God and consequently of mission in general. The missional God engaged his people in their state of bondage to liberate and restore them in the exodus and in the subsequent occupation of the promised land in which Israel's nationhood was established. However, for Wright, Israel's redemption and restoration were never intended to be ends in themselves; they were processes through which Israel would extend God's redemption and restoration to other nations. This extension was the fulfilment of the Abrahamic promise that was ultimately fulfilled in Christ. However, while God revealed himself through the exodus and supremely through Jesus Christ, his Son (Heb 1:1–3), he also reveals himself to the nations through the witness of his people.

Wright places the breadth of God's redemptive and restorative mission to the whole world in a monotheistic perspective. The missional God distinguishes himself from the idol gods, making it clear that he alone is responsible for the needs of his people and all creation. Repeatedly God declares that he himself is the only living God and that idol gods are dead human creations (e.g. Deut 4:35, 39). Wright emphasizes that there are no other gods besides YHWH and

---

5. Ibid., 48.

6. Ibid.

7. Ibid., 49. He succinctly states, "The [biblical] text in itself is a product of mission in action."

8. Ibid., 21–22, 51. Here Wright criticizes the tendency he witnessed in his younger days when there seemed to be little connection between theology and mission.

that all the false gods and idols that exist are delusionary human creations and do not have the "*divine* existence that the one living God alone possesses."[9] The implication is that human beings have no one else to depend on for their entire existence but the living God.

Wright takes cognizance of biblical monotheism in a manner that ultimately affirms the comprehensive nature of the mission of God. YHWH's monotheistic declaration that he is the only living God and the categorical forbidding of the worship of idols clearly show that YHWH expects humanity to be entirely and exclusively dependent on him for *all* its needs. God asserts himself as the only sufficient redeemer and provider of all the needs of human beings. The fact that the monotheistic God forbids idolatry and demands that his people depend exclusively on him affirms the comprehensive nature of missional work. Wright shows that God's act of redeeming Israel from their Egyptian bondage through the exodus event "provided the primary model of God's idea of redemption,"[10] which is key to understanding not just the Old Testament view of salvation but also the meaning and significance of the cross of Jesus Christ in the New Testament.

The Notion of "Public"

"Public" is used here to refer to the sphere of socioeconomic and political reality. This is the sphere often (mis)understood among evangelical Christians as secular, non-spiritual or the worldly realm, with which "good" Christians should not become entangled. Kretzschmar notes how some conservative Christians view Christian faith as a private thing that is only concerned with "personal [spiritual] concerns of individuals and separated from the needs and concerns of the wider society in which we live."[11] According to this privatized faith model, the lordship of Jesus Christ is viewed in purely private spiritual terms divorced from the public realm of socioeconomics and politics. An example of a privatized view of the public sphere is the view that politics is a dirty game or the distorted view that money is the root of evil (cf. 1 Tim 6:10).

---

9. Wright, *Mission of God*, 140, 151–162.

10. Ibid., 264.

11. L. Kretzschmar, "The Gap between Belief and Action: Why Is It That Christians Do Not Practise What They Preach?" *Scriptura* 62 (1997): 313.

To the influential South African Reformed theologian Dirkie Smit, *public* designates "life in general, everyday life in reality with all and everybody."[12] It captures the whole breadth of sociopolitical and economic life, which means the "totality of life with others in the world, in a variety of forms of social institutions and relations."[13] This means that Christian faith is equally relevant to personal life and to life within the broader world of economics, politics and the natural environment. Therefore, faith and spirituality are not exclusively concerned with private religion but also with how one relates to the public issues such as politics and the economy.

For Smit, the foundation of the Christian appreciation of the public sphere stems from the fact that "the gospel is in all respects a message *about* the whole of the world *for* the whole of the world."[14] He insists on the importance of grasping the holistic nature of the gospel and says that if this is missed it is impossible to truly understand the gospel. In other words, if we overlook the fact that the gospel message spoken to Christians concerned their relation to their socioeconomic and political contexts, we will miss the holistic nature of the gospel message. In highlighting that the gospel had implications in the public square in which the believers lived out their faith, Smit is underscoring Wright's view of the comprehensive nature of God's mission.

Smit shows that although the sociopolitical and economic involvement of the emerging earliest Christian community was not as extensive as we know it today, yet the gospel message brought about "a new kind of piety and way of life"[15] that affected every area of their socioeconomic and political life. Concurring with the New Testament scholar N. T. Wright, Smit affirms that it is impossible to read the Bible and not realize the profound implications of the Christian gospel of the triune God for the whole of reality and the entirety of life.[16] This means that the gospel does not address Christians only spiritually and privately, but also it addresses them socioeconomically and politically in relation to all the public social institutions and relations in which they live.

The Bible shows that God created and faithfully sustains all that he created (Acts 17:24–28), and that Jesus Christ reconciled the world with God and

---

12. D. Smit, "What Does 'Public' Mean? Questions with a View to Public Theology," in *Christian in Public: Aims, Methodologies and Issues in Public Theology* 1, ed. L. Hansen (Stellenbosch: African Sun Media, 2007), 34.

13. Ibid.

14. Ibid.

15. Ibid., 35.

16. Ibid.

restored all things to their rightful place (Acts 3:18b–21), and that the Holy Spirit groans alongside creation with the ultimate eschatological goal of renewal and recreation (Rom 8:18–27). This all demonstrates that the triune God is concerned about both the private and the public spaces of the socioeconomic, ecological and political realms. In essence, the gospel has public implications. From a comprehensive missiological perspective, God's mission is concerned about bringing the whole reality under his *shalom* reign, this being the liberating and empowering rule of his kingdom.[17]

Evangelicals and the Public Space in Zimbabwe

The EFZ emerged within the politically volatile decade of the1960s in which Zimbabwe's two major liberation political parties were formed to spearhead the liberation of black people from colonial and racial domination. The Zimbabwe African People's Union (ZAPU) was formed in 1960, while the Zimbabwe African National Union (ZANU) (now ZANU-PF and the current governing party) was formed in 1963.

In 1965, Ian Smith issued a Unilateral Declaration of Independence from Britain with the goal of defending white minority rule over the black majority. He enacted racist and oppressive laws that eventually led to a bloody and costly war in the mid-1970s. The EFZ's formation thus took place in a demanding socioeconomic and political context.

The other two main church bodies that emerged in the volatile 1960s were the Zimbabwe Council of Churches (ZCC) formed in 1964, and the Zimbabwe Catholic Bishops Council (ZCBC) formed in 1969. Both immediately became entangled in the fight for black freedom.[18] However, the EFZ's founding objectives suggest a serious lack of direct concern for the prevailing socioeconomic and political context. As listed by Bhebhe, the founding objectives of the EFZ were as follows:

1. To provide a spiritual fellowship among evangelical Christians as a means of united action in promoting Bible teaching, prayer and Evangelical ministries in accordance with the Evangelical faith outlined in the fellowship's statement of faith, directed toward the

---

17. K. Nürnberger, "The Task of the Church concerning the Economy in a Post-Apartheid South Africa," *Missionalia* 22, no. 2 (1994): 119.

18. C. F. Hallencreutz, "A Council in Crossfire: ZCC 1964–1980," in *Church and State in Zimbabwe*, eds. C. Hallencreutz and A. Moyo (Gweru: Mambo, 1988), 113.

perfecting of individual believers, the edification and revival of the Church of Jesus Christ, and the salvation of lost souls.

2.   To co-operate with other similar Evangelical bodies throughout Africa and other countries.

3.   To take common action with a view to awakening Christian people to the danger of modernism, false cults, and from ecumenicity that is achieved at the expense of vital Christian faith.[19]

This list of objectives highly prioritizes otherworldly spiritual concerns. The list seems designed to deliberately steer the EFZ away from sociopolitical and economic issues. As implied below, the EFZ seems to have distinguished between socioeconomic and spiritual concerns and given priority to spiritual issues. Kretzschmar shows how Christians make this distinction by highlighting the following statement from a pastor in a totally different situation but a similar context.

> As a church we are here to meet the needs of our people – first of all, *the spiritual need* – and many people are frustrated with the situation in churches where politics are emphasized instead of the word of God (italics added).[20]

This could epitomize the EFZ of the 1960s, particularly when it is considered that the EFZ grew out of the Rhodesian Christian Conference (RCC), which functioned as the churches' forum of engaging the government on social issues such as education and health care. Rather than becoming bogged down with socioeconomic and political controversies, the EFZ chose to focus on spiritual issues. As if to confirm this, in an interview Jake Shenk, a former bishop of the Brethren in Christ Church and a founding member of the EFZ, stated that the EFZ developed out of a felt need for fellowship among evangelical churches and for encouragement in discipleship, church growth and church leadership development. Affirming that the EFZ distinguished between spiritual and socioeconomic and political issues, Bhebhe notes that the RCC continued as a Christian platform for addressing sociopolitical and the poor socioeconomic conditions endured by Africans.[21] It is as if evangelicals withdrew from the

---

19. S. M. Bhebhe, "Church and State in Zimbabwe: An Evangelical Appraisal," in *Church and State in Zimbabwe*, eds. C. Hallencreutz and A. Moyo (Gweru: Mambo, 1988), 321.

20. L. Kretzschmar, "Privatization of the Christian Faith: Mission, Social Ethics and the South African Baptists," *Ecclesial Studies* 1 (1998): 12.

21. Bhebhe, "Church and State," 322.

public space and left it to the RCC. Furthermore, the evangelicals expressed a negative attitude to the African quest for democracy and even considered it their "Christian duty and confession to speak out and advise against the Liberation movement."[22] They saw African liberationists as communist terrorists and agents of Russia, attempting to destabilize a Christian country. The EFZ seems to have been unaware of the incongruence of prioritizing true Christian spirituality while upholding a Christian government that pursued racially oppressive policies.

By the time Zimbabwe attained political independence in 1980, the ZCC and ZCBC had developed a heritage of engaging the public space through active involvement in opposing colonial and racial oppression of Africans. Evangelicals, on the other hand, had no such heritage to speak of. Contrary to the evangelicals' fears that the Marxist-oriented regime would be anti-Christian, the new rulers announced a policy of national reconciliation and racial integration with the former white oppressors and allowed Christianity to thrive unhindered.[23] The new rulers also embraced the churches as strategic development partners.[24] Thus, while many white evangelicals still left Zimbabwe, the warm gesture from the new Marxist-oriented rulers seems to have prompted the remaining evangelicals to avoid antagonizing the new rulers by being too critical of their policies. Thus, compared to the ZCC and ZCBC, the EFZ was largely invisible in the public space in the first decade of Zimbabwe's independence, apart from food relief efforts like the *Dura raJoseph* (Joseph's Silos/Barns) and joining with heads of denominations to take a united stand against the Fifth Brigade massacres in Matebeleland and Midlands between 1983 and 1987.[25] By and large, the EFZ was invisible as a

22. Ibid., 324.

23. A. M. Moyo, "Religion and Political Thought in Independent Zimbabwe," in *Church and State in Zimbabwe,* eds. C. F. Hallencreutz and A. Moyo (Gweru: Mambo, 1988), 204; E. Chitando, "Beyond Phenomenology: Teaching African Traditional Religions in a Zimbabwean University," *Zimbabwe Journal of Educational Research* 13, no. 2 (2001): 178; E. Chitando, "Church and Land in Zimbabwe: A Phenomenological Investigation," *International Congregational Journal* 2, no. 2 (2002): 142.

24. J. C. Weller and J. Linden, *Mainstream Christianity to 1980 in Malawi, Zambia, and Zimbabwe* (Gweru: Mambo, 1984), 216; P. Gundani, "The Catholic Church and National Development in Independent Zimbabwe" in *Church and State in Zimbabwe,* eds. C. F. Hallencreutz and A. Moyo (Gweru: Mambo, 1988), 215–249; Moyo, "Religion and Political Thought," 209–213.

25. From interviews with P. Netha and J. Shenk conducted by the author on 5 December 2016.

public defender of the poor, the powerless and the unjustly brutalized in the first decade of Zimbabwe's independence.

There are however signs that evangelicals did agonize over the need to engage the public space. For instance, Bhebhe shows that in 1986 the EFZ added to its main objectives, "promotion and coordination of development and relief assistance in needy areas" and "providing member bodies with a representative voice in matters of church and National needs."[26] Furthermore, the evangelicals formed an Ethics, Society and Development Committee. However, a statement by the Reverend Gary Smith at the 1987 AGM shows that evangelicals still placed a higher priority on evangelism and church growth. Bhebhe highlights that the Reverend Smith announced:

> The role of Evangelicals is to preach Christ and exercise Apostolic evangelism. Efforts of the government (in social development) must be met with Evangelical preaching of the Gospel. Evangelicals must be conservative in preserving the word and radical in preaching the word. We must be Evangelical in faith and evangelistic in function. When you evangelize, you bring the kingdom of God to man and thus bring righteousness and justice.[27]

This statement shows that to the evangelicals, evangelism and church growth are crucial means of engaging and transforming the public space. Therefore, rather than deal with justice issues practically, evangelicals would prefer to evangelize and pray for divine intervention. This was made evident in the 1990s when Ngwiza Mnkandla led the implementation of the Disciple a Whole Nation (DAWN) programme dubbed Target 2000, which aimed at saturating Zimbabwe with churches by the year 2000. Target 2000 coincided with the government-led Give A Dam Campaign, to which, according to Pastor Patson Netha, the EFZ contributed nine dams in rural areas. Although a holistic approach appeared, evangelism and church growth still dominated the overall perspective. The idea seems to have been that having more Christians would translate into democracy and economic prosperity. The problem with this approach is that democracy and economic prosperity remained abstract concepts.

The socioeconomic and political turmoil of the late 1990s that eventually led to the constitutional referendum of 2000 forced the EFZ into the public sphere. Events leading to the referendum included university student riots,

---

26. Bhebhe, "Church and State," 327.
27. Ibid.

workers' strikes and public demonstrations. According to Pastor Netha, EFZ General Secretary from 1994 to 2001, the evangelical body actively participated in seeking peaceful solutions to these upheavals. To safeguard freedom of worship, the EFZ took a keen interest in the drafting of the new constitution, and even called for Zimbabwe to be declared a Christian state, which demonstrated the evangelical belief that evangelism and church growth are effective means of engaging and transforming the public realm.

However, after 2000, the EFZ's public role became very controversial. At the start of that year, the EFZ was staunchly pro-democracy and vehemently opposed to the undemocratic rule of President Mugabe and his ZANU-PF party.[28] On several occasions, the EFZ leaders called for national dialogue to resolve the socioeconomic and political crisis in Zimbabwe. This indicates the beginning of a shift within the evangelical movement towards social justice. They even made attempts to broker peace as they sought to bring the ruling ZANU-PF and the opposition Movement for Democratic Change to the negotiation table.[29] During the writing of the Kairos document *The Zimbabwe We Want*, a visionary blueprint for national reconstruction, Bishop Trevor Manhanga, the chairperson of the EFZ, seemed bitterly opposed to the ruling undemocratic regime. However, when the document was ready to be presented to the political leaders and to the public in 2006, Manhanga shifted towards a pro-Mugabe stance,[30] similar to that of other prominent church leaders within the EFZ such as Andrew Wutawunashe and Ezekiel Guti.

While Manhanga could be accused of having sold out, this turnabout needs to be considered from the Pan-Africanist philosophical perspective that views President Robert Mugabe and his ZANU-PF party as the African liberators and defenders from imperialist forces. From this perspective, Mugabe is the only one who can be trusted to protect African economic wealth and power from Western imperialists.[31] Opposition parties are viewed as puppets of Western imperialists. Raftopoulos argues that many church leaders have succumbed to

28. T. O. Ranger, Afterword to *Evangelical Christianity and Democracy in Africa*, ed. T. O. Ranger (Oxford: Oxford University Press, 2006), 237–240.

29. "Church Leaders Reveal Details of Mugabe Meeting," *Zimbabwe Independent*, 24 March 2005. Available online at https://www.theindependent.co.zw/2005/03/24/church-leaders-reveal-details-of-mugabe-meeting; E. Chitando, "Prayers, Politics and Peace: The Church's Role in Zimbabwe's Crisis," *Open Space* 1 (2011): 43–48.

30. J. Tarusarira, *Reconciliation and Religio-Political Non-Conformism in Zimbabwe* (London: Routledge, 2016), 112.

31. Chitano, "Prayers," 46; A. Wutawunashe, "Godly Counsel for Party of Christian Values," [Online], 2014. http://www.herald.co.zw/godly-counsel-for-party-of-christian-values; Tarusarira, *Reconciliation*, 113.

"Mugabe's nationalism."[32] Bishop Shenk agrees, observing that a politicization of church leaders leads them to be silent about injustices lest they condemn the political party they support.[33]

What emerges is that due to the lack of a sound socioeconomic and political framework that is sufficiently informed by the comprehensive mission of God, evangelicals have been swayed by shallow nationalism. This shallow Pan-Africanism is suspicious of criticism and calls for national leadership renewal, and evangelicals have fallen victim to it. For instance, in its 2016 AGM, the EFZ announced that it had aligned its developmental work to the controversial economic indigenization and empowerment programme known as the Zimbabwe Agenda for Sustainable Socioeconomic Transformation (ZimASSET).[34] This economic blueprint is based on the political ideology of ZANU-PF. The EFZ's action is tantamount to being co-opted by the ruling elite, because the EFZ does not really need to fit its prophetic, pastoral or priestly role to political party ideologies in order to be effective for God's holistic missional agenda. On other occasions, evangelicals have used Romans 13:1–7 to suppress national dissent against Mugabe's despotic regime.[35] This demonstrates that they have been co-opted by the ruling elites and have a shallow theological response to socioeconomic and political issues.

However, it is true that the EFZ does attempt to influence government policies. It sees prayer, evangelism and church growth as key strategies for transforming the public sphere, hence these are strongly emphasized.[36] In its 2016 AGM report, the EFZ reported that it had defended the space of the church and freedom of conscience[37] by resisting the implementation of the National Schools Pledge that threatened to replace prayer in schools. In addition to community and social programmes, the EFZ lobbied the governor of the Reserve Bank of Zimbabwe over monetary policies that negatively

---

32. B. Raftopoulos, "The Crisis in Zimbabwe, 1998–2008," in *Becoming Zimbabwe: A History from the Pre-Colonial Period to 2008*, eds. B. Raftopoulos and A. Mlambo (Harare: Weaver, 2009), 227.

33. Interview with J. Shenk conducted by author.

34. B. Makwara, "General Secretary's Report," *EFZ 2016 Annual Report*, 10.

35. L. Togarasei, "'Let Everyone Be Subject to Governing Authorities': The Interpretation of New Testament Political Ethics towards and after Zimbabwe's 2002 Presidential Elections," *Scriptura: International Journal of Bible, Religion and Theology in Southern Africa* 85 (2004): 73–80; C. Banda and B. Senokoane, "The Interplay between the Christian Sacralization of Human Authority and Political Repression in Zimbabwe," *Religion & Theology* 16 (2009): 207–245.

36. S. Munyeza, "President's Report," *EFZ 2016 Annual Report*, 2–5.

37. Makwara, "General Secretary's Report," 9.

affected the poor.[38] There are also efforts to revive discussions on the 2006 Kairos Document *The Zimbabwe We Want*.[39] To achieve a holistic agenda, five commissions have been set up, namely the Commission for Ministry Development, the Gender Development Commission, the Humanitarian, Relief and Development Commission, the Peace and Justice Commission and the Research and Development Commission.[40] These commissions are linked to the strategic priority areas of 2014–2018, namely holistic/integral ministry, strengthening organizational capacity, empowering youth and women, and maximizing impact on the nation.[41]

However, considering that the EFZ has since simplified its vision statement to read: "*A fellowship of Evangelicals fulfilling the Great Commission to impact the nation in all aspects of life*" and its mission statement to read: "*To mobilise, empower and network evangelicals for the accomplishment of the Great Commission in Zimbabwe*,"[42] the operations of the commissions and the strategic priorities still remain at the mercy of a narrow understanding of mission and salvation. This will not change as long as a critical socioeconomic theological-ethical framework is not formulated. Furthermore, the wording of the current vision and mission of the EFZ perpetuates the old idea, implicit in the body's founding objectives of 1962, that evangelism and discipleship will radically transform Zimbabwe's socioeconomic and political situation. In order not to appear to be driven solely by a desire for political relevance, the EFZ's commissions and strategic priorities must be anchored on a clearly articulated theological-ethical framework that is informed by the comprehensive mission of God.

Essential Aspects in the Church's Engagement of the Public Square

In order to transcend the evangelistic mode and operate from a position informed by the comprehensive mission of God in crisis-stricken Zimbabwe, evangelicals must consider the following three important questions, formulated by Dirkie Smit as a basis for meaningful engagement with the public sphere:

What constitutes a good and moral society?

---

38. Ibid., 9–11.
39. Munyeza, "President's Report," 4; Makwara, "General Secretary's Report," 10.
40. EFZ, EFZ Commissions, 2016. [Online], http://efzimbabwe.org.
41. Makwara, "General Secretary's Report," 15–16.
42. EFZ, *About EFZ*, 2016 [Online], http://efzimbabwe.org.

What constitutes good and moral people?

What constitutes good and moral decision-making.[43]

These questions, which will guide the discussion below, are useful in conceptualizing how evangelicals can formulate a process informed by a meaningful comprehensive mission of God in engaging the public square in Zimbabwe.

Smit's first question about what constitutes a good and moral society, is concerned with the vision of "a good society."[44] The question that the EFZ needs to ask is: "As evangelicals, what kind of society do we envision or dream of?" For Smit (and indeed Wright), belief in the just and loving Creator God who has explicitly declared his love for the poor and powerless, the widows and the orphans, calls for an evangelical Christian imagination of life in Zimbabwe inspired by God's *shalom* vision for his world. A mission-of-God-informed evangelical vision for a just and life-enhancing world must realize the theological seriousness of poverty,[45] seeing the world from the perspective of God's restlessness because of the suffering of his people and entire creation.[46] The EFZ's preoccupation with evangelism and church growth has an eschatological perspective to it, that of saving and preparing people for the coming kingdom of God. However, the EFZ needs to understand that saving and preparing people for the coming kingdom does not excuse them from addressing social injustice issues in a practical way. As Moltmann has highlighted, the integrity of our expectation of the coming kingdom is demonstrated in how we deal with present injustices.[47]

When the evangelical vision of a good society is informed by the triune Creator God who, based on his shalom vision for his world, has embarked on a comprehensive mission, the plan for socioeconomic and political prosperity will not be instructed by political ideology such as ZimASSET, or be subject to shallow Mugabean nationalism. Rather, it will be informed by the God of justice

---

43. D. Smit, *Essays in Public Theology: Collected Essays* 1, ed. E. M. Conradie (Stellenbosch: African Sun Media, 2007), 380.

44. Ibid., 381–385.

45. C. Banda, "Empowering Hope? Jürgen Moltmann's Eschatological Challenge to Ecclesiological Responses in the Zimbabwean Context of Poverty," PhD thesis Stellenbosch University, 2016, 180–183.

46. Nürnberger, "Task of the Church," 119.

47. See J. Moltmann, *Theology of Hope: On the Ground and the Implications of a Christian Eschatology* (Minneapolis: Fortress, 1967) and *The Church in the Power of the Spirit: A Contribution to Messianic Ecclesiology* (New York: Harper & Row, 1977), 190.

and peace, whose option is for the poor and the oppressed. Wright's notion of the comprehensive mission of God, when viewed in light of Smit's ethics of a good society, calls the EFZ to be a visionary body that is not satisfied with anything below God's abundant life (John 10:10). It means that evangelicals cannot be Christianly Pan-Africanist or nationalist and yet continue to uphold a government regime that inhibits the human flourishing of its citizens.

Smit's second question about what constitutes good and moral people focuses on who we are called to be as Christians. It emphasizes that we ought to faithfully embody our vision for a good society and demonstrate integrity by practically living out the vision.[48] It is disturbing that while claiming to be committed to justice and the welfare of the poor, the powerless and the oppressed, evangelicals in both colonial and independent Zimbabwe have been easily co-opted by the ruling oppressive elites. Evangelicals must boldly embody their vision of a just and fair society by being committed to it in word and action. The comprehensive mission of God has ecclesiological implications, calling the church to be a church that actually practices economic justice. Evangelicals need to have a well-articulated vision to which they are committed and by which they escape undemocratic and selfish tendencies. What is also needed is a critically discerning heart by which they avoid being co-opted by the ruling elites and avoid falling under the spell of uncritical nationalism and empty patriotism. This means that "there is need to increase the levels of political literacy of many [Zimbabwean evangelical] leaders."[49]

Smit's third question about what constitutes good and moral decision-making is concerned with "an ethics of doing," and captures the need for a fruitful theological-ethical framework for responding to issues. In its basic form, an ethics of doing raises the question: "What are we to do when we are faced with specific issues?"[50] It concerns theological-ethical methods and systems of analysing socioeconomic and political situations. The fundamental evangelical way of responding to crises is seeking "God's will" and "God's leading" in every situation. However, Mukonyora and Chitando and Manyonganise[51] rightly observe that evangelicals often turn to divine intervention in a manner that both underplays and stifles the development of critical skills and methods of

---

48. Smit, *Essays in Public Theology*, 385–392.

49. Chitando and Manyonganise, "Voices," 102.

50. Smit, *Essays in Public Theology*, 392.

51. I. Mukonyora, "Foundations for Democracy in Zimbabwean Evangelical Christianity," in *Evangelical Christianity and Democracy in Africa,* ed. T. O. Ranger (Oxford: Oxford University Press, 2008), 131–160; Chitando and Manyonganise, "Voices," 101.

engaging their socioeconomic and political context meaningfully. Reliance on prayer and fasting must not be employed in a superstitious, lazy and escapist manner that undermines God-empowered human agency.

Based on the work of Malcom Damon and Heinz Eduard Tödt, Smit suggests that a fruitful way of responding to issues requires a process that has three steps, namely, "seeing, judging and acting."[52] Similarly, Bedford-Strohm calls churches to a public theology model that holistically combines divine intervention and a deep appreciation of the dynamics of political and economic reality in order to engage the politicians and the political context meaningfully and prophetically.[53] This calls upon churches to develop a sound ecclesiology that recognizes the role of Christians who are informed about socioeconomic and political issues.

To a very large extent the problems in the EFZ are due to poor ecclesiology that is fixated on the glamorous role of self-appointed prophets and apostles resulting in an un[der]developed priesthood of all believers.[54] The growing trend of referring to churches as "ministries" has given rise to an entrepreneurial ecclesiology in which the centre of power lies with the founding leaders, the "anointed mighty" men and women of God who in many cases are self-appointed prophets and apostles, rather than a communal ecclesiology that recognizes the priesthood of all believers. An entrepreneurial ecclesiological framework allows church leaders to fill roles they are not technically suited to. It also ends up undermining the technical input and advice of technocrats, who are ignored or maligned as "fleshly advisers" and a hindrance to the vision of those who have faith in the God of no impossibilities. This approach essentially uses faith in a superstitious way that "absolve[s] human beings of their responsibility in creating the crisis as well as their role in its resolution."[55]

---

52. Ibid., 393.

53. H. Bedford-Strohm, "Poverty and Public Theology: Advocacy of the Church in Pluralistic Society," *International Journal of Public Theology* 2, no. 2 (2008), 144–162.

54. As an example of this, according to Raymond Motsi (2016), it was Bishop Trevor Manhanga during his term as president of EFZ who changed the concept of heads of denominations from individual church denominational heads to heads of the main church bodies, namely the heads of the ZCC, EFZ and ZCBC.

55. Chitando and Manyonganise, "Voices," 101.

The Implications of the Mission of God for Evangelical Theological Education in the Zimbabwean Crisis-Riddled Context

The problems surrounding the limited capacity of evangelicals to meaningfully engage the Zimbabwean context ultimately raise questions about the nature of theological training in the evangelical institutions in this country. Does theological training in Zimbabwe empower and liberate church leaders for meaningful engagement within the prevailing socioeconomic and political context? Mark Noll's book *The Scandal of the Evangelical Mind*, published in 1994, could have been bemoaning the poor state of theological reflection among Zimbabwean evangelicals.

Evangelical theological education in Zimbabwe is in crisis and therefore crippled when it comes to meaningfully empowering pastors to function in a liberating manner. Evangelicals tend to emphasize the notion of "being called" to the ministry and "having the anointing of God" in a manner which undermines and makes a mockery of the value of theological education. There is a sense that the "called" and "anointed" have no need to undergo a lengthy, demanding and rigorous theological programme of study. There is a need to be liberated from this dangerously crippling view of theological education if evangelicals are to produce theologians who can play an empowering and liberating role in the crisis-riddled context of Zimbabwe.

Furthermore, evangelicals in Zimbabwe have not sufficiently prioritized serious theological education by investing in it bountifully. Evangelicals continue to "have numerous elementary and often sub-standard and poorly staffed Bible schools all over the place."[56] The evidence of this is the recent closure of many evangelical theological colleges in the country by the Zimbabwe Council of Higher of Education for failing to fulfil government regulations for higher education institutions.[57] As things stand nearly four decades after national independence, ZAOGA's recently government-accredited Zimbabwe Ezekiel Guti University is the only evangelical institution of higher learning with its own independent accreditation. However, in light of the controversial nature of Ezekiel Guti among conservative evangelicals, time will tell how many evangelicals will be comfortable having theological qualifications that openly bear his name. Nonetheless, the growth of evangelical education in Zimbabwe has suffered greatly from internal rivalry and competition. It would

---

56. Bhebhe, "Church and State," 317.

57. "Govt Closes Chiyangwa Varsity," *Daily News*, 31 March 2014. Available online at www.dailynews.co.zw/articles/2014/03/31/govt-closes-chiyangwa-varsity.

be beneficial to pull resources together and build one high quality institution instead of having a string of poorly resourced individual institutions. A classic example of the disregard for good quality theological education among evangelicals is the EFZ's neglect and finally abandonment of the Theological College of Zimbabwe in 1998. In so doing, the EFZ abandoned a much needed wellspring of critical and vigorous reflection to empower the operations of the church.

A further crippling problem in evangelical theological education in Zimbabwe lies in its foreign and private nature. Evangelical education in Zimbabwe is predominantly reliant on foreign Western funding and can only be accessed in privately owned institutions. However, non-evangelical theological education is readily offered in public universities, where students are exposed to influential indigenous scholars and a curriculum that is pertinent to the socioeconomic and political context in Zimbabwe and are thus empowered to function publically. Furthermore, many Zimbabwean evangelicals with doctorates have scarcely published, nor have they undertaken a career in public universities where they can influence the theological curricula of public universities. This means that evangelical theology is by and large not influencing top Zimbabwean evangelical scholarship.

The serious weaknesses confronting evangelical theological education in Zimbabwe highlight an urgent need for theological education to be empowered and liberated by the comprehensive mission of God. When theological education in Zimbabwe is itself empowered and liberated, it will in turn enable evangelicals to function in an empowering and liberating manner in Zimbabwe. It is my view that evangelical Christianity has not taken Africanness seriously to the point of effectively dialoguing with it respectfully in order to bring about the needed socioeconomic and political transformation. "Instead of a dialogue in order to bring about transformation, Africanness is often wished away as if non-existent, or as if amassing more evangelical doctrines will transform the African worldview."[58] The result is that, instead of addressing specific raging socioeconomic and political dilemmas, evangelical theology in Africa gives priority "a defence of evangelical doctrines and correct hermeneutical biblical interpretation,"[59] as if these alone are sufficient to heal the crises in Africa.

---

58. Banda, *Empowering Hope*, 208.

59. Ibid.

Conclusion

Wright's notion of the comprehensive mission of God challenges evangelical Christians in Zimbabwe to reflect critically on the way they have existed and been engaged in the crisis-riddled Zimbabwean context. They ought to consider how their theological understanding of mission can be liberated from the simplistic view of evangelism and church growth as the means of transforming the socioeconomic and political crises that beset Zimbabwe. Evangelicals in Zimbabwe must develop a holistic theological framework that engages their socioeconomic and political context in an empowering and liberating way.

References

Banda, C. "Empowering Hope? Jürgen Moltmann's Eschatological Challenge to Ecclesiological Responses in the Zimbabwean Context of Poverty." PhD thesis, Stellenbosch University, 2016.

Banda, C., and Senokoane, B. B. "The Interplay between the Christian Sacralization of Human Authority and Political Repression in Zimbabwe." *Religion & Theology* 16 (2009): 207–245.

Bedford-Strohm, H. "Poverty and Public Theology: Advocacy of the Church in Pluralistic Society." *International Journal of Public Theology* 2, no. 2 (2008): 144–162.

Bhebhe, S. M. "Church and State in Zimbabwe: An Evangelical Appraisal." In *Church and State in Zimbabwe,* edited by Carl Hallencreutz and Ambrose Moyo, 313–333. Gweru: Mambo, 1988.

Chitando, E. "Beyond Phenomenology: Teaching African Traditional Religions in a Zimbabwean University." *Zimbabwe Journal of Educational Research* 13, no. 2 (2001): 177–195.

———. "Church and Land in Zimbabwe: A Phenomenological Investigation." *International Congregational Journal* 2, no. 2 (2002): 138.

———. "Prayers, Politics and Peace: The Church's Role in Zimbabwe's Crisis." *Open Space* 1 (2011): 43–48.

Chitando, E., and M. Manyonganise. "Voices from Faith-based Communities." In *Zimbabwe in Transition: A View from Within*, edited by T. Murithi and A. Mawadza, 77–111. Pretoria: The Institute of Justice and Reconciliation, 2011.

Daily News Zimbabwe. "Govt closes Chiyangwa Varsity." *DailyNews Live* (Harare). 31 March 2014 [Online]. Available: http://www.dailynews.co.zw/articles/2014/03/31/govt-closes-chiyangwa-varsity.

Dorman, S. R. "'Rocking the Boat?': Church – NGOs and Democratization in Zimbabwe." *African Affairs* 101, no. 402 (2002): 75–92.

EFZ. EFZ Commissions. [Online]. Available: http://efzimbabwe.org/?page_id=1418.

EFZ. *About EFZ*. [Online]. Available: http://efzimbabwe.org/.

Gundani, P. "The Catholic Church and National Development in Independent Zimbabwe." In *Church and State in Zimbabwe*, edited by Carl Hallencreutz and Ambrose Moyo, 215–249. Gweru: Mambo, 1988.

Hallencreutz, C. F. "A Council in Crossfire: ZCC 1964–1980." In *Church and State in Zimbabwe*, edited by Carl Hallencreutz and Ambrose Moyo, 51–113. Gweru: Mambo, 1988.

Kretzschmar, L. "The Gap between Belief and Action: Why Is It That Christians Do Not Practise What They Preach?" *Scriptura* 62 (1997): 311–321.

———. "Privatization of the Christian Faith: Mission, Social Ethics and the South African Baptists." *Ecclesial Studies* 1 (1998).

Makwara, B. "General Secretary's Report." *EFZ 2016 Annual Report*, 8–16.

Moltmann, J. *Theology of Hope: On the Ground and the Implications of a Christian Eschatology*. Translated by M. Kohl. Minneapolis: Fortress, 1967.

———. *The Church in the Power of the Spirit: A Contribution to Messianic Ecclesiology*. Translated by M. Kohl. New York: Harper & Row, 1977.

Moyo, A. M. "Religion and Political Thought in Independent Zimbabwe." In *Church and State in Zimbabwe*, edited by C. Hallencreutz and A. Moyo, 197–214. Gweru: Mambo, 1988.

Mukonyora, I. "Foundations for Democracy in Zimbabwean Evangelical Christianity." In *Evangelical Christianity and Democracy in Africa*, edited by T. O. Ranger, 131–160. Oxford: Oxford University Press, 2008.

Munyeza, S. "President's Report." *EFZ 2016 Annual Report*, 2–5.

Noll, M. *The Scandal of the Evangelical Mind*. Grand Rapids: Eerdmans, 1994.

Nürnberger, K. "The Task of the Church concerning the Economy in a Post-Apartheid South Africa." *Missionalia* 22, no. 2 (1994): 118–146.

Raftopoulos, B. "The Crisis in Zimbabwe, 1998–2008." In *Becoming Zimbabwe: A History from the Pre-Colonial Period to 2008*, edited by B. Raftopoulos and A. Mlambo, 201–232. Harare: Weaver, 2009.

Ranger, T. O. "Afterword." In *Evangelical Christianity and Democracy in Africa*. Edited by T. O. Ranger. Oxford: Oxford University, 2006. [Online]. Available: http://www.oxfordscholarship.com/view/10.1093/acprof:oso/9780195174779.001.0001/acprof-9780195174779-chapter-9. Accessed on 11 December 2016.

Smit, D. "What Does 'Public' Mean? Questions with a View to Public Theology." In *Christian in Public: Aims, Methodologies and Issues in Public Theology* 1, edited by L. Hansen, 11–46. Stellenbosch: African Sun Media, 2007.

———. *Essays in Public Theology: Collected Essays 1*. Edited by E. M. Conradie. Stellenbosch: African Sun Media, 2007.

Tarusarira, J. *Reconciliation and Religio-Political Non-Conformism in Zimbabwe*. London: Routledge, 2016.

Togarasei, L. "'Let Everyone Be Subject to Governing Authorities': The Interpretation of New Testament Political Ethics towards and after Zimbabwe's 2002 Presidential Elections." *Scriptura: International Journal of Bible, Religion and Theology in Southern Africa* 85(2004): 73–80.

Weller, J. C., and J. Linden. *Mainstream Christianity to 1980 in Malawi, Zambia, and Zimbabwe.* Gweru: Mambo, 1984.

Wright, C. J. H. *The Mission of God: Unlocking the Bible's Grand Narrative.* Nottingham: IVP, 2006.

Wutawunashe, A. "Godly Counsel for Party of Christian Values." *The Herald*, 17 November 2014. Available online at www.herald.co.zw/godly-counsel-for-party-of-christian-values/.

Zimbabwe Independent. "Church Leaders Reveal Details of Mugabe Meeting." 24 March 2005. Available online at www.theindependent.co.zw/2005/03/24/church-leaders-reveal-details-of-mugabe-meeting/.

5

The Impact of Langham Scholars on Theological Development among Romanian Evangelicals

Danut Manastireanu

Danut Manastireanu *is a member of the Academic Advisory Council of Osijek Institute for Mission Studies. He holds a PhD in Theology from Brunel University, London. His thesis was published in 2012 as "A Perichoretic Model of the Church: The Trinitarian Ecclesiology of Dumitru Staniloae." He is also the author of various articles and studies on evangelicalism in Romania. He previously served as director for faith and development for World Vision International (Middle East and Eastern Europe Region) and as lecturer in theology at Emmanuel Bible Institute (now Emmanuel University), Oradea, Romania. He is also involved in the Lausanne Movement, being a member of the Theology Working Group.*

Becoming a Langham Scholar

Before 1997, when I had the privilege of joining the Langham Scholars' community, I knew very little about Langham Partnership. Of course, every evangelical in Romania knew the name John Stott. The Romanian translation of his little book *Basic Christianity* had been smuggled into the country during the 1970s, and many of us read it countless times and shared it with our friends who were seeking God.

I will never forget my first face-to-face meeting with "Uncle John," when he visited Oradea, Romania, in 1988. We spent a few days in Bible study at the back of a Baptist church there, hiding from the eyes of the communist secret police. A few years later, when I had just finished my Master's studies at London Bible College and started teaching hermeneutics at Emmanuel Bible Institute in Oradea, Stott visited us again. He was in Romania to participate in an important consultation on theological education in Central and Eastern Europe after the fall of communism. This time I had the privilege of being his translator for a series of courses he taught at the Bible school.

Over the next ten years, I was engaged in part-time doctoral studies while working full-time teaching theology, and then serving in a regional position for World Vision International. I was able to visit the London School of Theology for periods of two to four weeks, and at those times All Souls, Langham was my "home church."

Two special encounters with "Uncle John" will always stay fresh in my mind. The first was a meal I ate in his modest apartment close to the church, together with a group of people that included another Langham Scholar, my friend Silviu Rogobete (who did a PhD on Dumitru Staniloae's ontology of love.[1]). The second encounter was also a visit to Uncle John, this time in the company of another dear friend, the Orthodox Fr. Stelian Tofana, an important Romanian biblical scholar, who was supported financially by John Stott so that he could spend two months at Tyndale House in Cambridge.

As to Chris Wright, Uncle John's worthy successor at Langham, I was certainly aware of his work while I was doing my theological studies. However, as my specialty was systematic theology with an emphasis on interaction with Eastern Orthodoxy, I must confess that I did not interact very much with his theological thinking during my doctoral studies.

The opportunity to know Chris Wright personally and to interact actively with him as a theologian and church leader came through the work of the Lausanne Theology Working Group, which he led prior to the Cape Town Congress in 2010. I joined the working group in 2007 at the recommendation of Peter Kuzmic, one of the senior Lausanne leaders, and probably the most respected evangelical leader in Central and Eastern Europe. The working group

---

1. Dumitru Staniloae (1903–1993) was the most important Romanian theologian and one of the key Orthodox scholars of the twentieth century. Both Silviu Rogobete and I focused on his theological work in an attempt to bridge the theological gap between evangelicals and the majority ecclesial tradition in our country.

was the most rewarding Lausanne process in which I was ever involved, and that was due to a large extent to the wise and able leadership of Chris Wright.

In what follows, I would like to share with you what I have learned about our leader, whom we jokingly referred to as "OT Wright," in contrast to the famous biblical scholar and former bishop N. T. Wright who teaches at the University of St Andrews.

Chris Wright is undoubtedly one of the most articulate conservative Old Testament scholars alive. His commitment to the trustworthiness and authority of the Bible is beyond any doubt. At the same time he has been able to keep a firm distance from the often useless, rationalistic, inerrantist debates haunting American evangelicalism. His non-involvement in these debates has made him much more useful for us in the Majority World, where we are worried about the intentional or unintentional attempts of American evangelicals to export those debates to our lands and to turn them into shibboleths of biblical orthodoxy.

Chris Wright's biblical scholarship is not dry academism but is imbued with genuine Irish passion, tempered by his typical British gentleman's manner. Chris is passionate about understanding profoundly and expounding relevantly the written Word of God, but he ably steers away from the fundamentalist temptation to idolize the text. His supreme allegiance is to Christ, the incarnate Word of God, to whom the Scripture bears witness.

Chris is also a student of culture, and a scholar who is committed to seeing the message of the gospel thoroughly incarnated in every culture in which it takes root. This became obvious during the meetings of the LTWG. Under Chris's able leadership, the cultural and theological diversity of this group became a source of strength and reciprocal enrichment, as is obvious in the various documents we created. In these, nobody will ever discern any trace of Western voices dominating the voices from the Majority World, as unfortunately is still the case in much of evangelicalism, including the Lausanne Movement.

During our meetings, but especially during the Lausanne III Congress in Cape Town, we witnessed another very important gift of our leader: his prophetic spirit, clothed in great diplomatic garments and accompanied by genuine humility, yet still uncompromising and sharp as a razor. Chris never shied away from speaking truth to power, whether informally or officially from the platform, as anybody can witness in the recordings available from this important event. There were delicate moments during the congress, as when "holy misogyny" tried to have its way, or when a Western leader preaching about people groups declared that all Orthodox diaspora communities were "unreached with the gospel." Chris Wright listened to our legitimate concerns, and acted promptly and wisely. Many of the participants were very thankful for his actions.

We, in the LTWG, could not have had a better leader, as is proven by the fact that this Lausanne task force has been struggling since Chris left to dedicate himself to the demanding task of leading the Langham Partnership.

When Uncle John's health started deteriorating, we, the direct beneficiaries of his vision for training evangelical leaders for the Majority World, started wondering who was going to continue his legacy. When Chris Wright was appointed as his successor, we all rejoiced. With his proverbial wisdom, John Stott had made the right choice. This, I believe, is obvious now to all who benefit, directly or indirectly from the diverse ministry of the Langham Partnership in more than seventy countries worldwide. Among these beneficiaries are Romanian evangelicals, to whom I now turn my attention.

Evangelicals in Romania

On an optimistic estimate, evangelicals represent about 4 percent of the population of Romania, a country dominated by Eastern Orthodoxy (accounting for 86 percent of the population). The oldest evangelicals in Romania are the Baptists, who recently celebrated 160 years of existence in the country. For most of their history, Romanian evangelicals have been a marginalized minority, persecuted either by the state or by the Orthodox hierarchy. Even today, more than twenty-five years after the fall of communism, evangelical denominations like the Baptists, Brethren and Pentecostals are referred to as "sects." Together with Jehovah's Witnesses and Mormons, they are viewed by the majority population as something foreign, even dangerous, to the national identity.

Evangelicals are virtually ignored in official histories and are practically invisible to the majority of Romanians. As a Romanian political scholar argues, "Romanian Protestantism [which is basically evangelical] is interesting to the public eye only as long as it is not pertinent from a social point of view."[2]

---

2. Daniel Barbu, "Invizibilitatea politica a omului evanghelic" [The Political Invisibility of the Evangelical], in *Omul evanghelic. O explorare a comunitatilor protestante romanesti* [The Evangelical: An Exploration of Romanian Protestant Communities], eds. Dorin Dobrincu and Danut Manastireanu, a collective work by some twenty authors, evangelicals and non-evangelicals, that will be published in 2017 by Polirom. This may well be the first academic work exploring evangelical communities in Romania from a variety of perspectives.

The last few years have seen a slight change as Polirom, the leading Romanian publisher, has issued three novels by young writers who have family connections to the evangelical community. The first, written by Dan Lungu, who is now a senator in the Romanian parliament, was inspired by the context of the evangelical church to which his wife belonged.[3] The second, published in 2016, came from a young and quite controversial author, Vasile Ernu, who is a leftist political and social activist, who comes from a Baptist family. His novel is a piece of pseudo-fiction, tracing the history of three generations of evangelicals in the south of Bessarabia (now the Republic of Moldova, a Romanian territory occupied by Stalin's Soviet Union in 1940).[4]

The latest title in this unusual group of books was written by Ioan T. Morar, whose father was a Baptist pastor and who knows evangelicalism very well from the inside, even if he is not a member of one of our churches. He is a former diplomat, and a right-leaning political thinker, living in self-imposed exile in France. Like Vasile Ernu's book, his novel is pseudo-fiction. It gives a very subjective account of the history of an evangelical musical group that he and his father knew personally.[5] The group was part of a revival movement in Romania in the early 1970s and called themselves "the awakened ones."[6] They were led by a very gifted musician, Jan Gligor, and so were also known as the *Janisti*.[7] In the course of their spiritual quest, they were in turn Baptist, Pentecostals, and Seventh-Day Adventists, before finally embracing Judaism (including circumcision), immigrating to Israel and joining a kibbutz. After the fall of communism, some of them returned to Romania and established a sort of messianic congregation. This incredible story has special significance for me personally because one of my aunts was associated with this revival movement. This led to her being excommunicated from our Baptist church in Iasi by order of the communist secret police, with the full cooperation of the pastor of that church who was a collaborator. My aunt was then accused of

---

3. Dan Lungu, *Cum sa uiti o femeie* [How to Forget A Woman] (Iasi: Polirom, 2009). The Christian community is called Nehemiah Church, and is an independent evangelical church of Brethren extraction. I know the pastor there well.

4. Vasile Ernu, *O trilogie a marginalilor. Sectantii* [A Trilogy of the Marginals: The Sectarians] (Iasi: Polirom, 2015). In one chapter Ernu describes his experience during the few years when he was involved in my discipleship ministry in Iasi, Romania. The chapter is dedicated to me under the name "Uncle Dan." Vasile dedicates other pages in the book to "Uncle Iosif," who is Iosif Ton, the most important Romanian evangelical leader alive. Many other key leaders and important events for the Romanian evangelicals feature in this book.

5. Ioan T. Morar, *Sarbatoarea corturilor* [The Feast of Tabernacles] (Iasi: Polirom, 2016).

6. "*Trezitii*" in Romanian.

7. In the novel, the character who represents him is called Jac.

"religious delirium" – a very serious charge at that time, and sentenced to ten years' imprisonment in a psychiatric ward. When she came out in the mid-1980s, she was a broken human being.

These three books have stirred up a previously unheard of level of debate and interest in evangelicalism in Romanian society. I am reminded of an Old Testament instance when a prophet refused to speak in God's name, and God had to use other, more unusual, means of communication.[8]

Because the majority of Romanian evangelicals came from the lower classes, their level of general education was not high, and their leaders too lacked theological education. Some evangelical denominations did have their own theological schools (the Baptists since 1921 and the Pentecostals since 1976), but these were strictly controlled by communist authorities and the level of education they offered was quite basic. It was only after the fall of communism in 1989 that they began to become university-level theological institutions.

Things have changed quite a lot since then. In an article published in 2007 for *East-West Church & Ministry Report* (EWCMR), I counted about fifty Romanian evangelicals with doctorates in theology.[9] I plan to repeat this research in 2017 and I am sure the number is no way beyond one hundred theological doctorates. To be fair, not all of these doctoral degrees are of equal value, nor have all those who hold these degrees gone on to significant careers as professors or writers in the field of theology. Yet, there has never been a time in the history of Romanian evangelicalism when so many or our leaders have had post-graduate theological education.

Evangelicals in Romania owe a lot to evangelicals in the West. We could not have made such progress in theological education without their assistance. However, relationships between Westerners and the Majority World have seldom been completely smooth, and that has also been the case when it comes to theological cooperation. We have seen such things as Western paternalism at work and the fostering of irrelevant theological debates.[10] Yet I

---

8. See Num 22:22–39.

9. "Romanian Evangelicals with Doctorates in Theology," *East-West Church & Ministry Report* 15, no. 1 (2007): 7–12, available online at http://eastwestreport.org/22-english/e15-1/357-romanian-evangelicals-with-doctorates-in-theology-danut-manastireanu-compiler (accessed 15 December 2016).

10. For further discussion of this painful reality, see the articles I have written for *EWCMR*: "Western Assistance in Theological Training for Romanian Evangelicals to 1989," *East-West Church & Ministry Report* 14, no. 3 (2006): 1–4; "Western Assistance in Theological Training for Romanian Evangelicals Since 1989 – Part I," *East-West Church & Ministry Report* 14, no. 4 (2006): 6–9; and "Western Assistance in Theological Training for Romanian Evangelicals since 1989 – Part II," *East-West Church & Ministry Report* 15, no. 1 (2007): 5–6.

am convinced that, at the end of it all Romanian evangelicalism continues to mature theologically, even if it may still be in its teenage years.

We have not yet been very successful in developing thoroughly enculturated versions of evangelical theology, as has happened in Latin America and is currently happening in Africa and Asia. Nevertheless, we in Eastern Europe have a unique opportunity: we are called to develop evangelical theology in the context of Eastern Orthodoxy.

Evangelicalism is a Western ecclesial reality and developed in the context of the Western theological paradigm and its debates. The juridical paradigm that underlies the understanding of salvation and spirituality, the institutional framework, the rationalism of the Enlightenment with its underlying individualism and its implications for biblical hermeneutics, the conflict between liberalism and fundamentalism and the so-called "culture wars" in which the church is involved, especially in the United States – all these are Western phenomena and they affect, in varying degrees Catholicism, Protestantism and Evangelicalism. The Orthodox mindset, be it Eastern (Chalcedonian) or Oriental (non-Chalcedonian), is radically different. It is more relational and communitarian, more speculative and mystical, more process-oriented, more incarnational and organic. Such a worldview results in a very different theological paradigm from that in the West. As a result, even when the two "halves" of the church are using the same theological terms, the meanings attached to the words can be quite different.

Let me give just one example. When it comes to understanding salvation and conversion, the West emphasizes the wrath of God towards sin, which is an offence against his honour and involves complex issues of justice, with conversion being viewed as a (more or less) instantaneous event meant to deal with those problems. As a result, conversion and discipleship are perceived as two rather distinct phases of the Christian life. Not so in the East. For the Orthodox, the problem of sin is one of a broken relationship between creature and Creator. The heart of God is broken by the rebellion of his children, as in the parable of the prodigal son. Conversion, therefore, is not viewed as an event but as a process, a constant reorientation (*metanoia*) in relation to Christ. Thus conversion and discipleship are not separated but are two sides of the same coin.

Both perspectives have their strengths and weaknesses, like all human ideas. Nevertheless, an evangelical paradigm that grows organically from within the Eastern context would unavoidably look very different from its Western counterpart. This issue has never been explored before, and the result of such an endeavour may well be a source of renewal in the context of the current identity struggles in world evangelicalism, especially in its Western expressions. Romanian Langham Scholars have much to contribute in this regard, but they also face considerable difficulties as they seek to do so.

Langham Scholars in Romania

Romanian Langham Scholars face unusual problems because of the post-communist pathologies that still affect evangelical communities in our country. Most leaders run their institutions in an authoritarian manner, for that was the only leadership paradigm they witnessed during the communist era. Furthermore, the failure of leaders and of churches to deal with the tragedy of collaboration with the communist regime has had all kinds of spiritual and relational repercussions, with victims still hoping for restitution while perpetrators deny their crimes or lack the courage to confess them for fear that they will be rejected by the community. In the meantime, the innocent blood of the victims cries out from the ground like that of Abel, the sins of the traitors are not atoned for, and the guilty ones are not restored through the love of the community.

It does not help that theological institutions tend to be ambitiously oversized, which leaves them dependent on financial support from abroad, particularly from the West. As so often happens, financial dependence results in foreign control and manipulation and the importation of theological and political conflicts from the West into Romania. Very few Romanian evangelical leaders have the guts to resist such pressures and temptations.

All of us in the Romanian Langham community have felt the impact of these pathologies, as will become clear when I recount the experience of the Romanian evangelicals who have participated in the Langham Scholars programme.

Three of those Langham Scholars who did their doctoral studies in the United States and Great Britain are no longer counted as members of the programme because for various reasons, mostly related to their family situations and the impossibility of finding a teaching position in Romania, they remained in the West and were unable to fulfil their commitment to return and minister in their own country.

Of those who did attempt to stay in Romania, two of us were forced out of academia and instead found ourselves working, still in theological roles, for international Christian organizations like World Vision International and the British Bible Society. In these capacities we are able to serve the Christian communities in our own countries and beyond, promoting integral mission and a relevant involvement of the body of Christ in society. Both of us have served as members of the Lausanne Theology Working Group and one of us has also become involved in the core group of the Lausanne–Orthodox Initiative. In addition, we continue to use every available opportunity to teach theology in Romania and abroad, and to publish academically in our areas of expertise.

Other Langham Scholars have found that they could get teaching posts only outside Romania or in areas other than theology. Thus two Romanian Langham Scholars are involved in university-level theological education in Hungary, while another scholar had to accept a post as lecturer in political science, with an emphasis on human rights, particularly because of his interest and expertise in anthropology and sociology. From that position he was able to support the accreditation of a master's programme in theology and social work at the state university in Timisoara. He continues to be a bridge between academia and the church, playing an essential role in promoting a robust public theology in a secular context.

Sadly, other Romanian Langham Scholars who have clashed with the legalism and dogmatism of denominational leaders have also found themselves excluded from academia. As a result, they have channelled their energy into planting and nurturing vibrant life in local churches while doing theological teaching unofficially, through various extension programmes.

The upshot is that of the fourteen Romanian Langham Scholars, only two are actually teaching in evangelical theological institutions in Romania! One is teaching Old Testament theology at the Pentecostal Theological Institute in Bucharest, while the other has taken over the academic leadership of a Pentecostal theological degree programme at the state university in the west of Romania.

The problems that the Romanian scholars were having in finding teaching positions led the Langham Partnership Regional Council for Europe to organize a consultation in Bucharest in December 2006. It was a painful time for us all, as all cards were put on the table. Chris Wright came to understand the complicated context in which we are called to serve. He was surprised to learn that in less than ten years, twenty-five evangelical scholars, many of international standing, had been forced to leave one of the most prominent evangelical theological schools in Romania. And the situation was not much better in other theological schools.

A Few Conclusions

So what can we learn from this very difficult situation?

1. *Context determines the form and aims of our ministry.* Ministry is not done in a vacuum. It has to respond to concrete issues and needs arising from the particular context in which our churches are called to witness for Christ. Our theological training, done with the support of Langham scholarships, has prepared us thoroughly for the challenging realities in which we live.

2. *The importance of theological dialogue with Orthodoxy.* Since Orthodoxy is the faith of the majority of Romanians, we cannot ignore this great ecclesial tradition. We can learn much from it, particularly in terms of the historical and patristic rootedness of the Christian faith, the centrality of Trinitarianism, and the central role of community. At the same time, to the extent that there is openness for it, we can contribute by enriching that tradition with evangelical strengths such as our commitment to the Bible, our emphasis on the need for personal conversion, and our passion for witnessing.

3. *The principle of incarnation as a model for ministry.* By following the living example of highly committed servants of God like John Stott and Chris Wright, and by learning from our theological mentors, we have realized that we cannot serve people "from above" but have to become "like them," with the exception of sin. We have found in Langham a great model of servanthood, and we try by God's grace to live it out ourselves and pass it on to others. I would also call this the principle of multiplication.

4. *You win some, you lose some.* Because God has created us as free moral agents, we will always lose some of those with whom we work. Langham hoped that all Romanian Langham Scholars would be able to stay and teach in Romania, serving the Romanian evangelical community with their expertise and personal example. For a number of complex reasons, often objective but at times also subjective, this was not always possible. Sad as this may be, we have to continue to trust God and to honour our commitment to Romania as best as we can, by his grace and through the power of the Spirit.

5. *Building towards the future.* Evangelicalism does not have a long history in Romania. Yet in spite of the pathologies of the communist

past that still haunt our society, we now have a relatively well-trained leadership. It is time to start laying a more solid foundation for the future. There is much to do: we need a more up-to-date scholarly translation of the Bible;[11] we need original Bible commentaries that are scholarly, accurate and contextually meaningful; we need to develop a contextual systematic theology that is both evangelical and Eastern; and a new generation trained in ethics and public theology who will be willing and able to engage with the great challenges confronting Romanian society. This task may sound overwhelming, but for the first time in history we have hope that we can successfully tackle it and make a difference in our world.

In a little book I wrote a few years ago for World Vision I argued that we in the post-communist world may need to go through forty years in the desert of transition before being able to enter the promised land of normality – whatever that is.[12] The communist ideology caused such damage that two or more generations may pass before we can see any degree of normal life in our land. But "the land of milk and honey" will not just fall into our lap. We will have to fight for it. In this respect, we can learn by studying how Moses prepared his people for crossing the River Jordan, and how Joshua led Israel in the conquest of the holy land. This is a task for all theologians, biblical scholars, dogmatic theologians or specialists in ethics and pastoral theology. Out time has come, and we are grateful to Langham for giving us the tools and supporting us in getting ready for the task. Now it is our turn to give back. May God be honoured through our faithful response!

---

11. At the moment, a small group of Romanian evangelical scholars are working together to produce a major revision of the Cornilescu translation of the Bible, which was funded by the British Bible Society and is used by all evangelical denominations in Romania.

12. Danut Manastireanu, *After Liberation, Then What? Enabling and Protecting Communities in Post-Authoritarian Contexts* (Monrovia, CA: World Vision International, 2012).

6

Unity in Diversity: The Slavic Bible Commentary

Peter Penner

Peter Penner *was born in Kazakhstan and grew up in Germany. He is director of advanced studies at the Eurasian Accrediting Association. He earned a ThD from the University of South Africa, Pretoria, in 1998 and a Dr Habilitus from the Károli Gáspár University in Budapest, Hungary, in 2012. He has served as principal and later dean of St. Petersburg Christian University in Russia, director of biblical studies and contextual missiology at the International Baptist Theological Seminary in Prague, and dean and later director of advanced studies at TCM International Institute in Heiligenkreuz, Austria. He was the New Testament editor of the Slavic Bible Commentary.*

The launch of the Slavic Bible Commentary in October 2016 was the culmination of a successful partnership between Langham and the Eurasian Accrediting Association (EAAA), both organizations that have been inspired by the leadership of Christopher Wright.

The partnership began to take shape after stimulating conversations with Christopher Wright, Riad Kassis, and Pieter Kwant at the International Council for Evangelical Theological Education (ICETE) consultation in 2009 in Sopron, Hungary.[1] The EAAA then began to discuss the possibility of producing a contextually relevant commentary for Russian-speaking readers and churches.

Chris Wright's contribution to the project was significant. His visits to the Commonwealth of Independent States (CIS – also called the Russian Commonwealth) contributed to the growing trust between the Langham

---

1. www.icete-edu.org/hungary/index.htm.

team and the group of leaders and theologians from the former Soviet Union that would sustain the project through difficult times in the region. He also contributed theologically through his advocacy of a missional hermeneutic in which the Bible is read and interpreted from a mission perspective in mind. This approach guided the editorial team when it came to drawing up guidelines for those writing the commentary. Moreover, his paper at the 2009 ICETE gathering, which emphasized community building,[2] inspired this community of writers in the EAAA to embark on preparing a Eurasian community-driven commentary using community hermeneutics.

In this paper I will outline the facts and processes involved in the creation of the SBC as well as the underlying contextual issues and methodological discussions that contributed to the commentary's hermeneutical framework.

What Is the Slavic Bible Commentary?

The SBC, the latest contribution to the Langham series of contextual commentaries, was born on 1 October 2016 as 9,000 freshly printed copies left the press: 6,000 copies in Ukraine and 3,000 copies in Russia. The need to print the commentary in two countries reminds us that it was the continuing tensions between Russia and Ukraine made it impossible to have one print run to serve all those who would be reading this commentary in the Russian language.

The ninety-four contributors represent diverse backgrounds including Anglican, Brethren, Christian Missionary Alliance, evangelical Christians, Baptists, Mennonite, Messianic Jews, New Life Charismatic, and Pentecostal.[3] They come from Australia, Austria, Belarus, the Czech Republic, Germany, Israel, Kyrgyzstan, Moldova, Russia, Ukraine and the United States. This list of countries is a good representation of where Russian-speaking evangelical Christians currently live: some in the expansive territory of the former Soviet Union and many others in the diaspora. The list of contributors also reflects the dominant role of men in the Russian-speaking Christian community, for only a seventh of the contributors are female, while the editorial board is entirely male.[4] Despite some issues and tensions, the unifying impact of the project was and continues to be immense.

---

2. Chris Wright, "Wrapping Up and Moving Forward," *ICETE* 2009, 5–9.

3. Peter Penner, "Slavic Bible Commentary," *East-West Church & Ministry Report* 25, no. 1 (Winter 2017): 3.

4. Sergei V. Sannikov, ed., *Славянский Библейский Комментарий [Slavic Bible Commentary]* (Kiev: EAAA, Knigonosha, 2016), 5–8.

The need for a Slavic commentary had long been obvious, but the Soviet context and its wide-ranging implications prevented it from being produced sooner.[5] Even though the term Slavic may be misleading – for the commentary is written in Russian – it was the Russian Bible and the Russian language as a *lingua franca* that has been uniting Christians in the region. For some two hundred years the Russian Synodal Bible has created a common foundation for the church throughout the region, including for those who are non-Slavic.[6] Much later, the Bible was translated into Ukrainian and other regional languages. The translations into Uzbek, Tatar, Crimean Tatar and Turkmen languages were only printed in 2016 and 2017.[7]

Times are changing, and the need will arise to translate this commentary, in a contextually relevant way, into the different languages of the former Soviet Union. This need will emerge as Bibles and other Christian literature become available in those languages, to help these ethnic churches develop their own identity as part of the overall Christian identity. The collapse of the Soviet Union, the growth of churches and denominations in various countries and language groups, and access to theological education over the last quarter century[8] created a foundation on which God cultivated the fruit of the SBC. The commentary is a celebration of how God has intervened in history, throwing open the door to religious freedom, and blessing the church with a relevant commentary.[9]

The SBC is the result of cooperation between Eastern and Western Christians who have agreed to serve the churches together. It was launched thanks to the generosity of Western sisters and brothers, and particularly of Langham Literature, who inspired the Euro-Asian editorial team and walked alongside the authors helping them to be servants of God's people.

The SBC is written by evangelical ministers in the CIS for pastors, preachers, teachers, leaders of small groups, and those involved in various types of ministry in the local church or mission. It offers a contextual evangelical perspective that should help readers interpret and apply biblical truths to

---

5. Mary Raber, "Remembering the Russian Bible Commentary," in *History and Mission in Europe: Continuing the Conversation* (Schwarzenfeld: Neufeld Verlag, 2011), 304.

6. Sannikov, *Славянский Библейский Комментарий [Slavic Bible Commentary]*, 18.

7. The complete Uzbek, Tatar, Crimean Tatar and Turkmen Bible translations were presented to the wider public for the first time during the Central Asian Consultation in February 2017.

8. See announcement (http://www.e-aaa.info) of the 25th anniversary celebration of EAAA (16–21 октября 2017: Юбилейное общее собрание [Anniversary General Assembly]).

9. Celebrating the SBC: http://sbc.e-aaa.info.

various aspects of life. It reflects the traditional way of reading the biblical text in local evangelical churches in the CIS. The commentary also includes more than seventy articles that are contextually relevant and touch on important issues of spiritual and practical Christian living in the CIS. The team of authors tried to meet the readers where they are and lead them to the next level of Bible interpretation, while giving them material and tools for their ministry.

Missional hermeneutics, as presented by a variety of authors and especially by Chris Wright, was a major influence, as also was community hermeneutics, which is important given the religious context and tradition of the region. Lengthy discussions on hermeneutical lenses and contextual issues resulted in consensual decisions about the hermeneutical framework and contextual emphases of the commentary. One of the key goals set before the authors and editors was to identify the common needs and understandings of the readers and how they could be helped to become better ministers. The SBC as a tool will help individual readers and communities to change their church so that it becomes missional and relevant in and for their region.

Contextuality

Contextuality often seems like a magic buzzword, but is in fact difficult to do. A contextual commentary should respond to the needs experienced by the readers and explain the biblical text in such a way that it applies to issues that are relevant to where readers live in terms that relate to them and their situation.[10] So an indepth understanding of the context is vital, as well as a missional attitude that is keen to connect biblical truths with the present context of the church.

The church in the former Soviet Union is still at a transitional stage. The revival experienced in the 1980s and 1990s was succeeded by a period of stagnation, with the result that there is now debate about whether and how to work towards evangelism and church renewal.[11] Following the break-up of the Soviet Union and before the turn of the millennium, the church experienced

---

10. A number of books have recently dealt with the contextualization of the message of the Scriptures – see chapter 10 in Harriet S. Hill, *The Bible at Cultural Crossroads: From Translation to Communication* (Manchester: Kinderhook; New York: St. Jerome, 2006), 178–192.

11. See the conversation on revival at the Central and Eastern European Association of Mission Studies, triggered by Anne-Marie Kool's paper, "The Relation between Evangelism, Revival and Church Renewal in Four Mission Documents in the Light of the Ministry of James A. Stewart in Central and Eastern Europe," CEEAMS Conference 13–17 February 2017, Osijek, Croatia.

both an exodus as many Christians emigrated to the West and an influx of previously unchurched people.

Tensions and wars between the newly established countries that had been part of the Soviet Union paralyzed the church in its mission. The conflict in Eastern Ukraine received the most press coverage,[12] but for decades there have been armed collisions, sometimes flaring up into outright war, between Azerbaijan and Armenia. Many in Azerbaijan, a Muslim country, are rejecting Christianity on the grounds that "Christian" Armenia has taken their land. Armenia, on the other hand, suffers from severe poverty, although the evangelical church is growing in the midst of crisis. Since the 1990s, Moldova has been divided into two, Transnistria and Moldova, as a result of war between Russia and Moldova. The North Caucasus area is full of ethnic conflicts. A few years ago ethnic conflict also erupted between Kyrgyz and Uzbeks in Kyrgyzstan.[13]

These conflicts have hindered the effectiveness of the churches in their outreach, and have separated and estranged members of the same denomination in different countries. For this and other reasons, evangelical churches have reached a plateau in their growth. The context of the CIS has rapidly changed from a predominantly hostile socialist society to a culture of rampant capitalism and materialism. At the same time, majority religious communities intentionally limit the activities and impact of evangelical churches. In some countries there is outright persecution; in others Protestant and evangelical churches and their members are a small minority, a diaspora among their own people, as governments give majority religions preferential treatment. Issues like these have to be reflected in the interpretation of Scripture, for the biblical text portrays similar situations and offers guidelines and help for the people of God. Contributors to the SBC attempted to let the biblical text speak into such contexts.[14]

A contextual Bible commentary such as the SBC also needs to investigate what resources for Bible study are already available in the region. The first full

---

12. Mykhailo Cherenkov, "'Maidan Theology' in Experience and Reflection of the Younger Generation of Ukrainian Protestants," *Acta Missiologiae: Journal for Reflection on Missiological Issues and Mission Practice in Central and Eastern Europe* 6 (2017): 18; Roman Lunkin, "Religious Politics in Crimea, 2014–2016," *East-West Church & Ministry Report* 25, no. 1 (2017): 1–3.

13. Dominic Lieven and John McGarry: "Ethnic Conflict in the Soviet Union and Its Successor States" in *The Politics of Ethnic Conflict Regulation: Case Studies of Protracted Ethnic Conflicts*, eds. John McGarry and Brendan O'Leary (London: Routledge, 1993).

14. Some of this contextuality may need to be more focused when the SBC is translated into other languages of the region.

Bible commentary written in the Russian language appeared about a century before the advent of the SBC. This work, which is known as the Lopukhin Bible Commentary, is still heavily used by both Orthodox believers and evangelicals. Even though Bible interpretation was not been the first priority of the Orthodox Church, a number of resources and books were developed before and after the 1917 Revolution, and some of this material has been reprinted.[15]

One of the first evangelical commentaries to be translated into Russian was William Barclay's Daily Study Bible Series. The New Testament books were completed and printed by 1985, and the Old Testament books by 1994.[16] Since the 1990s, many other individual commentaries and commentary series have been translated, including the Bible Speaks Today series, a number of commentaries by John McArthur, and several volumes of the so-called "C-Series" from Germany published by Light in the East. Resources like Bible introductions, New and Old Testament theologies, word study handbooks, linguistic keys, dictionaries, etc., have provided for a modest biblical studies library. The SBC refers to these resources in order to point readers to additional literature that is available in Russian.[17] In this, it is different from translated commentaries or dictionaries in which references usually point exclusively to Western sources written in a language that is not accessible to the reader.

A commentary usually develops over a long period of time and grows out of the writer's experience of teaching and preaching on a particular Bible book. It is shaped by ideas and responses to conversations within a classroom, church or other group. Usually those conversations take place in a Western context. Because it is often impossible to comment on all aspects of the biblical text due to the length limits set for a commentary, authors need to make choices in the process of writing. Often such choices are determined by the most frequent questions raised by the author's target audience. Study Bibles especially reflect such selection processes.[18] Thus the majority of published commentaries are focused mainly on a Western audience and respond to questions from that

---

15. Orthodox seminaries in the diaspora were important repositories for such literature in the time of the Soviet Union.

16. Raber, "Remembering the Russian Bible Commentary," 323–325.

17. Unpublished document setting out the principles, goals and guidelines for the SBC, developed by the editorial team and presented to the authors in 2013.

18. The festschrift for Grant R. Osborne was recommended to the editorial team as a helpful tool for looking at different approaches and decisions when writing a Bible commentary, see *On the Writing of New Testament Commentaries: Festschrift for Grant R. Osborne on the Occasion of His 70th Birthday*, Texts and Editions for New Testament Study, eds. Stanley E. Porter, Eckhard J. Schnabel, and Grant R. Osborne (Leiden; Boston: Brill, 2013).

background, making them contextually relevant primarily for the Western church. Yet, they often claim to present objective truth and to be relevant to contexts all over the world.

The SBC, however, draws on the experience of this commentary's authors in their Euro-Asian context. Interpretations are based on the questions that are frequently asked of particular Bible passages in this context and on the discussion topics raised in Bible studies in churches, youth work, society, and so on. To test the relevance of the SBC's contextual interpretation, prospective readers were also asked to respond to drafts of various commentary texts and to identify issues that needed to be addressed. These discussions with believers' communities, pastors, missionaries, denominational leaders, and teachers in various seminaries helped to focus the commentary. Because the context and the communities are so diverse, more conversation needs to happen around the interpretation in order to make the commentary still more relevant, especially to the overall Eurasian context.[19]

The seventy articles interspersed with the commentary texts add tremendous value to SBC's contextuality. They function almost like an excursus, an in-depth discussion of a topic that has been raised in the commentary, adding a primarily theological reflection of it. The articles pick up and expand issues and themes discussed and relevant to the context. They build a bridge between the Bible text and the context of the reader, and help the reader to understand the concept in the Bible and how it translates into the present context. The articles sometimes arise from a particular Bible text, but then, like a theme in biblical theology, discuss all scriptural input on this topic and give a fuller understanding of it. They also help readers to think through and understand hermeneutical issues and questions regarding the use of Scripture; they address issues of relevance and application. The short articles of between 500 and 1500 words are quick to read, summarize the key points of the topic, and in their simple language help practitioners in the church and mission to fulfil their calling in ministry.[20]

Scripture was not written free from a culture and context, and the commentary becomes an instrument for interpreting biblical truths in and for a particular context. Contextualization is, therefore, an important matter that needs to be implemented wisely and formulated within a well-reflected hermeneutical framework.

---

19. Unpublished document setting out the principles, goals and guidelines for the SBC; see also Penner, "Slavic Bible Commentary," 4.

20. Sannikov, *Славянский Библейский Комментарий [Slavic Bible Commentary]*, 10–11.

Hermeneutical Framework

When working on the interpretation of Scripture in a particular context, like the Euro-Asian context, it is important to clarify thought through and intuitive views of Scripture and recognize Scripture as such. For the editorial team and for all SBC authors, it was thus important to formulate a clear common position on Scripture. Since the changes in the former Soviet Union, Western Bible teachers have brought their own understanding of Scripture to the CIS and there they have continued their battles against those whom they believe hold a wrong view of Scripture. Thus documents such as the Chicago Statement on Biblical Inerrancy were introduced at CIS Bible schools as foundational.[21] It seemed, in some discussions, that the battles of Western biblical scholars were simply being transplanted into a different context, even though the relationship of Eastern European and Central Asian churches and Christians to Scripture had always been different from that in the West and Western debates had not affected the Eastern churches' high view of Scripture. This is true for both evangelicals in the Russian-speaking world and the Orthodox Church, for both hold similar positions on Scripture.[22]

This high view of Scripture held by the Eastern church is reflected in the commentary. This is evident in the decision to limit the length of the introductions to each Bible book so that the commentary would not waste space dealing with introductory questions (who wrote what when) and talking *about* the text, but would instead focus on interpreting the Bible text itself. It is also apparent in the decision to provide background information about particular passages only it contributes to a fuller understanding of the passage. Attention is thus focused on the explanation of words and phrases, presentation of the passage's theology and its application to current challenges in church and society.[23]

---

21. In the 1990s, there were many Westerners teaching in the new Bible colleges and seminaries in the CIS, and they often took their battles on inerrancy and other issues from the West to the East. Students and pastors were not particularly interested in these debates, saying, "We love the Bible and God's church and we are interested in the message of the Bible." Similar debates were introduced into the EAAA general assemblies with the goal of pushing schools to sign on to modernistic Western positions and labeling those who were not interested as liberals. (See the minutes of the EAAA General Assembly in 2001).

22. Alexander I. Negrov, *Biblical Interpretation in the Russian Orthodox Church: A Historical and Hermeneutical Perspective*, Beiträge Zur Historischen Theologie (Tübingen: Mohr Siebeck, 2008).

23. Following the paragraph on «Библия в славянском контексте» [The Bible in Slavic Context], the SBC comments on its view of how to interpret the Bible [Истолкование Библии]. Sannikov, *Славянский Библейский Комментарий [Slavic Bible Commentary]*, 18.

Evangelicals in Eurasia agree with the Orthodox Church that the Old and New Testament Scriptures are the trustworthy and sufficient Word of God as well as the highest authority for life and conduct for every believer and for the whole people of God.[24] At the same time, the authors of the commentary connect to the international community of evangelicals and embrace the Lausanne Covenant and its statement on Scripture, which uses terms such as "inspiration, truthfulness and authority."[25] In the study guide found on the Lausanne Movement's website, John Stott stresses that "God's words are not like our words" but that they are reliable and initiate action. He comments that the Word "illumines the minds of God's people in every culture to perceive its truth freshly through their own eyes and thus discloses to the whole church ever more of the many-coloured wisdom of God."[26] And concludes by saying, "Thus the whole church is needed to receive God's whole revelation in all its beauty and richness."[27] These words became a guideline and a motto in the interpretation of Scripture for Russian readers of the SBC.

A high view of Scripture is closely connected to the canonical approach of the commentary, which recognizes the Protestant text of the Bible that includes 39 Old Testament books and 27 New Testament books, but follows the order of these books in the Russian Synodal Bible.[28] Therefore the SBC does not include an interpretation of the texts known as Old Testament apocrypha and pseudepigrapha. The text of the Bible is understood to be given to the whole church, with the understanding that Scripture is clear and interprets itself. When authors worked with particular topics or issues, intertextuality was important in showing how different parts of Scripture shed light on each other and on the issues. At the same time, each book's distinctiveness and coherent message were maintained in order to show the diversity within the unity of the canon.[29]

---

24. Ibid.

25. See Section 2 of the Lausanne Covenant, "The Authority and Power of the Bible." See also John Stott, *The Lausanne Covenant: Complete Text with Study Guide*, with a preface by Chris Wright (Lausanne Movement, 2012), 16ff.

26. John Stott, "The Lausanne Covenant: An Exposition and Commentary by John Stott," Lausanne Occasional Paper 3, https://www.lausanne.org/content/lop/lop-3#2, March 2017.

27. Ibid.

28. Sannikov, *Славянский Библейский Комментарий [Slavic Bible Commentary]*, 15. The Russian Synodal Bible follows, for instance, the LXX structure of the book of Psalms, or places after the Gospels and Acts the Epistle of James, then 1 and 2 Peter, etc., instead of continuing with Romans.

29. Ibid., 16–17.

Community hermeneutic was one of the key principles in the hermeneutical framework. It informed how authors and editors worked together with their local communities, with the wider community of Bible interpreters, and with the editorial board. It was the simple and familiar approach known in the region for many years, when the church under communism had little access to theological education and literature and so read the Bible together. The challenges faced by the evangelical church in the former Soviet Union were similar to those early Anabaptists experienced, and so they arrived at a similar application of community hermeneutics.[30] The approach involves asking one main question as we sit around the table with the Bible: "Do you see what I see in the text?" This opens up a conversation in which the interpretation of a particular text is widened and, at the same time, corrected. So in the process of writing the commentary, an intentional hermeneutical community was created, not only as editorial team members engaged with the authors, but also among the authors themselves and, sometimes, even including other groups, such as theology students, church members and Christian professionals. In some cases, the commentary offers several possible interpretations of texts in order to invite the reader to also participate in the hermeneutical community.[31]

As previously mentioned, it was important to contextualize the powerful message of God through his word by using appropriate language, literary associations, and the cultural experience of a variety of Eurasian contexts. When talking about the missional context of the commentary, it was important to recognize the predominantly Orthodox and Muslim context in which evangelical communities live and witness as a minority. The commentary, therefore, needed to be written in a way that respected and considered the surrounding context and majority religious communities.[32] As regards the Orthodox Church, the commentary needed to recognize not only its involvement in preserving the early church tradition but also its participation in the mission of God.[33] At the same time, it was important to recognize the

---

30. John Yoder, *Preface to Theology Christology and Theological Method* (Grand Rapids: Baker, 2002); Stuart Murray, *Biblical Interpretation in the Anabaptist Tradition* 3, Studies in the Believers Church Tradition (Kitchener, Ontario: Pandora, 2000).

31. Sannikov, *Славянский Библейский Комментарий [Slavic Bible Commentary]*, 10–11.

32. Walter Sawatsky, "Orthodox-Evangelical Protestant Dialogue on Mission – Challenges and Shifting Options," *Acta Missiologiae: Journal for Reflection on Missiological Issues and Mission Practice in Central and Eastern Europe* 1 (2008): 183–184.

33. Father Leonid Kishkovsky, "The Mission of the Russian Orthodox Church after Communism," *East-West Church & Ministry Report* 1, no. 3 (1993): 1–2; Holy and Great Council, "The Mission of the Orthodox Church in Today's World. Official Documents of the Holy and

different faces of Islam in Eurasia, for example in Central Asia, North Caucasus, and other places in order to evaluate what would attract those readers to the commentary and how it could become for them an understandable witness to the Christian Scripture.[34] However, the dominant influence looming over the entire commentary was the post-communist context, with its overall influence on majority and minority religions and world views. This influence needs to be kept in perspective in order to arrive at a relevant, contemporary interpretation, moving from the "then and there" of Bible times to the "here and now" of Eastern Europe and Central Asia.

The intentional hermeneutical community is understood as a missional community, and so an important lens for reading the Scriptures is missional hermeneutics. Both the community and the Bible text are partakers in the mission of God. Chris Wright defines missional hermeneutics in the first two chapters of his book *The Mission of God* (which has also been translated into Russian)[35] as well as through the list of six ingredients of a missional reading of a Bible text that he presented when teaching at Heiligenkreuz in Austria in July 2016.[36] The discussion on missional hermeneutics has been picked up on a wider scale, beyond the SBC, as some Russian language publications show.[37] In discussing the hermeneutical framework, missional hermeneutics has been understood by the editorial team as involving the use of the following three lenses: (1) Identifying the meta-narrative of the Scripture text in each book and in each text portion that is being interpreted in relation to the *missio Dei* and the author of the Bible text.[38] (2) Mission is the purpose behind the Bible

---

Great Council of the Orthodox Church," https://www.holycouncil.org/-/mission-Orthodox-Church-Todays-World. Pentecost 2016.

34. Mihai Malancea, "Евангельская миссия на территории постсоветской Средней Азии [Evangelical Mission on the Territory of the Post-Soviet Central Asia]," in *Новые Горизонты Миссии [New Horizons in Mission]* (Черкассы: Коллоквиум, 2015), 269–272.

35. Christopher J. H. Wright, *The Mission of God: Unlocking the Bible's Grand Narrative* (Nottingham: IVP, 2006).

36. Six ingredients of a missional reading of a Bible text: some questions to ask:
    1. How is this text or book linked to the overall biblical grand narrative – the "drama of Scripture"?
    2. How does it reveal the God of the Bible?
    3. What aspects of the human condition does it illustrate?
    4. What aspects of the biblical gospel does it illustrate?
    5. What does it show about God's people?
    6. What does it show about God's universal involvement with all nations, or all creation?

37. Peter Penner, *Миссиология и Герменевтика: Прочтение библейских текстов в контексте миссии [Missiology and Hermeneutics]* (Черкассы: Коллоквиум, 2014).

38. This is similar to Chris Wright's approach of an overall grand narrative.

text. Scripture is written and preserved to this day to identify God and his work with his people. The text speaks of God's mission throughout time and the *missio Dei* in the text needs to be identified, understood and interpreted for the present reader.[39] (3) The missional context and the mandate of the reader is carried in the Bible text, which invites the reader to participate in the mission of God. This needs to be reflected in the contextual application.[40] Reading and interpreting the Bible missionally became a roadmap for the commentary, helping us to identify the different voices in the text of Scripture and to keep the focus clearly on the missional community. The missional hermeneutic has brought together and united the readers and interpreters around the text to recognize in the Bible God's purpose in history and time and God's calling through the Scriptures.

Some Concluding Observations and Perspectives

In the former Soviet Union, the Bible was the book that guided evangelicals through different stages of their history.[41] A Bible commentary such as the SBC needs to meet readers where they are and strengthen their rootedness in the Bible. It needs to confirm what the Bible has been in this region – a precious book that individuals and communities need to read and listen to in order to continue the faithful journey in following the Lord. In the dark days of the Soviet Union, the Scripture, its teachings and preaching, was a rare good. God has provided for the church and, in his grace and goodness, has blessed it with many competent Russian-speaking authors who are equipped to write a Bible commentary.[42] In a tremendously changed world with new challenges, the church needs the Scriptures as a light on its way. The Bible commentary can be a bridge that connects Scripture with the people and

---

39. As the text is written as a missional text to the readers, this has implications for the interpretation of the Scriptures.

40. Peter Penner, "Missional Hermeneutics," *Acta Missiologiae: Journal for Reflection on Missiological Issues and Mission Practice in Central and Eastern Europe* 4 (2015): 11–16.

41. Raber, "Remembering the Russian Bible Commentary," 304–307.

42. Marina Sergeyevna Karetnikova, "The Missionary Movement in Russia: The Nineteenth and the Twentieth Centuries," in *Mission in the Former Soviet Union* (Schwarzenfeld, Germany: Neufeld Verlag, 2005), 71–73. Marina Sergeyevna was a contributor to the SBC but died before the commentary was officially published. She was the soul of Russian-speaking evangelicals and one of the first Russian faculty who communicated to the younger generation the value of the Scriptures in her teaching of the history of evangelicals in the former Soviet Union. A number of authors and members of the editorial committee had been her students and later her colleagues.

also helps to unite the people of God, independently of their denominational, ethnic, or other backgrounds. The SBC commentary harks back to the memory of Bible interpretation under persecution and makes the Bible understandable for readers in the twenty-first century.

While the launch of the commentary was due to an effective partnership between the Eurasian Accrediting Association and Langham Partnership, there are many others who supported the team and are not even mentioned in the commentary. It is indeed a great model of cooperation in the global mission context. As the celebration of this commentary continues, it is important to take the next steps and strengthen the multicultural church in the CIS by expanding the impact of the SBC.[43] While for now the majority of the church still uses Russian, the younger generation in many CIS countries are losing this ability and using their national languages. So it is important that we translate, contextualize and help formulate a biblical and theological language for those ethnic communities, especially those that experience pressure and even persecution.

References

Cherenkov, Mykhailo. "'Maidan Theology' in Experience and Reflection of the Younger Generation of Ukrainian Protestants." *Acta Missiologiae: Journal for Reflection on Missiological Issues and Mission Practice in Central and Eastern Europe* 6 (2017): 18.

Hill, Harriet S. *The Bible at Cultural Crossroads: From Translation to Communication.* Manchester; Kinderhook, NY: St. Jerome, 2006.

Holy and Great Council. "The Mission of the Orthodox Church in Today's World. Official Documents of the Holy and Great Council of the Orthodox Church." https://www.holycouncil.org/-/mission-Orthodox-Church-Todays-World. Pentecost 2016.

Karetnikova, Marina Sergeyevna. "The Missionary Movement in Russia: The Nineteenth and the Twentieth Centuries." In *Mission in the Former Soviet Union,* 64–73. Schwarzenfeld, Germany: Neufeld Verlag, 2005.

Kishkovsky, Father Leonid. "The Mission of the Russian Orthodox Church after Communism." *East-West Church & Ministry Report* 1, no. 3 (1993): 1–2.

Lunkin, Roman. "Religious Politics in Crimea, 2014–2016." *East-West Church & Ministry Report* 25, no. 1 (2017): 1–3.

Malancea, Mihai. "Евангельская миссия на территории постсоветской Средней Азии [Evangelical Mission on the Territory of the Post-Soviet Central Asia]."

---

43. Sannikov, *Славянский Библейский Комментарий [Slavic Bible Commentary]*, 9–11.

In *Новые Горизонты Миссии [New Horizons in Mission]*, 261–273. Черкассы: Коллоквиум, 2015.

McGarry, John, and Brendan O'Leary, eds. *The Politics of Ethnic Conflict Regulation: Case Studies of Protracted Ethnic Conflicts.* London; New York: Routledge, 1993.

Murray, Stuart. *Biblical Interpretation in the Anabaptist Tradition* 3. Studies in the Believers Church Tradition. Kitchener, Ontario: Pandora, 2000.

Negrov, Alexander I. *Biblical Interpretation in the Russian Orthodox Church: A Historical and Hermeneutical Perspective.* Beiträge zur Historischen Theologie. Tübingen: Mohr Siebeck, 2008.

Penner, Peter. "Missional Hermeneutics." *Acta Missiologiae: Journal for Reflection on Missiological Issues and Mission Practice in Central and Eastern Europe* 4 (2015): 7–25.

———. "Slavic Bible Commentary." *East-West Church & Ministry Report* 25, no. 1 (Winter 2017): 4–5.

———. *Миссиология и Герменевтика: Прочтение библейских текстов в контексте миссии [Missiology and Hermeneutics].* Черкассы: Коллоквиум, 2014.

Porter, Stanley E., Eckhard J. Schnabel, and Grant R. Osborne, eds. *On the Writing of New Testament Commentaries: Festschrift for Grant R. Osborne on the Occasion of His 70th Birthday.* Texts and Editions for New Testament Study. Leiden; Boston: Brill, 2013.

Raber, Mary. "Remembering the Russian Bible Commentary." In *History and Mission in Europe: Continuing the Conversation.* Schwarzenfeld: Neufeld Verlag, 2011.

Sannikov, Sergei V., ed. *Славянский Библейский Комментарий [Slavic Bible Commentary].* Kiev: EAAA, Knigonosha, 2016.

Sawatsky, Walter. "Orthodox-Evangelical Protestant Dialogue on Mission – Challenges and Shifting Options." *Acta Missiologiae: Journal for Reflection on Missiological Issues and Mission Practice in Central and Eastern Europe* 1 (2008): 11–31.

Stott, John. *The Lausanne Covenant: Complete Text with Study Guide.* Preface by Chris Wright. Lausanne Movement, 2012.

Wright, Christopher J. H. *The Mission of God: Unlocking the Bible's Grand Narrative.* Nottingham: IVP, 2006.

———. "Wrapping Up and Moving Forward." *ICETE* 2009.

Yoder, John. *Preface to Theology Christology and Theological Method.* Grand Rapids: Baker, 2002.

7

Developing a New
Way of Thinking

Brian Wintle

Brian Wintle *holds a PhD from the University of Manchester and has been principal of the Union Biblical Seminary, Pune, as well as the first regional secretary of the Asia Theological Association (India chapter). He was the general editor of the South Asia Bible Commentary (2015) and is currently serving as the academic coordinator of the PhD degree programme in Christian Studies offered by the Centre for Advanced Theological Studies, Sam Higginbotham University of Agriculture, Technology and Science (SHUATS), Allahabad.*

I consider it an honour and privilege to be invited to make a contribution to this festschrift being presented to Dr Christopher Wright on the occasion of his seventieth birthday. I congratulate Chris on his reaching this milestone and pray that the Lord will grant him many more years of fruitful service.

Chris and I were colleagues in the Biblical Studies department of the Union Biblical Seminary, Pune, in the 1980s, and I greatly enjoyed working with him. His love for the Old Testament was contagious, and it was very apparent that the students thoroughly loved his teaching. UBS was truly privileged to have him on its faculty.

A glance at the list of books that Chris has written suggests that besides having a broad concern for the mission of God in the world, he is also interested in the subject of ethics.[1] What did it mean for Israel to be God's chosen people

---

1. *Walking in the Ways of the Lord* (1995) and *Old Testament Ethics for the People of God* (2004) are two titles that come to mind immediately.

among the nations? How was she expected to be different? And how did the law relate to her call to be a light to the nations?

As one considers this matter of ethics, which Dr Wright has explored so thoroughly and effectively, one becomes impressed by the vital role of the mind in the lives of those who seek to live as the people of God. The mind of the disciple is of a particular quality and is centrally important to the fulfilment of his or her calling. Dr Wright, of course, has concentrated on the Old Testament, but a similar emphasis is found in the New Testament writings. In Matthew 28:19–20, commonly called the Great Commission, is the phrase, "teaching them to obey everything I have commanded you." How do we learn to obey? In this article, I have focused my attention on the change in thinking that is a necessary part of the process of learning to obey.

I

In his exposition of the theme "The one who is righteous through faith shall live" in Romans 1–8, the Apostle Paul makes two references to the eschatological goal of salvation: In Romans 5:2 he says, "We boast in the hope of the glory of God," and he goes on to say that hope does not disappoint us because God has given us his Spirit. Then in Romans 8:1–30, where he describes life in the Spirit in more detail, he first says that "those God foreknew he also predestined to be conformed to the image of his Son" (8:29), and then describes this eschatological goal as being "glorified." In other words, Paul describes the climax of salvation in terms of attaining the glory of God and then elaborates this further as being conformed to the likeness of Christ.

This idea is repeated elsewhere in the Pauline writings. In Galatians 4:19, for example, he tells the Galatians that the goal of his ministry among them is that Christ be formed in them. Then in 2 Corinthians 3:18 he describes believers as "being transformed into his image with ever-increasing glory, which comes from the Lord, who is the Spirit." Most commentators agree that the reference here is to the image of Christ, who himself bears the glory of God, and that the agent of this transformation is the Spirit.

II

It is significant that Paul uses the language of transformation in another context in his writings as well. In Romans 12:2, as he transitions from the theological section of his letter to the practical exhortation,[2] he says, "Do not conform to the pattern of this world, but be transformed by the renewing of your mind." He adds, "Then you will be able to test and approve what God's will is – his good, pleasing and perfect will."[3] There are various terms used here that need to be understood correctly in order to appreciate the point the apostle is making, but it is clear that the transformation he is referring to relates to the believers' way of thinking. He is contrasting the way of thinking of believers and that of "the world," and the context suggests that the latter is a description of the believers' former way of thinking.

This contrast between a former and a new way of thinking is also found in Ephesians 4:17–24. Here Paul describes the former way of thinking of the Ephesian believers, who were Gentile converts, as futile and darkened in understanding. Such thinking is reflected in a lifestyle that is ignorant, insensitive, sensual, impure and full of greed. In contrast, the way of life they were taught in Christ involves being "made new in the attitude of their minds" – created to be like God in true righteousness and holiness. Being "made new in the attitude of their minds" is part of a thorough reorientation of life in accordance with the truth learned in Christ. The Christian *nous* (mind) is primarily determined by acknowledgment of the lordship of Christ crucified, from which comes acceptance of the cross as a way of life.[4]

Similarly, in the letter to the Colossians, Paul challenges his readers as follows: "Since you have been raised with Christ, set your hearts . . . (and) minds on things above, not on earthly things." His rationale for his challenge is "For you died, and your life is now hidden with Christ in God. When Christ, who is your life, appears, then you also will appear with him in glory" (Col 3:1–4). The context suggests that the references to dying with Christ and being raised with him are related to the rite of baptism, and this is confirmed by the fact that the apostle proceeds to use the related concepts of taking off the old self and putting on the new self (Col 3:9–10).

Paul makes use of baptismal imagery in Ephesians 4 too. There he reminds his readers that they had been taught, "with regard to your former way of life,

---

2. Morna D. Hooker notes that "what he [Paul] is going to say next depends on the case he has set out in the previous eleven chapters" ("Interchange in Christ and Ethics," *Journal for the Study of the New Testament* 25 [1985]: 4).

3. Ibid. "In order to understand what Paul means by transformation, we need to turn back once again to his earlier argument, this time to ch. 8, where he explains that their destiny is to be conformed to the image of God's Son, and to be glorified with him."

4. Horace E. Stoessel, "Notes on Romans 12:1–2," *Interpretation* 17, no. 2 (1963): 166.

to put off your old self . . . to be made new in the attitude of your minds, and to put on the new self" (Eph 4:22–24).

In the following verses (Eph 4:25–5:2), Paul describes the new way of thinking. It means putting off falsehood and speaking truthfully; it involves a forgiving spirit so that the devil will not be given a foothold in the community; it involves making oneself useful, providing for one's own needs as well as having something to share with those in need; and it calls for speech that is not unwholesome but helpful for building others up according to their needs, that it may benefit those who listen. He closes by making it clear that he is setting before them the example of Christ, who loved them and gave himself for them, and the example of God, who forgave them in Christ.

The classic passage in Paul's writings in which he draws out the implications of faith publicly attested in baptism is Romans 6. In this passage, the apostle describes the symbolism of the baptismal rite. When baptizands enter the water, they are identifying with Christ in his death (all of us who were baptized into Christ were baptized into his death – Rom 6:3) and when they rise out of the water, they rise that they too "may live a new life" (Rom 6:4). However, the new life in Christ to which baptizands rise is described in the future tense, that is, it is a matter of potential or possibility. In his exposition of this new life in Christ in Romans 6–8, Paul describes believers as having been delivered from the power of sin (Rom 6) and from the penalty of sin (Rom 7:1–4) before moving on to describe the new life in Christ as one empowered by the Spirit (Rom 8:1–30).[5]

However, to realize this potential, believers must appropriate the enablement of the Spirit. In the second half of Romans 6, Paul draws out the implications of the realities symbolized in baptism.[6] It is up to believers "to count themselves dead to sin but alive to God in Christ Jesus" (Rom 6:11). This is then followed by a number of imperatives ("Do not let sin reign in your mortal body;" "Do not offer any part of yourself to sin" but rather offer yourself

---

5. John Webster states, "Any account of 'life in Christ' will be deficient if it does not seek to describe the ways in which human beings act in response to obligation, and how their actions are intrinsic to what we understand of their character as persons" ("The Imitation of Christ," *Tyndale Bulletin* 37 [1986]: 104).

Ibid., 112. "The thrust of Paul's understanding of baptism is to say that human identity is not achieved through human acts but is the gift of God through union with Jesus Christ. Baptism dramatically portrays the origins of the Christian life *extra nos*, in a way which makes plain that that life is the fruit of the creative act of God and not simply of human moral dispositions."

6. See Hooker, "Interchange," 7: "Through baptism, believers are united with Christ in death and resurrection. And though resurrection is still a future hope, death and resurrection are already being worked out in their lives."

to God; "Offer every part of yourself to him as an instrument of righteousness") together with a number of indicatives, summed up in 6:17 as follows: "You have come to obey from your heart the pattern of teaching that has now claimed your allegiance." Hooker points out that "this is Paul's use of the so-called 'indicative-imperative,' which has been neatly summed up as the command to 'be what you are.' Those who are 'in Christ' must behave accordingly."[7] This emphasis on obedience is significant, for in two other passages, Paul sums up the work of Christ in the concept of obedience.

In Romans 5:12–21, Paul widens his discussion of how God has provided a solution to the problem of human sin in Christ by contrasting Christ with Adam. In 5:18–19, in summary manner, he contrasts the one trespass (disobedience) of Adam, which resulted in many being made sinners, with the one act of righteousness (obedience) of Christ, through which the many will be made righteous.

Similarly, in Philippians 2:1–11, Paul sums up the life of the incarnate Son in one word: obedience. In this letter, Paul is seeking to deal with the problem of disunity in the Philippian church. He challenges his readers to be "like-minded, having the same love, and being one in spirit and of one mind." Rather than acting out of "selfish ambition" and "vain conceit," he urges them to show "humility" by being sensitive to the interests of others. He bases his appeal on the fact that the very basis of their being in Christ was the incarnation, which revealed the mindset of the eternal Son of God.[8] Though Christ was equal with God, he did not consider his equality with God as something to be used to his own advantage, but became a human being in humble obedience to the saving will of the Father and eventually went to his death on a cross. Paul's point appears to be that, given these facts, it is expected that those who are in Christ will reflect a similar mindset to that of the incarnate Son of God.[9]

In his book *The Mind of Christ in Paul: Light from Paul on Present Problems of Christian Thinking*, F. C. Porter says, "The Christ of Paul's description of

---

7. Ibid. Allen Verhey states that "participation in Christ's cross and resurrection (the important priority of the indicative) and anticipation of God's unchallenged sovereignty (the important finality of the indicative) are constituted here and now by obedience to God's will (the imperative)," in *The Great Reversal: Ethics and the New Testament* (Grand Rapids: Eerdmans, 1984), 104–105.

8. Webster, "Imitation," 110: "Jesus Christ is not here envisaged simply as a lordly redeemer whose authority is confessed, but as one whose human history is to be impressed on the histories of those who participate in his life."

9. Hooker, "Interchange," 10: "The behaviour which is required of those who are in Christ and who wish to be like him conforms to the attitude which he himself showed in becoming like us: he was obedient, he emptied himself; he humbled himself; he became poor."

the ideal of Christ-likeness is the Jesus of the gospels."[10] This is an important insight, as we shall now attempt to show.

III

In the synoptic tradition, the obedience of the Messiah may not be a prominent theme, but it is nevertheless present. The primary focus of the temptation narrative in both Matthew and Luke is the temptation Jesus faced to follow an alternative path to the one the Father willed for him. But Jesus successfully resisted this temptation, insisting that his relationship to the Father was his priority (Matt 4:1–11; Luke 4:1–13).

About six months before he was eventually put to death, Jesus began to prepare his disciples for his rejection by the nation, and his subsequent passion. In the synoptic tradition, we have the threefold prediction of his passion and subsequent divine vindication (Mark 8:31–33; 9:30–32; 10:32–34 and parallels). The words, "the Son of Man must suffer many things" suggest that Jesus sensed a necessity relating to his upcoming suffering. In the light of the Old Testament, this is generally understood to mean that he saw his passion as predicted in prophecy and as willed by the Father. Similarly, in the parable of the tenants (Mark 12:1–12), the quotation of Psalm 118:22 in Mark 12:10–11 clearly implies that his rejection by the builders and subsequent positioning as the cornerstone of the building were God's will for him.

Likewise at the Last Supper, Jesus tells the disciples around the table that one of them will betray him and then adds, "The Son of Man will go just as it is written about him" (Mark 14:21), implying that his suffering, including being betrayed by one of his inner circle of disciples, is the Father's will for him. And finally, in Gethsemane, in an intense struggle he finally submits to the Father's will with the words, "Father, if you are willing, take this cup from me; yet not my will, but yours be done." (Luke 22:42).

This emphasis on Jesus's submission to the Father's will throws light on Jesus's calling prospective disciples to "follow" him (Mark 1:17; 2:14 and parallels). The word "disciple" means "pupil" or one engaged in learning,[11] but it is interesting that Jesus's call to discipleship involved following him. Unlike the Jewish rabbis, Jesus offered himself rather than his outstanding gifts, and

---

10. F. C. Porter, *The Mind of Christ in Paul: Light from Paul on Present Problems of Christian Thinking* (New York: Charles Scribner's Sons, 1930), 28.

11. *TDNT*, Abridged, 1985, 555.

claimed allegiance to himself rather than to a cause that he represented.[12] And just as he was obedient to the Father's will, his disciples were called to obey his teaching (Matt 28:19–20). This idea is found in Mark 8:31–9:1 too, when, just after his first passion prediction Jesus went on to tell the crowds and his disciples, "If anyone would come after me, he must deny himself and take up his cross and follow me." The reference to the cross here is significant – it is Jesus's willingness to be obedient, even to the point of death on the cross (see Phil 2:8) that disciples are being called to emulate.

IV

We now return to the references in Paul's writings to his following the example of Christ. As noted above, Paul's exemplar is the Christ whose mindset was shaped by his obedience even to the point of death on a cross. And even as he follows Christ's example, Paul challenges his readers and others under his pastoral oversight to follow his own example. "There is a certain accent that keeps recurring in the passages on imitation. It is the accent on humility, self-denial, self-giving, self-sacrifice for the sake of Christ and the salvation of others."[13]

In one of his earliest writings, the Letter to the Galatians, Paul says, "I have been crucified with Christ and I no longer live, but Christ lives in me. The life I now live in the body, I live by faith in the Son of God, who loved me and gave himself for me" (Gal 2:20). We can immediately detect in this text echoes of the baptismal language that we have examined above. The life Paul lives in Christ is the new life to which he has been raised and is lived in the power of the Spirit. In other words, the life in Christ is not merely a matter of following the example of Christ. It is lived in the power of the Spirit and by virtue of the relationship of believers to the risen Lord.[14]

In 1 Corinthians 4:8–17, Paul deals with a different problem that had arisen in the church in Corinth. The Corinthians had mistakenly adopted the position that they had all that they needed as Christians: they had already

---

12. *TDNT*, 556.

13. Willis Peter De Boer, *The Imitation of Paul: An Exegetical Study* (Kampen: J. H. Kok, 1962), 207.

14. Webster, "Imitation," 100: "The call to 'follow Christ' should not be interpreted to suggest that Christ becomes a model to be imitated in such a way that the disciple comes to be like the Lord. Rather, the calls to obedient following presuppose election by the Lord: the possibility of hearing and obeying resides not in the disciples' act of allegiance but in the creative initiative of the Lord himself. To 'follow Jesus' is thus not merely to engage in moral striving but to participate in the salvation accomplished by Jesus," 95–120.

become rich, they had already begun to reign (1 Cor 4:8). To put it differently, there was no eschatological dimension to their thinking. They thought they had already arrived spiritually! Consequently, there were those in the church who felt that Paul's difficulties as a minister of the gospel indicated that he was not a true apostle.

In response, Paul uses irony to set things in proper perspective. I wish that you really had begun to reign, he tells them, but the truth is that "God has put us apostles on display at the end of the procession, like those condemned to die in the arena. We have been made a spectacle . . . we are fools for Christ . . . we are weak . . . we are dishonoured" and so on (1 Cor 4:9–13).

Paul goes on to remind them that he is the one who had brought them to faith in Christ: "I became your father through the gospel" (1 Cor 4:15), and as their spiritual father, his desire was not to put them to shame but to warn them against their faulty thinking. The qualifier "through the gospel" also serves to underline the point that their new existence in Christ is not based upon Paul as their father but upon the word of the cross of which Paul is the servant and agent.[15] Paul then urges them to imitate him. He tells them that he is sending his colleague, Timothy, who will *remind them* of his way of life in Christ Jesus (1 Cor 4:17). The entire thrust of the passage is on the suffering involved in the apostolic ministry of the gospel and on Paul's appeal to the Corinthians to recognize that suffering has a legitimate place in following the crucified Messiah. "It is this correct embodiment of Christian leadership and existence, as typified in the apostles' acceptance of worldly disapproval and suffering, that Paul hopes his converts will imitate. Humility and the way of the cross are diametrically opposed to the triumphalism of the Corinthians."[16]

Further in the letter (1 Cor 8–10), Paul deals with an issue that the Corinthians had written to him about, seeking his advice – the issue of food offered to idols. Paul deals with the issue, and then widens the discussion somewhat in his concluding paragraph (1 Cor 10:31–11:1). And once more, his appeal is based on his own example. He begins with the matter of eating or drinking, but then widens the discussion to "whatever you do," and urges his readers to "do it all for the glory of God." He goes on to say, "Do not cause anyone to stumble" and then appeals to his own example – "even as I try to please everyone in every way. For I am not seeking my own good but the good of many, so that they may be saved." His closing appeal is "Follow my example,

---

15. B. Sanders, "Imitating Paul: 1 Cor. 4:16," *Harvard Theological Review* 74, no. 4 (1981): (353–363), 356.

16. Robert L. Plummer, "Imitation of Paul and the Church's Missionary Role in 1 Corinthians," *JETS* 44, no. 2 (2001): (219–35), 231.

as I follow the example of Christ." From 1 Corinthians 9:12, 19–23, we get a clearer picture of what Paul means by his attempts to "please" all people (10:33). The apostle adjusts his behaviour in inconsequential matters so as not to put an unnecessary barrier between a non-believer (or person of questionable faith) and the gospel.[17]

It is clear that the primary concern of the apostle is to impress on the Corinthians that as those who are in Christ, they must seek the good of others rather than their own interests. In doing this, they will be following the example of the Lord Jesus Christ, and his own example. "Paul seems to be saying that Christ was a model for him in that Christ did not seek his own advantage, but that of others – for their salvation."[18] This understanding of Christ as selflessly giving himself for others' salvation corresponds with Paul's presentation of Christ in his other letters, and with the gospel tradition.[19]

In the Thessalonian correspondence, too, we find Paul appealing to the example of the Lord and to his own example. In his opening thanksgiving he refers to the gospel as having come to them "not simply with words but also with power, with the Holy Spirit and with deep conviction." He then goes on to say, "You became imitators of us and of the Lord" and that they in turn had become a model for believers in Macedonia and Achaia (1 Thess 1:5–7) in that they had "welcomed the message in the midst of severe suffering with the joy given by the Holy Spirit."

We look, finally, at the letter to the Philippians once again. Having reminded them in 2:5 that the very basis of their being Christians is the mind of Christ reflected in the incarnation and in the life of obedience of Jesus that led him to the cross,[20] Paul holds up before them other examples as well. In Philippians 2:19–24, he appeals to the example of Timothy, "who will show genuine concern for your welfare." Unlike others who "look out for their own interests," Timothy looks out for the interests of Jesus Christ. Similarly, he holds up as an example their own church member, Epaphroditus, who, though he was ill and almost died, risked his life to fulfil the task of taking care of Paul's needs on behalf of the church (Phil 2:25–30).

---

17. Ibid., 226.

18. Charles A. Gieschen, "It appears that it is primarily Jesus' sacrificial servanthood that Paul has in mind when he speaks of imitating Christ, and not a list of specific behaviours of Jesus" in "Christian Identity in Pagan Thessalonica: The Imitation of Paul's Cruciform Life," *Concordia Theological Quarterly* 72 (2008): 14.

19. Plummer, "Imitation of Paul," 225.

20. Webster, "Imitation," 111: "Christ's action is more than vicarious: it is also evocative, or, perhaps better, provocative, in that it summons to a properly dependent mimesis."

As a final point, Paul appeals to his own example in that he forgets what is behind and strains towards what is ahead. He presses on towards the goal to win the prize for which God has called him heavenward in Christ Jesus (Phil 3:12–14). In the light of other passages that we have looked at, we may confidently conclude that Paul is saying that his goal is to be fully conformed to the image of Christ. As he says a few verses later, his mind is not set on earthly things, but he eagerly awaits the Saviour who "will transform our lowly bodies so that they will be like his glorious body" (Phil 3:19–21).

Paul was a thinker, and he wanted those under his pastoral oversight to learn to develop a Christian mindset. This involves recognizing that God is at work in the lives of those who are "in Christ," conforming them to the image of his Son. If the challenge before those who are "in Christ" is rightly described as "become what you are," it is up to us to discern what it means to be conformed to the likeness of Christ and to allow the Lord to change us. However, Paul makes it amply clear that this is not a matter of mere passivity on our part. Rather, we need to learn to think in a way that is consistent with what God has in mind for us. And the way we think determines how we conduct ourselves, and, ultimately, what kind of persons we are. As Paul puts it in Philippians 2:12b–13, "Continue to work out your salvation with fear and trembling, for it is God who works in you to will and to act in order to fulfil his good purpose."

References

De Boer, Willis Peter. *The Imitation of Paul: An Exegetical Study.* Kampen: J. H. Kok, 1962.

Gieschen, Charles A. "Christian Identity in Pagan Thessalonica: The Imitation of Paul's Cruciform Life." *Concordia Theological Quarterly* 72 (2008): 14.

Hooker, Morna D. "Interchange in Christ and Ethics." *Journal for the Study of the New Testament* 25 (1985): 4.

Plummer, Robert L. "Imitation of Paul and the Church's Missionary Role in 1 Corinthians. *JETS* 44, no. 2 (2001): 231.

Porter, F. C. *The Mind of Christ in Paul: Light from Paul on Present Problems of Christian Thinking.* New York: Charles Scribner's Sons, 1930.

Sanders, B. "Imitating Paul: 1 Cor. 4:16." *Harvard Theological Review* 74, no. 4 (1981): 356.

Stoessel, Horace E. "Notes on Romans 12:1–2." *Interpretation* 17, no. 2 (1963): 166.

Verhey, Allen. *The Great Reversal: Ethics and the New Testament.* Grand Rapids: Eerdmans, 1984.

Webster, John. "The Imitation of Christ." *Tyndale Bulletin* 37 (1986): 104.

8

Reflection on Article 9 of the Cape Town Confession of Faith: Loving the People of God

Frew Tamrat

Frew Tamrat is vice-president of the Evangelical Theological College of Addis Ababa. He holds a Master's in New Testament Studies from Gordon-Conwell Theological Seminary, and a PhD in Christian Higher Education Leadership from Columbia International University. He is a member of one of the largest evangelical denominations in Ethiopia, the Ethiopian Kale Heywet Church, and is highly involved in training church leaders. He serves the Lausanne Movement, as a member of the Global Theological Education Steering Committee and the Theology Working Group. He is the country coordinator for Langham Preaching in Ethiopia and a fellow of the Global Associates for Transformational Education.

It gives me great pleasure to be among those contributing an article to this work in honour of Chris Wright and the godly service he has rendered to the global church. I am grateful to God for the impact that Chris Wright has had on my life through his writings and the ministry of Langham Partnership International.

I came to know Dr Wright a decade ago when he came to Ethiopia to be the keynote speaker at the Frumentius Lectures. These annual lectures at the Ethiopian Graduate School of Theology commemorate Bishop Frumentius, the church father who officially introduced Christianity to Ethiopia in the fourth century. I have also had many opportunities to hear Dr Wright as he has been a regular keynote speaker at the ICETE gatherings that are held every three years. One of the things that has drawn me to these gatherings has been the solid, thought-provoking theological issues addressed by Dr Wright. As a keynote speaker, he set the tone and the agenda for the whole event in his introductory speech. He also has a great gift for summarizing and highlighting the main points made by the plenary speakers. I am always impressed by how he uses the Scriptures to give theological foundations for all his presentations, whether it is about missions or the issue of brain drain from the Majority World to the West.

I have also benefitted greatly by being part of the Langham Preaching Movement in which Dr Wright serves as one of the international facilitators. I had the privilege to sit at his feet and learn the skills of preaching from the Old Testament. It was an honour and a blessing for us in Ethiopia to have him facilitate the 2015 Langham Preaching Seminars. More than forty pastors and preachers attended his session on preaching from the Old Testament in which he gave us a new lens through which to view the Old Testament writings and a new skill in preaching from them. He helped us to fall in love with the Law, the Prophets and the Writings!

The Ethiopian Langham Preaching participants so loved his new book *Sweeter than Honey* that focuses on preaching from the Old Testament, that it is being translated into Amharic and will be the standard textbook for Langham Preaching in Ethiopia. It will also be used as a textbook in our Amharic Bible Schools.

When I think of Chris Wright's impact and contribution to the global church, I think also of his involvement in the Lausanne Movement. I was one of the fortunate people who attended the third Lausanne Congress in Cape Town, South Africa in 2010. In that great gathering of more than 4,000 people from all over the world, it was clear that Chris Wright was the master architect of the confession of faith and call to action that has become known as the Cape Town Commitment. The document clearly shows Dr Wright's conviction about God, his word, and his mission to the world.

I have been particularly challenged by the first part of the document, which outlines ten things we love because of the Lord we love. These are confessions of our faith that we need to embrace as evangelical Christians. Though these ten confessional statements were drafted by the Lausanne leadership and embraced by the participants at the third Lausanne Congress, I believe that Dr Wright played a great role in articulating clearly our evangelical identity that distinguishes us from other Christian traditions.

Since the publication of the Cape Town Commitment as an official document in 2011, I have been studying and reflecting on the contents of the document. Specially, I have been reflecting on Article 9 of the first section of the Confession of Faith: "*We love the people of God.*"

When I was invited to contribute to this festschrift the first thing that jumped to my mind was to reflect on Article 9 and explain what it means to be "the people of God" and "to love the people of God" according to the Word of God. I am very grateful to Dr Wright for triggering my mind to reflect more on this issue and draw out the implications of the concept "we love the people of God" for my life and for the wider body of Christ, the church.

We Love the People of God

In the Bible, the phrase the "people of God" always indicates a relationship with God. The people of God are the people chosen by God for his own possession and purposes. In Genesis 12, God called Abram (later Abraham) to leave his land for a new one that God would show him, so that he would become the father of the nation that would become the people of God. God's promise to Abraham in Genesis 12:2, "I will make of you a great nation, and I will bless you and make your name great, so that you will be a blessing" was God's commission to Abraham to establish this new humanity. Therefore, in the Old Testament, the people of God are those who are associated with God's purposes and promises to Abraham. They were the people related to the nation Israel, and specifically to the God of Israel. Israel became the people of God because he chose them to be his own possession (Exod 6:6–7; 19:5–6).

In the New Testament, the people of God are people from all nations whom God in Christ has loved, chosen, called, saved and sanctified for his own possession. These are people who have come to faith in Israel's promised Messiah, Jesus Christ, and who are members of the body of Christ, the church, God's new creation. Peter, referring to this new people of God (that is, to all of us who have believed in Christ), says to us "You are a chosen race, a royal priesthood, a holy nation, a people for his own possession, that you may proclaim the excellences of him who called you out of darkness into his marvellous light" (1 Pet 2:9). According to Peter, today the church is the new people of God, the new Israel.

As people of God, loved and chosen by God, we are commanded to love one another. For the new people of God who are under the new covenant, love for one another has become their distinguishing mark. In John 13, Jesus says to his disciples "A new commandment I give to you, that you love one another: just as I have loved you, you also are to love one another. By this all people will know that you are my disciples, if you have love for one another" (John 13:34–35). According to Jesus, for the new people of God to be called his disciples, loving one another was not optional; it was commanded. None of those who profess faith in Jesus Christ are exempted from showing love to their brothers and sisters in Christ. Though the command to love one's neighbour was not new (Lev 19:18), what makes the love of the new people of God to one another new, is that we are commanded to love as Jesus loved us. Christ's love, shown to his people in his person and work, is the model for us to love one another. God showed his unconditional love through Christ, by allowing Jesus to die for sinners who do not deserve his mercy. Furthermore, Christ has made this love for one another the means whereby his people will demonstrate to the world their relationship with him as his disciples. As New Testament believers, when we confess "We love the people of God," we are professing that we have love for one another, we are imitating Christ's love, and we are showing to the unbelieving world that we belong to Christ as his disciples.

The source of our love for one another is God himself. John reiterates the words of Jesus when he writes, "Dear friends, let us love one another, for love comes from God. Everyone who loves has been born of God and knows God. Whoever does not love does not know God, because God is love" (1 John 4:7–8). The new people of God, who are recipients of God's love, love others because the love of God is in them. It is the indwelling presence of God that enables the people of God to show love for one another. As the ultimate source of love, God continually shows his love to his people, and his people in turn are required to display this love to others. It is not sufficient to profess to be a Christian; as the people of God, we must also display this divine attribute of love, just as our heavenly Father displayed his love for us.

John helps us understand how we can demonstrate love for one another by describing how God's love for us was manifested. In 1 John 3:16–18, he says, "By this we know love, that he laid down his life for us, and we ought to lay down our lives for the brothers. But if anyone has the world's goods and sees his brother in need, yet closes his heart against him, how does God's love abide in him? Little children, let us not love in word or talk but in deed and in truth." God's love for us was manifested by sending his Son to die for us.

We too are expected to demonstrate love to others by our actions and not just our words. As the new people of God, we are expected to live out love in kindness, generosity, and service to others. Christian love is self-sacrificing and self-giving. It is not indifferent to the needs of brothers and sisters in Christ. As the new people of God, we are called to the same standard of love that God showed us.

The love we have for one another is not limited to meeting the needs of others in the family of God; it is also an instrument that God uses to draw others to this loving God. The ultimate purpose of our love for one another is to reveal to all who Christ was and is. When Jesus issued his command to his disciples to love one another in John 13:35, he said, "By this all people will know that you are my disciples, if you have love for one another." The key word in this verse is "*my*", which refers to the Lord Jesus Christ. The Lord's purpose was that non-Christians will come to know of his love through his disciples' loving relationship with one another. Christ's purpose has not changed. His command is still binding on those of us who profess faith in his name. It is through our love for one another that the unbelieving world will come to know the love of Christ. Our love for another is missional. It is not only "self-oriented" among the people of God; it is also "other" oriented. It has a ripple effect, reaching those who have not yet been reached by the love of Christ and included in his fold (John 10:16).

In light of the missional nature of our love and relationship to one another as people of God, there are areas to which we need to pay serious attention as we endeavour to attract people to Christ.

First, as stated in Article 9, when we say we love the people of God, we are admitting that we are called to unity. In his high priestly prayer in John 17, Jesus prayed for his disciples to be unified as a powerful witness to the reality of God's love among them. His great desire for his disciples was that they would become one as a reflection of the unity that has eternally existed between the Father and the Son (John 17:11). There is no more powerful testimony to the world than the unity of God's people. The unity that is demonstrated among us is one of the ways we witness to the world, so that the world may believe in Jesus (John 17:21).

This call for unity among the people of God requires all of us to work together to destroy any barriers that hinder the spread of the gospel of Jesus Christ. As the new people of God, our Christian unity should not be based on our race, colour, gender, social class, economic status, or political inclination. Unities that have been forged around these markers of identity in the past have hindered the preaching of the gospel rather than advancing it, and in some cases have led even to the defaming of the name of Jesus. Today our unity as the people of God is threatened by a kind of "party spirit" that mirrors the unbelieving world. Political parties in the world indulge in character assassination, tearing down those who belong to other parties in order to show their allegiance to their own party. This attitude ought not to be found among us since we share the same mission of spreading the gospel of Jesus Christ. Rather, we should be united and should show our love by having a common mind and purpose in the mission of God.

As people of God, we have far more in common than we have differences that divide us. So we should focus on the things that unite us rather than on those that divide us. In Ephesians 4:3, the Apostle Paul tells us that we do not create unity; rather we are called to preserve the unity that is already established among us. To preserve this unity, we need to work for things that will bring peace among us, not division and enmity. Regardless of our traditions and denominational background, we should focus on those doctrinal truths that we commonly confess so that we can foster our spiritual unity and be a witness of Christ to the world.

Second, when we say we love the people of God, it means we are called to overlook offences among us. In 1 Peter 4:8, Peter says "Above all, love each other deeply, because love covers over a multitude of sins." How we handle offences in the family of God is the litmus test of our spiritual love for one another. The love that we have for one another should be demonstrated by forgiving offences done against us. As members of God's family, we should try our best to handle them in love among us. True brotherly love does not rejoice in exposing the sins of family members to the world. Rather, it shows integrity by not aggravating the weaknesses of others but by working towards the restoration of the sinning brother or sister to the family of God.

It is sad that our Christian witness to the world has been marred by the ways we choose to use to disclose the weaknesses among us. Rather than offering forgiveness and calling people to repentance so that they can be restored to the service of God's mission, we tend to expose our weaknesses in a way that destroys the ministry of God's people to the world. When we do this and take harsh disciplinary actions against sinning brothers and sisters in the church, our actions are sometimes not done in love. They can drive away people from repentance, rather than inviting them to repent as a way of drawing them back and restoring their relationship with the Lord. Love for God's people calls the church of Christ back to her prophetic role of calling God's people to repentance when they sin, offering them forgiveness, and restoring them to their God-given service, so that the saving beauty of the gospel of Christ can shine in the world.

Third, when we say we love the people of God, it means we are called to show our solidarity with our needy Christian brothers and sisters. In Matthew 25:34–40, Jesus closely identifies himself with those who are needy, saying that their suffering is his suffering and any compassion shown to them is compassion shown to him. He commends those disciples of his who respond in compassion to the hungry, the thirsty, the stranger, the naked, the sick, and the imprisoned. One of the fruits of our salvation is helping those who are needy both in the church and in the world. Evangelism and social action need to go hand in hand in Christian mission to the world. A gospel that fails to address the physical needs of people is not the "whole gospel." As the people of God, we are called to take the "whole gospel to the whole world" and this calls us to share the sufferings of the needy by meeting their needs.

More than at any time in history, millions of Christians in the world today are passing through some kind of persecution and suffering. Those of us who are living in relative ease need to share the burden carried by our brothers and sisters in the suffering church. We should demonstrate our love and solidarity with them through our prayers, advocacy, and financial support. We should be alert to hear and follow up the needs of the suffering and persecuted churches in the world so that we can respond to their needs in a timely manner. Our efforts in this regard will be more far-reaching if we do not only respond individually to the needs of the suffering church but coordinate our efforts by establishing a network of like-minded brothers and sisters in our regions.

Fourth, when we say we love the people of God, it means we are called to be sensitive and not hurt the consciences of our brothers and sisters when we practise our freedom in Christ. In Romans 14 Paul calls for mutual acceptance between the strong and the weak Christian in the Roman church, saying "If your brother is grieved by what you eat, you are no longer walking in love. By what you eat, do not destroy the one for whom Christ died" (Rom 14:15). Paul believes that both strong and weak Christians can cause their brothers and sisters to stumble by acting insensitively when they practise their Christian liberty. According to Paul, when we are not sensitive to the consciences of our brothers and sisters as we practice our external observances, it means we are not acting in love to one another. Furthermore, Paul says, when we harm one another by abusing our freedom in Christ, it will give unbelievers grounds to deny the goodness of the gospel (Rom 14:16). But as people of God, for the sake of love, we need to be sensitive to one another by forgoing our legitimate rights in order not to cause others to stumble in their faith.

It is a sad thing that Christian mission in the past has been characterized at times by Christian groups despising one another. We have sometimes rejected people whom God has accepted because they have not followed our practices in secondary or non-essential things such as dress codes or eating habits. We have failed to give the gospel first place in our effort to reach the unreached by focusing too much on such matters. It has been difficult for many of us to forgo our rights for the sake of love. As a result, many unbelievers have identified the gospel with the cultures of certain nations and people groups. But love calls us to be sensitive to those who have a different culture than us in our effort to reach them by the gospel of Jesus Christ.

As people who profess to love the people of God, we need to distinguish between those things that are essential for salvation and those which are non-essential. We need to know the difference between gospel and culture in missions. If something is worth dying for, let it be biblical truths such us the uniqueness of Christ, the authority of the Word of God and the like. Let us forgo our liberty in non-essentials so that we can build the faith of those brothers and sisters who have not yet reached the same maturity level in handling secondary issues. This will also give us a stronger witness to the unreached.

It is my prayer and hope that as the new people of God we will embrace the Cape Town Confession of Faith, "We Love the People of God." Like the Apostle Paul who passed on what he had received from the Lord and entrusted the preaching of the gospel to his spiritual son Timothy (2 Tim 2:2), so Chris Wright has passed on to us what he has received from the Lord during his many years of faithful Christian ministry. Now it is up to us who have been taught and mentored by Dr Wright to demonstrate that we are reliable people who will be faithful to the gospel and will in turn pass the message on to others so that the true gospel and the spirit of the Lausanne Movement may continue to exist for many years and generations to come.

Dr Wright has proved to be one of the distinguished fathers of the Lausanne Movement. As a father, he will rejoice to see his legacy continued by those who follow in his footsteps. May the Lausanne family continue to bear testimony to the mission of God and the gospel of Christ!

9

Creation Care and the Mission of God

Las Newman

Las G. Newman *is the global associate director for regions for the Lausanne Movement. He is a member of the International Fellowship for Mission as Transformation and former president of the Caribbean Graduate School of Theology (CGST) in Kingston, Jamaica. He holds a Master of Arts (MA Hons) in History from the University of Waterloo, Ontario, Canada, and a PhD in Mission History from the Oxford Centre for Mission Studies (OCMS)/University of Wales. He has spent more than thirty years working with students in the campus ministry Students Christian Fellowship and Scripture Union in Jamaica, and the International Fellowship of Evangelical Students (IFES).*

Chris Wright is, in my view, the consummate scholar–mission leader. He has authored and published several scholarly books, articles, and essays covering a wide range of biblical, theological, and pastoral subjects and collaborated with several mission organizations. His magnum opus is *The Mission of God: Unlocking the Bible's Grand Narrative.*[1] This book presents Chris's analysis of the biblical story, which he determines is centred in the *missio Dei*, as well as a definitive statement of a biblical hermeneutic linking the Old and New Testaments. This book has given me insight into the link between the theology underlying the missionary enterprises of the church and the theology of God's intention for his people and for the world.

---

1. Christopher Wright, *The Mission of God: Unlocking the Bible's Grand Narrative* (Nottingham: IVP, 2006).

As a Christian, I grew up knowing that there should be a biblical basis for everything we do, for Scripture is "the final authority on all matters of faith and conduct." Chris's scholarship as an outstanding Old Testament scholar has helped me tremendously through its focus on the grand narrative of Scripture in both the Old and New Testaments. The insights I have obtained from Chris have grounded my own worldview of the Bible and how it should be read.

What Is the Mission of God in the World?

The mission of God, according to Chris, is broad, comprehensive, and holistic. It is the activity of God, the originator of everything, who "has a goal, a purpose, a mission that will ultimately be accomplished by the power of God's Word and for the glory of God's name. This is the mission of the biblical God."[2] This mission encompasses all the great themes of the biblical story – monotheism, creation, humanity, election, redemption, covenant, ethics, and future hope. And while Chris wrestles with whether or not this book is to be regarded as a biblical theology of mission or a missiological way in which the story of the Bible should be read, his leaning towards the latter comes through very clearly and with great persuasiveness. As he puts it at the beginning of the book, "Mission is, in my view, a major key that unlocks the whole grand narrative of the canon of Scripture."[3]

Part IV of *The Mission of God*, "The Arena of Mission" is the most captivating section of the book for me. There Chris devotes several pages to the arena in which the mission of God is enacted and offers an exquisite exposition of the centrality of Christ.[4] This arena involves the whole of creation, human and non-human. Taking his cue from Deuteronomy 10:14, "To the LORD your God belong the heavens, even the highest heavens, the earth, and everything in it," he argues for the goodness and sanctity of creation and that the whole earth is the field of God's mission and will one day find its ultimate redemption in the atoning work of Christ.

That chapter provides a missiological warrant for the church to embrace creation care as a central part of its endeavours. It identifies six biblical,

---

2. Ibid., 64.

3. Ibid., 17.

4. Ibid., 414.

theological and practical reasons that forge an integral link between creation care and Christian mission:[5]

- Creation care is an urgent issue in today's world.
- Creation care flows from love and obedience to God.
- Creation care exercises our priestly and kingly role in relation to the earth.
- Creation care tests our motivation for mission.
- Creation care is a prophetic opportunity for the church.
- Creation care embodies a biblical balance of compassion and justice.

Living Out the Mission of God in the World

Chris's scholarship and piety have contributed to the amazing growth and impact of the Langham Partnership which he has led, and to other organizations he has served. One of his most outstanding contributions to the Lausanne Movement, and by extension to the global church, was his work on the Cape Town Commitment that emanated from the third Lausanne Congress on World Evangelism in South Africa in 2010.

Prior to the congress, Chris was invited to lead the Theology Working Group for the Lausanne Movement. Under his leadership, a group of young evangelical theologians from around the world came together to wrestle with and help shape the theological themes that would guide the third congress. This was no easy task, for nineteen years had elapsed since the second Lausanne Congress in Manila in 1989. The group met several times in different locations on different continents. They identified a number of themes on which they developed and published small pamphlets.

I have vivid memories of a meeting in December 2009 at which a select group of theologians from different continents met in Minneapolis to work on drafting a statement to be issued by the third Lausanne Congress, perhaps something akin to the Lausanne Covenant, which was the statement of the first congress in 1974. After two and half days, little progress had been made. Time was running out. A major snowstorm was looming, and we all had to catch flights out of Minneapolis before it descended. The meeting ended without agreement – except for the statement, "Let's leave it all to Chris Wright." In the elevator returning to our rooms to collect our bags, Chris turned to me and

---

5. Ibid., 412–420.

said, "What a burden! Why me?" He wondered aloud what Uncle John (John Stott) would have done.

As he tells the rest of the story, early in the new year (2010), after the Christmas holiday break was over, he went to the retreat known as the Hookses on the south coast of Wales for a time of quiet and meditation. It was there that he received the inspiration that framed the confession of faith in Part 1 of the Cape Town Commitment, "For the Lord We Love."[6] And what a marvellous document the Cape Town Commitment (CTC) turned out to be!

As a confession of faith and call to action, the CTC is, in my view, the missiological document of the twenty-first century. It is a major tool for missional practice and theological engagement that will last well through this century, and is a guide to living out the mission of God in the world. And the imprint of Chris Wright is stamped on it.

One of the strongest and perhaps the most courageous sections of the CTC document is Part 1.7 – "We Love God's World." Rarely in global ecumenical, let alone evangelical, statements has such a clear and unequivocal link been made between the gospel and a social issue such as creation care. The CTC categorically states that creation care is "a gospel issue within the lordship of Christ." Chris had upheld and argued this point in *The Mission of God*, where he argued that the gospel is indeed good news for the whole of creation.

When it comes to living out the mission of God in the world, two principal actions resulted from the seed sown in *The Mission of God* and the CTC. The first was the Lausanne Global Consultation on Creation Care and the Gospel that was held in Jamaica in October 2012 with over fifty selected participants from twenty-three countries as diverse as Argentina, Bangladesh, Benin, Kenya, Uganda, Singapore, the UK, the USA, and Canada. Theologians, scientists, writers, and environmental practitioners met for five days to pray, talk, and reflect on the state of the planet, the home on which we live, and on the role and ministry of the church in caring for God's creation. The programme, developed in partnership with four organizations (the WEA, Tear Fund, World Vision, and Arocha) was structured around God's Word (*Bible reading*), God's world (*science*), and God's work (*church and mission*). Out of that consultation came a call to action (2012)[7] and a major book, *Creation Care and the Gospel:*

---

6. He tells the story in his keynote address to the ICETE International Consultation for Theological Educators in Nairobi, Kenya, 2012, "Alertly Rooted! Energetically Engaged!" http://www.icete-edu.org/pdf/Wright%20Rooted%20and%20Engaged.pdf.

7. See www.lausanne.org/content/statement/creation-care-call-to-action. Used by permission.

Reconsidering the Mission of the Church (2016), for which I was invited to write the foreword.[8]

The call to action affirmed the CTC's statement that creation care is indeed "a gospel issue within the lordship of Christ" and asserted that "love for God, our neighbors and the wider creation, as well as our passion for justice, compel us to 'urgent and prophetic ecological responsibility (CTC I.7.A).'" Specifically, a call was made to the global church for:

1. **A new commitment to a simple lifestyle.**

   Recognizing that much of our crisis is due to billions of lives lived carelessly, we reaffirm the Lausanne commitment to simple lifestyle (Lausanne Occasional Paper # 20), and call on the global evangelical community to take steps, personally and collectively, to live within the proper boundaries of God's good gift in creation, to engage further in its restoration and conservation, and to equitably share its bounty with each other.

2. **New and robust theological work.**

   In particular, we need guidance in four areas:
   - An integrated theology of creation care that can engage seminaries, Bible colleges and others to equip pastors to disciple their congregations.
   - A theology that examines humanity's identity as both embedded in creation and yet possessing a special role toward creation.
   - A theology that challenges current prevailing economic ideologies in relation to our biblical stewardship of creation.
   - A theology of hope in Christ and his Second Coming that properly informs and inspires creation care.

3. **Leadership from the church in the Global South.**

   As the Global South represents those most affected in the current ecological crisis, it possesses a need to speak up, engage issues of creation care, and act upon them. We the members of the Consultation further request that the church of the Global South exercise leadership among us, helping to set the agenda for the advance of the gospel and the care of creation.

---

8. Chris Wright was the guest speaker at the launch of the book in London on 6 June 2016. The book, edited by Colin Bell and Robert White, has been given exposure in the public media in Jamaica, reviewed in *The Sunday Gleaner*, 5 March 2017, Arts and Education, E7. http://jamaica-gleaner.com/article/art-leisure/20170305/book-review-fresh-look-christian-perspective.

4. **Mobilization of the whole church and engagement of all of society.**
Mobilization must occur at the congregational level and include those who are often over-looked, utilizing the gifts of women, children, youth, and indigenous people as well as professionals and other resource people who possess experience and expertise. Engagement must be equally widespread, including formal, urgent and creative conversations with responsible leaders in government, business, civil society, and academia.

5. **Environmental missions among unreached people groups.**
We participate in Lausanne's historic call to world evangelization, and believe that environmental issues represent one of the greatest opportunities to demonstrate the love of Christ and plant churches among unreached and unengaged people groups in our generation (CTC II.D.1.B). We encourage the church to promote "environmental missions" as a new category within mission work (akin in function to medical missions).

6. **Radical action to confront climate change.**
Affirming the *Cape Town Commitment's* declaration of the "serious and urgent challenge of climate change" which will "disproportionately affect those in poorer countries", (CTC II.B.6), we call for action in radically reducing greenhouse gas emissions and building resilient communities. We understand these actions to be an application of the command to deny ourselves, take up the cross and follow Christ.

7. **Sustainable principles in food production.**
In gratitude to God who provides sustenance, and flowing from our conviction to become excellent stewards of creation, we urge the application of environmentally and generationally sustainable principles in agriculture (field crops and livestock, fisheries and all other forms of food production).

8. **An economy that works in harmony with God's creation.**
We call for an approach to economic well-being and development, energy production, natural resource management (including mining and forestry), water management and use, transportation, health care, rural and urban design and living, and personal and corporate consumption patterns that maintain the ecological integrity of creation.

9. **Local expressions of creation care, which preserve and enhance biodiversity.**
   We commend such projects, along with any action that might be characterized as the "small step" or the "symbolic act," to the worldwide church as ways to powerfully witness to Christ's Lordship over all creation.

10. **Prophetic advocacy and healing reconciliation.**
   We call for individual Christians and the church to prophetically "speak truth to power" through advocacy and legal action so that public policies and private practice may change to better promote the care of creation and better support devastated communities and habitats. Additionally, we call the church to "speak the peace of Christ" into communities torn apart by environmental disputes, mobilizing those who are skilled at conflict resolution, and maintaining our own convictions with humility.

This statement obviously encompasses a wide range of missiological actions aimed at caring for God's creation in ways that enhance human life and glorify God. It has the potential to unleash a new environmental missions and environmental awareness, motivated and guided by the gospel of Christ.

The second action arising from *The Mission of God,* the CTC, and the Jamaica Call to Action was the formation of a global movement for creation care known as the Lausanne/WEA Creation Care Network. This network has been engaged in action plans and a series of consultations and conferences in Latin America, Africa, Europe, the Middle East, Eurasia, East Asia, Canada, and the United States. Led by Ed Brown, these regional and national consultations use the same programme structure as the Jamaica consultation in 2012, focusing on God' word (*Bible reading),* God's world (*science),* and God's work (*church and mission).*

In the summer of 2016, the Lausanne Movement hosted its third global Younger Leaders Gathering in Jakarta, Indonesia. Chris Wright was a speaker and part of the mentoring team. One of the most encouraging things about that event was witnessing more than a thousand leaders under thirty-five years of age from every continent in sober reflection on the state of the world and making a fresh, passionate, commitment to global mission. The workshop on creation care attracted a number of young Christian professionals who shared their hopes, dreams, and engagement with missional activities aimed at creation care in their home countries. Every available copy of *Creation Care and the Gospel* was sold.

Creation Care and the Caribbean

Earth Day has now been observed in April for nearly fifty years.[9] It is supported by the United Nations as a way to draw attention to the state of the planet, our habitat and common home. Each year more than one billion people around the globe participate in Earth Day activities calling attention to the state of the earth and the need for creation care. But in the Caribbean (and elsewhere), Earth Day often goes unnoticed by the Christian community.

In our hymns we praise God for the beauty of his creation. I remember singing,

> For the beauty of the earth, for the glory of the skies,
> For the love which from our birth over and around us lies,
> Lord of all to Thee we raise, this our hymn of grateful praise.

However, I must confess that I have often wondered whether Christians and institutional religion, such as churches, are not among the greatest abusers of the environment. As we look around at the wanton pollution and degradation of the natural environment, the question needs to be asked – where is our concern for environmental justice and for God's creation? Are we in the church in the Caribbean concerned about promoting sustainable living? How can every church demonstrate its commitment to caring for God's creation in some meaningful way?

At the Caribbean Graduate School of Theology (CGST) in Jamaica, Earth Day has been observed in a chapel service since 2010. Each year, a distinguished fellow of the college is invited to speak on a topic related to the environment. On other occasions, guests from government or NGOs and the university are invited to participate in a symposium on an environmental topic. In this way, as a community involved in theological education and the equipping of leaders for the church, we highlight the biblical mandate to care for the earth and make students and the public aware of the current environmental crisis.

We have also encouraged individuals and congregations to develop action plans to guide their activities. Action plans may include any of the following:

1.   READ the Jamaica Statement on Creation Care and Call to Action.

---

9. The first Earth Day was observed in the United States on 22 April 1970. It drew 20 million Americans from all walks of life into a public display of concern for the state of the planet earth and is widely credited with launching the modern environmental movement. It is now observed on every continent each year on April 22. See www.earthday.org/about/the-history-of-earth-day/.

2. ENSURE your own environment (i.e. your household, your church, your workplace, your lived community) is green, energy efficient, healthy, and life-affirming.

3. JOIN the search for alternative energy sources. Explore and utilize renewable sources of energy. Apply technological innovation for new fuels, electricity generation, etc. Necessity has always been the mother of invention.

4. ADVOCATE for the protection and preservation of our mountains, rivers, watersheds, wetlands, coastlands, and green spaces. Join and support conservation groups that are advocates for protection of our heritage sites (UNESCO recognized).

5. MOBILIZE community education and action groups (e.g. clubs, schools, churches engaged in reforestation/tree planting, banning of bush fires, protection of wild life and endangered species). Preserve public health. Prevent the spread of vector-borne diseases.

6. PLAN appropriate proper human settlements/better shelter policy for the poor. "Squatters" should be discouraged from settling in watersheds, river courses, swamp lands, vulnerable and fragile environments.

7. ADVOCATE for appropriate public transportation policies to cut emissions, improve efficiency, improve air quality, create a healthier public environment.[10]

Why Creation Care Matters

Thanks to Chris Wright, therefore, the Lausanne Movement's proclamation that "creation care is a gospel issue within the lordship of Christ" has been awakening the global church in remarkable ways to the call for urgent action to deal with the global ecological crisis and environmental challenges.

---

10. At the commencement of the new academic year, 2012–2013, the CGST Faculty of Theology and Religious Studies held its first Theology Workshop on the topic: "The Church in Search of a Viable Theology of Environment." Presenters included Dr Barry Wade, "Environmental Justice and the Poor: Problem of Squatting, Landlessness, and Environmental Refugees in a Christian Society," Professor Elizabeth Thomas-Hope, "Concepts of a Moral Relationship within Earth," and Dr Garnet Brown, "Contours of Environmental Theology." This is adapted from my presentation "Faith and Environment: Black Mass and the End of Time: What Shall We Do?"

Creation care matters for very practical reasons. Changing precipitation patterns and climate variability are causing serious harm to human habitat, biodiversity, and ecological balance. For example, The National Climate Assessment in the United States and the US Centers for Disease Control and Prevention assess that climate change is causing wide-ranging impacts on all these areas, including human health.[11] These impacts include:

- rising sea-levels that threaten coastal living.
- severe droughts in some areas and severe flooding in others due to extreme weather events.
- rising levels of food insecurity resulting from severe damage to farm infrastructure and losses in agricultural production and disruptions in the food chain.
- public health pandemics and the spread of vector-borne diseases such as chikungunya and the Zika virus.[12]
- significant air pollution and degradation of air quality that impacts on human health.[13]
- ocean acidification, coral blights will affect beaches and impact the tourism industry.
- greater public and private expenditure on disaster-risk management and recovery.
- A need for new climate-based urban planning and land use policies.

These are realities that churches and communities in vulnerable environments are unable to ignore and are struggling to come to terms with. While many are engaged in relief and development work (after the fact), everyone must be

---

11. For the full report of the National Climate Assessment in the United States see http://nca2014.globalchange.gov/report.

12. According to the US Centers for Disease Control and Prevention (CDC), a vector is "any organism – such as fleas, ticks, or mosquitoes – that can transmit a pathogen, or infectious agent, from one host to another." Because warmer average temperatures and longer warm seasons, earlier spring seasons, shorter and milder winters, and hotter summers create conditions that tend to prove more hospitable for many carriers of vector-borne diseases, changes in climate are having an impact on the public health environment.

13. The National Climate Assessment Report assesses that "frequency of wildfires is expected to increase as drought conditions become more prevalent. Exposure to allergens will cause health problems for many people. When sensitive individuals are simultaneously exposed to allergens and air pollutants, allergic reactions often become more severe. The increase in air pollutants makes the effects of increased allergens associated with climate change even worse. People with existing pollen allergies may therefore be at increased risk for acute respiratory effects" –http://nca2014.globalchange.gov/report/sectors/human-halth#intro-section-2.

fully aware of recommended preventative actions, in addition to measures for adaptation to new climate realities.

For example, in Latin America and the Caribbean, we have experienced the impact of climate change. Extreme weather events such as severe hurricanes, droughts, floods and wildfires are now frequent occurrences. For example, in 2016 Hurricane Matthew ripped through the Caribbean at category five strength, narrowly by-passing Jamaica and slamming into Haiti. Matthew was the thirteenth storm of the 2016 Atlantic hurricane season. It caused widespread destruction and catastrophic loss of life, including over 1,000 dead in Haiti, 1 in Colombia, 4 in the Dominican Republic, 4 in Cuba, 1 in St Vincent and the Grenadines, and 47 in the United States. It was the costliest Atlantic hurricane since Hurricane Sandy in 2012, with evacuation of over 1 million people in Cuba and damages estimated in excess of US$15 billion.[14] The already over-burdened nation of Haiti bore the brunt of Hurricane Matthew with damages amounting to over US$1.89 billion and 80 percent of the coastal city of Jeremie destroyed.[15]

As Small Island Developing States (SIDS), the beautiful countries of the Caribbean have joined in the global fight for a more sustainable climate future. Such a future, they believe, can be secured if global leaders agree to strive to reduce greenhouse gas emissions, limit the increase in global average temperature to below two degrees, monitor our carbon future, and limit the burning of fossil fuels.[16] Leading up to the Paris Climate Summit in 2015 and since then, the Caribbean's plea for "1.5 to Stay Alive" has been a plea for ecological and economic survival. Caribbean leaders are strongly opposed to and will never allow the overwhelming scientific and experiential evidence of the realities of climate change to be obscured, denied, and by-passed by those who for selfish political and economic gain are seeking to inject their own climate "facts." Global leaders, including church leaders, must firmly commit to the protection of the environment to save the planet, the only home for our common humanity. As Chris Wright has shown, we must embrace what God has embraced. "Trashing someone else's property is incompatible with

---

14. https://en.wikipedia.org/wiki/Hurricane_Matthew.

15. Reported by Nick Bryant, BBC, 6 October 2016. http://www.bbc.com/news/world-us-canada-37576996.

16. This was the agreement made in Paris in December 2015 by 195 countries participating in the UN Framework Convention on Climate Change, known as the Climate Summit. http://unfccc.int/paris_agreement/items/9485.php.

any claim to love that other person," he says in *The Mission of God.*[17] "We care for the earth, most simply, because it belongs to the one whom we call Lord."[18]

Facing the Challenge

Chris Wright recognizes that arguing so boldly for Christian embrace of creation care and engagement in the mission of God in the world risks conflict with powerful forces that are antithetical to God's mission in the world.

> If the church awakens to the urgent need to address the ecological crisis and does so within its biblical framework of resources and vision, then it will engage in missional conflict with at least two other ideologies (and doubtless many more). 1. Destructive global capitalism and the greed that fuels it. 2. Pantheistic, neo-pagan and New Age spiritualties.[19]

Chris recognizes that there are many people, even inside the church, whose attitude towards God's creation is exploitative and uncaring. They are among those who cause damage to creation and danger to humanity. So the challenge for the Christian is to face these risks, firm in the biblical conviction that the creation belongs to God and is loaned to human beings as stewards and managers with moral responsibility for it. Proper environmental care and justice for the earth are therefore required.[20]

I rather like how Karri Munn-Venn, senior policy analyst at Citizens for Public Justice in the US, concluded her article in the *Huffington Post* entitled "Climate Justice as a Matter of Faith." Just ahead of the COP21 summit in Paris she wrote:

> The engagement of faith communities in the work of climate justice is important as it brings added dimension – both moral and spiritual – to an issue once considered the purview of environmental science alone. As institutions of faith, churches

---

17. Wright, *Mission of God*, 414.

18. CTC 1.7a.

19. Wright, *Mission of God*, 417.

20. For example, organizations like Bring Climate Criminals to Justice (BCCJ) in France and the UK are working to highlight and prosecute those whose deliberate actions contribute to climate-related deaths. http://www.climatecriminals.co.uk.

See also Bill McKibben, "The coral die-off crisis is a climate crime and Exxon fired the gun." *The Guardian*, 17 August 2016. https://www.theguardian.com/environment/2016/aug/17/the-coral-die-off-crisis-is-a-climate-and-exxon-fired-the-gun.

have significant resources at their disposal. These include practical actions (greening), political engagement (advocacy), as well as spiritual endeavours (built around prayer) that are available to people from all walks of life. For many, prayer serves as a gateway to action. As faithful citizens, Christians, Muslims, Jews, Buddhists, Hindus, and others respond to the pains of the Earth and the cries of those most marginalized, by living into a calling to love and care for the Earth, to make choices that support the flourishing of creation – and to press their governments to do the same.[21]

---

21. Karri Munn-Venn, "Climate Justice as a Matter of Faith," Huffington Post 12/07/2016. http://www.huffingtonpost.ca/karri-munnvenn/climate-justice-a-matter-_b_8721354.html.

10

Mission as Making (and Wearing) New Clothes

C. Rosalee Velloso Ewell

C. Rosalee Velloso Ewell *is a Brazilian theologian from São Paulo. She earned a PhD from Duke University (USA) and taught for seven years in a cross-confessional seminary in Londrina, Brazil. She is the author and editor of various books and articles and the New Testament editor for the forthcoming* Latin American Bible Commentary. *She currently serves as executive director of the Theological Commission for the World Evangelical Alliance and lives in Birmingham, England.*

Chris Wright has contributed vastly to the fields of missiology, biblical theology and preaching. But two themes stand out in his many works and from the testimony of his life: love and integrity. I have had the privilege of working with Chris in Brazil and through Langham. We were both part of the team drafting the Cape Town Commitment (CTC) for the Lausanne Movement. It was his suggestion that the CTC begin with God's love – God first loved us; we respond and participate in God's mission through love. At the Third Lausanne Conference in Cape Town, Chris delivered a powerful message on integrity and service to God's kingdom. It is thus a privilege and an honour to have this chance to reflect more deeply on these two themes that are so central to all Chris is and has been to so many people around the world.

At first glance, there do not appear to be many links between Genesis 3 and Colossians 3. Genesis 3 narrates the so-called "fall" – that infamous occasion when Eve took the forbidden fruit of the tree of the knowledge of good and evil, ate it, and shared the fruit with Adam. Colossians 3 contains Paul's extraordinary description of our new lives, hidden in Christ and then revealed with Christ in all his glory. But with a little bit of imagination, we can see that together these texts preach to us about what we wear, where our clothes come from, and the musicological implications of these ideas in the contemporary world.

Genesis 3

As Chris notes, the narrative in Genesis 3 exposes the root of idolatry – it shows humans trying to blur the distinction between Creator and creature in that they eat of the tree in order to be "like God." Once Adam and Eve have eaten the fruit, they are not only able to distinguish good and evil, but they take it upon themselves to determine what actually counts as good or evil – a moral prerogative that belongs to God alone.[1]

Dietrich Bonhoeffer describes the two alternatives that Adam has in terms of a choice between two truths – God's truth and the serpent's truth. God's truth is that Adam is a creature made in God's image (*imago Dei*), existing and having his "being for God and neighbour, in its original creatureliness and limitedness."[2] The serpent's truth is that Adam can be similar to God, without limits, knowing good and evil for himself, acting independently for himself and alone in his essential being. The *imago Dei* is bound to the word of God and is "the creature living in the unity of obedience," whereas the *sicut Dei*, the being like God, is bound to the depths of its own knowledge and is the "creator-human-being who lives on the basis of the divide between good and evil."[3]

These two choices have dramatic implications for mission. In some ways, Genesis 3 can be described as the first public square in history. What is mission in the public square? What do the people of God look like as they act out in this space? The text reads:

> Now the serpent was more crafty than any other wild animal that the Lord God had made. He said to the woman: "Did God say that you shall not eat from any tree in the garden?" The woman said to the serpent, "We may eat of the fruit of the trees in the garden, but God said 'you shall not eat of the fruit of the tree that is in the middle of the garden, nor shall you touch it, or you shall die.'" But

---

1. Christopher J. H. Wright, *The Mission of God: Unlocking the Bible's Grand Narrative* (Downers Grove: InterVarsity Press, 2006), 163–165.

2. Dietrich Bonhoeffer, *Creation and Fall: A Theological Exposition of Genesis 1–3* (Minneapolis: Augsburg Fortress, 1997), 113.

3. Ibid.

the serpent said to the woman, "you will not die, for God knows that when you eat of it your eyes will be opened and you will be like God, knowing good and evil." So when the woman saw that the tree was good for food and that it was a delight to the eyes, and that the tree was to be desired to make one wise, she took of its fruit and ate; and she also gave some to her husband, who was with her, and he ate. (Gen 3:1–6)

Adam and Eve were already in the centre of the garden, close enough to that tree to take and eat. They were in the public square of the garden of Eden. The narrative gives us three reasons for why they take the fruit: (i) food is good; (ii) it is a delight to the eyes; (iii) it makes one wise. Food, delight and wisdom are all good things; they are all gifts from God. But the cost of this engagement in the public square went far beyond what Adam and Eve hoped or desired. It was a transformative encounter, though perhaps not in ways that they had planned.

This is the first time in the book of Genesis that a conversation happens without God. The story of creation that began with God is disrupted by a conversation in the public square between Eve and the serpent talking about God, but without God. It is a conversation about gardening without the gardener. It is a conversation about making the world a better place without the world's Creator. Indeed, why would you not want more wisdom?! The serpent's promise is that Eve and Adam will make the world better, *their* world better by having wisdom and independence apart from God, by creating it on their own terms. Their mission becomes about themselves rather than about God; their participation in mission becomes participation in their own plans, their self-sufficient plans, rather than participation in what God has prepared for them.

The problem is not that Eve and Adam were in the public square or engaged in mission. It is also not a problem that they wanted to make the world a better place, or even that they were talking with the serpent. Mission in the public square is a good thing. The problems came when they decided to engage in such mission on their own terms. In doing so, they forgot God's goodness – that God created all things and said that all things were good.

Participation in mission has to be on God's terms, not ours – we are to do and to be as God desires, not as we would like. It is important to remember that though God is not in this conversation between Eve and the serpent, God is also in the public square, but God is often doing things in ways we do not expect or want.

In the Genesis narrative, God as a loving parent comes to his naked children and asks them what is going on. In doing so, says Bonhoeffer, "The Creator is now the preserver; the created world is now the fallen but preserved world. In the world between curse and promise, between *tob* and *ra*, good and evil, God deals with humankind in a distinctive way. 'He made them cloaks,' says the Bible."[4]

God makes something new out of the mess Adam and Eve have created, and in so doing he preserves them and enables them once more for mission. God makes them clothes, he protects them and the garden, offering them a new way to begin. The new beginning, the new way of participating in mission, is once more on God's terms and with limits set by God. The good news is that God is still in the business of making new garments.

In Orthodox theology, the garments of skin that God makes for Adam and Eve represent, among other things, the mortality with which humans are clothed following the fall. According to Gregory of Nyssa and others, it is bad theology to equate the garments with the body as this leads to a gnostic understanding of the human being and therefore a gnostic missiology. Rather, as Panayiotis Nellas explains Genesis 3, life is no longer a characteristic proper to the human being precisely because Adam has chosen to define himself, his life and his mission, apart from God. So in the place of life, the first humans receive death. "Life has been transmuted into survival."[5] Wearing the garments of skin becomes a sign, a symbol of God's care for Adam even after Adam attempted to create himself autonomously "without God and before God and not in accordance with God."[6]

From the biblical narratives to patristic theology to Bonhoeffer, Genesis 3 opens up a story of "being dressed for mission" for contemporary theological reflection on mission and the Scriptures. Despite the fall of humanity and Adam's giving in to the serpent's version of the truth, God is still working to redeem his creation and to enable it to participate with him in the work of redemption. Jesus is not only the "answer" to Adam's fall but is before Adam, creating and enabling us to be part of something new. To understand what it means to be fully and truly human and thus engaged in God's mission, we are called to look to Jesus, not to Adam. And in Jesus, the fullness of our call to

---

4. Ibid., 139.

5. Panayiotis Nellas, *Deification in Christ: Orthodox Perspectives on the Nature of the Human Person* (New York: St Vladimir's Seminary Press, 1997), 47.

6. Ibid., 47–48.

mission, to engagement with God in the world, is realized and made new in radically different ways.

Colossians 3

The context of Colossians is nearly as important for mission as its content and gives us a backdrop for the depth and significance of Paul's words in chapter 3. This is because, unlike many of his other letters such as Philippians or First and Second Corinthians, this letter is written to people Paul does not actually know, to a congregation he had not started. He writes to them from prison because he had heard about them from his friends and learned of some of the struggles they were facing from false teachers, from misunderstandings, and from misguided definitions of what it means to live as God's people in the world. The text is an extraordinarily missiological text. From an empty prison cell, the apostle writes of the fullness of Christ and about the identity and role of God's people in and for the society in which they find themselves.

Many have suggested that the theme of the letter to the Colossians is fullness: the fullness of our knowledge of God, or our fullness in Christ.[7] The concept of fullness is expressed many times in the book: "In Him the *fullness* of God was pleased to dwell" (1:19); "I became a servant [of the church] to make the word of God *fully* known" (1:25); "you have come to *fullness* in him, who is the head of every ruler and authority" (2:10); "Let the word of Christ dwell in you *richly* [or even *fully*!]" (3:16). In fact, we are to be so full of Christ that we have no need of anything or anyone else. But then come the questions: what Christ fills you? What Christ fills us? What Christ is the centre of our missionary and evangelistic practices? What difference does fullness make? Indeed, fullness is a dominant theme in Colossians, but it is fullness with a purpose, with an impetus towards mission and the implications of living out one's identity in society. Just as Adam and Eve were working out the purpose of their being in the public square of Eden, so also the people in Colossae were trying to understand both the source of their identity and the implications of this for their lives in the Roman Empire.

In Latin America, images of Christ vary from a chubby, white, helpless infant in his mother Mary's arms to a full-bearded, dark-skinned revolutionary warrior. In the beginning of chapter 3 of Colossians, Paul says that our life is

---

7. Solomon Andria, "Colossians," in *Africa Bible Commentary* (Jos and Nairobi: Hippo; Grand Rapids: Zondervan, 2006), 1449.

hidden with Christ in God and that when Christ, who is our life, is revealed, we also will be revealed (3:3–4). So it matters a great deal what sort of Christ we are hidden with.

In *The Mission of God*, Chris Wright sets out to offer us a reading of the biblical narratives seen through the eyes of mission. His massive work presents mission as a key theme for better understanding the biblical worldview and God's calling on us as we participate in his works of redemption made possible in Christ and through the Spirit. The biblical narratives that Chris draws out reveal a constant defining and redefining of the people of God. Mission belongs to God and when the people get this wrong and try to define their roles on their own terms, trouble ensues. Redefining our identity suggests that prior definitions of peoplehood were insufficient, lacking or just wrong and idolatrous. Perhaps this was one of the challenges facing those in Colossae. If our understanding is wrong, the first step in mission is repentance for not seeing our identity in Christ and for not letting the Word of God dwell in us fully, as Paul puts it more plainly in his letter to the Colossians.

A reminder of what it means to live in Christ

According to Colossians, if we are going to redefine ourselves as God's people, then we must ask the question, what does it mean to live in Christ? This is important because "living in Christ" is one of the major identity markers that Paul gives us for what it means to be the people of God. As God's holy ones, chosen and beloved (Col 3:12), we are called to be a people of integrity. Receiving Christ, living and walking in Christ are all inseparable for the Christian: "As you therefore have received Christ Jesus the Lord, continue to live your lives in him" (2:6). As the people of God living in the large cosmopolitan city of Colossae, the Colossians are called to live in Christ – to lead lives of integrity and love, fully pleasing to God. For this Paul and his companions pray all the time: "We have not ceased praying for you . . . so that you may lead lives worthy of the Lord, fully pleasing to him" (1:9–10).

In Colossians 3 Paul succinctly defines our identity as the people of God. Yet while these identity markers are timeless and in a way universal, they are not without context and should not be abstracted from the grander biblical narrative. In this very letter, Paul urges the Colossians (and us) to think more carefully about redefining ourselves as God's people in a world of constant change, in a world ruled by death, in a world waiting for us to proclaim the good news of life in Jesus Christ. Just as God had given his people, Israel, a set of laws by which they should live – laws that were to guide their lives so that the peoples around them might come to know God, so Paul gives the Colossians a series of guidelines, new clothes, the wearing of which have radical implications for their witness in that place.

As was mentioned previously, one of the ways Paul defines the identity and the integrity of the people of God in Colossians, is precisely by talking about our life in Christ. Chapter three starts with the words: "So if you have been raised with Christ, set your heart on the things that are above, where Christ is, seated at the right hand of God" (3:1). Paul had already written in 2:6, 9–10, "As you therefore have received Christ Jesus the Lord, continue to live your lives in him . . . for in him the fullness of deity dwells bodily, and you have come to fullness in him." The argument follows an "if . . . then" pattern:

If you have been raised in Christ . . . then set your hearts on things above.

If you have received Christ . . . then continue to live in him.

Paul is explaining two key points to the Colossians: (i) Jesus has come to you and been proclaimed to you and you have received the gospel; and (ii) since you have died and been raised in him, it is not an impossible request to say "put on Christ," or live in Christ. It is Jesus himself who has already enabled the Colossians to do this. There is nothing to boast about – it is Jesus who has already died for us, risen from the dead, and sent his Spirit to enable us to live in him. Just as in Genesis 3 the fullness of life that God promises is based on the terms set by God, and life and mission itself dwell fully in God, so here Paul urges the Colossians to see their identity as being in Christ. This identity is distorted when it is seen as being in oneself, independent from God and from one's neighbour.

A change of clothes and a reorientation of desire

"Set your minds on the things that are above, not on things that are on earth" (Col 3:2) is far better translated as "seek the things" (NRSV, KJV) or even "keep seeking" (NASB), "work at it," "keep practising!" Even though we are enabled by Christ in the Spirit to live accordingly, it is an ongoing, daily practice. One does not simply or easily "have" integrity or love; rather, one works at this with the help of others. We are called to keep seeking this way of being over and over and over again. Redefining ourselves as God's people means we must continually work at developing the practices that lead us to integrity and holiness, loving God and our neighbour.

The distinction between things that are above and things that are on earth is also not a dualistic or gnostic understanding of the human person. Patristic theology reads Colossians 1:18 ("Christ is the head of the body, the church") as the very opposite of Gnosticism. Christ is the head of humanity and therefore, only through being in Christ – in union with the Word that became flesh – do we attain "real substance." Real humans were born when Christ came into this life and was born. For this reason Basil the Great calls the day of Christ's birth truly and not metaphorically "the birthday of humanity."[8] The Christ in whom we are hidden is the Word who became flesh and through Jesus we are transformed into the image of God.

Paul's teaching to the Colossians has much broader implications than just the reversal of what was lost in Adam. Being united with Christ is about redemption and about mission. Christ accomplishes the salvation of humanity not only in a negative way, liberating us from the consequences of original sin, but also in a positive way,

> completing our iconic, prelapsarian being . . . It is no accident that in his letter to the Colossians . . . St Paul calls on every person to become mature in Christ (Col 1:28) and to attain the fullness of Christ. St Paul does not do so for reasons of external piety and sentiment; he speaks ontologically. He is not advocating an external imitation or a simple ethical improvement but real Christification. For, as St Maximus says, "God the divine Logos wishes to effect the mystery of His incarnation always and in all things."[9]

Paul in his prison cell knows that such living is not easy and so he gives his readers some basic guidelines. He gives us a new wardrobe, as it were, and shows us the set of clothes we are to dispose of. One way to think about this has to do with desire. Keep seeking the things that are above. Work at desiring the things that are of God's kingdom. That does not mean a denial of our bodies or a spiritualizing of the Christian life that forgets God's good creation in all its flesh and bone. Not at all! Paul has already said that the fullness of deity was pleased to dwell *bodily* in him, who is ruler over all.

Setting our minds on things that are above is not a guessing game. We do not have to sit around wondering what God wants us to think about or what God wants us to do. He has made it clear in his word, through his prophets,

---

8. Nellas, *Deification*, 38.
9. Ibid., 38–39.

and most importantly, in the life and teachings of Jesus. What is God's will: seek justice, do mercy, take care of the widow and the orphan, tell the truth. Set your mind on these things, practise these things and you will find yourself in the fullness of Christ.

Seek the things that are above. What Paul is saying is that "thinking about the realm of Christ will affect how we live in this present world."[10] It is not just a mind game or a mental exercise; it is not just an ethical code or set of rules, but has to do with the day-to-day stuff of life here on this earth, in many contexts with all their various challenges and joys. It is a reorientation of desires and learning how to desire the things that are of God. It is changing clothes and role playing that has no return for clothes that affects the very being of who we are as individuals and as God's people.

To help us out in our changing of clothes, Paul even gives us a list of some of the old clothes we must set aside daily if we are to live in Christ's realm: fornication, impurity, greed, anger, wrath, malice, and abusive language. Paul's list is not exhaustive or comprehensive, but it is a great start. It is worth noting how many of the things on this list have to do with how we talk: anger, wrath, malice, slander, filthy language. In Brazil, my father had a saying: "either you're also a Christian on the football field or you're not a Christian at all. The alternative is to be a Pharisee."

Redefining ourselves as people of integrity very much includes the way we talk and act towards one another and towards those to whom we witness. As Paul himself says later in Colossians, "Let your speech always be gracious, seasoned with salt, so that you may know how you ought to answer everyone" (4:5). This is being in Christ and being for mission.

A change of clothes and a reorientation of power

There is a tendency for those in Christian ministry and leadership to think they need to change the world in great ways, with wonderful projects and big plans for Christians to secure power and then bring change to this troubled earth. Chris Wright's integrity and his faithfulness to the Scriptures offers the church a beautiful contrast to such tendencies and a reminder that being hidden and clothed in Christ is our first calling, from the very beginning.

The lists that Paul gives us in Colossians 3 point far less to big schemes and grand plans to change the world and remind us instead that it is the little

---

10. Andria, "Colossians," 1455.

things that matter. Changing the world is about changing one life at a time, one story at a time and doing so on God's terms rather than on those we set for ourselves. It is in the daily, rather mundane activities of being careful about the words we use, the things we desire, and the people we serve, that we define or redefine our identity as God's holy people. And it is these little things that the world and those around us will notice.

These small things also direct us to the type of power and authority that characterize the people of God. Paul not only lists for us the types of clothes we need to tear up and dispose of, he also guides the Colossians towards particular practices and virtues that the Spirit gives in order for us to live as the holy, beloved and missionary people of God.

Again there is a reminder about our speech – we must not lie to one another because we have put on new clothes that are being renewed in knowledge in the image of the Creator (3:9–10). The renewal of our identity is only possible because of Christ in and through whom power, authority and desire are redefined and reoriented. Paul explains this reorientation in Colossians 3:12–15.

> Put on compassion, kindness, humility, meekness and patience.
> Bear with one another, and if anyone has a complaint against
> another, forgive each other. Just as the Lord has forgiven you, so
> you also must forgive. Above all, clothe yourselves with love . . .
> and let the peace of Christ rule in your hearts, let the word of
> Christ dwell in you. Be thankful.

The power and authority of being in Christ lie precisely in the gifts of kindness, humility, patience, putting up with one another. If the world's public square is what is shaping our desires and dreams, then the risk for the Colossians (and us) is that our identity and mission will be centred on ourselves – we will be like Adam, trying to be like God. When we follow the world's way, we become the centre, we become full of ourselves and not full of Christ. But in these texts Paul is saying, "It's not about you! It's about Jesus." We are to be filled with Christ – with Christ's peace, with Christ's word, with Christ's love, and we are to do everything in the name of Jesus. This is a radical shift in power because at its very core it is a reorientation of our lives in light of one who served, who was tried and executed on a cross. Servants are hidden, and in Colossians Paul argues that our lives are to be of such service that we are not known precisely because we are hidden with Christ. Christ can and should be known, but only through our service. This is about giving up power and not listening to the serpent, about putting on clothes that the world does not think are pretty.

Mission and Story

One of the gifts Chris has given the church in his writings and preaching is the emphasis on the biblical narratives as stories. He not only draws key principles for life and mission from the texts, but also directs us to reflect more deeply and to take more seriously the narratives themselves. We learn about obedience and faithfulness through walking with Abram from one land to another; we learn of suffering and patience through the stories of Israel in the desert and in exile; we are encouraged to have ears to hear through the stories of the prophets, through John the Baptist and the crowds listening to Jesus on the hillside.

In Genesis 3 we read of the terrible consequences of what happens when we do not listen to the stories of God and turn our attention to the narratives of others. In Colossians 3 we read of the wonder and the challenge of participating in a story far greater than our own and being transformed in and through that greater story. In these ways, the missiological impetus of the Scriptures is about participating in God's story. As Stephen Shoemaker puts it,

> Our lives must find their place in some greater story or they will find their place in some lesser story . . . To give ourselves over to these lesser stories and images (sex, money, ambition, fame) is to live a life diminished and fragmented. The purpose of Scripture is to unite us to our Maker and to invite us into God's world of justice, grace, peace, order, hope, mercy, where God is making us and all the world whole. It is the story itself that moves us into its sacred sphere.[11]

The God of the Bible is the God who continually makes new garments for his people, teaching them how to dress, how to be, so that the world might know who is the one true God. This missiological view of Scripture also highlights that we are not alone in this story. It matters who is on the journey with us. Being God's people and participating in God's mission implies being with others, and especially with others whom we might not have chosen to be with if mission were on our own terms. It is in the messiness of the narratives

---

11. H. Stephen Shoemaker, *God Stories: New Narratives from Sacred Texts* (Valley Forge: Judson, 1998), xix.

that God works out our salvation. In the stories of imperfect churches and broken relationships, God gives us new clothes and a new way to be God's people in this world.

As we draw closer to Christ and are hidden in Christ (the "Christification" of which patristic theology writes), we are drawn closer to one another – we are not alone when hidden in Christ. The missiological expression of this is precisely in being a people who show in words, deeds, and character that another world is not only possible but is already here in Jesus and his kingdom. We are to wear the clothes of this kingdom and rejoice in God's promises to bless us and to raise us up with Christ in all his glory.

References

Andria, Solomon. "Colossians." In *Africa Bible Commentary*. Jos and Nairobi: Hippo; Grand Rapids; Zondervan, 2006, 1449–1458.

Bonhoeffer, Dietrich. *Creation and Fall: A Theological Exposition of Genesis 1–3*. Minneapolis: Augsburg Fortress, 1997.

Nellas, Panayiotis. *Deification in Christ: Orthodox Perspectives on the Nature of the Human Person*. New York: St Vladimir's Seminary Press, 1997.

Shoemaker, H. Stephen. *God Stories: New Narratives from Sacred Texts*. Valley Forge: Judson Press, 1998.

Wright, Christopher J. H. *The Mission of God: Unlocking the Bible's Grand Narrative*. Downers Grove: InterVarsity Press, 2006.

11

Election, Ethics, Mission and the Church in India

Paul Swarup

Paul Swarup *is a Langham Scholar who holds a ThM from Princeton and a PhD from Cambridge. He is ordained in the Church of North India and is currently presbyter in charge of the Cathedral Church of the Redemption in the Diocese of Delhi. He was a major contributor to the* South Asia Bible Commentary, *and one of the Old Testament editors for that volume.*

It gives me great joy to write for this festschrift as Chris Wright was the one who made the Old Testament exciting and alive during his lectures at Union Biblical Seminary, Pune, from 1983–1987 and was also my guide for my BD thesis. His inspirational teaching encouraged me to delve deeper into the texts.

One of the things that has been etched in my mind is the paradigm he taught using triangles to show how the election of Israel was for the sake of the nations and how election, ethics and mission are interlinked. That paradigm has helped me to understand the theology of both the Old and New Testaments. In this paper, I will highlight these three aspects and look at how they make a difference in the Indian context.

Election

The dictionary defines *election* as "A formal and organized choice by vote of a person for a political office or other position."[1] So it seems to refer to a formal

---

1. https://en.oxforddictionaries.com/definition/election.

and organized choice for any position. In the Old Testament we see election at work in regard to Abraham and Israel.

Abraham

In Genesis 12 Abraham is called by God to leave his country:

> Go from your country, your people and your father's household to the land I will show you. "I will make you into a great nation, and I will bless you; I will make your name great, and you will be a blessing. I will bless those who bless you, and whoever curses you I will curse; and all peoples on earth will be blessed through you." (Gen 12:1–3)

Abraham is promised posterity, land, and that he will be a blessing to the nations. In Genesis 15, this promise is confirmed as God unilaterally enters into a covenant with Abraham. It will be another twenty-five years before the promise of posterity begins to be fulfilled with the birth of Isaac to the aged Abraham and Sarah.

The context of the covenant with Abraham is significant. If we look back in the biblical text, we note that God had created everything good, but with the entry of sin human beings became alienated from God and had to leave the garden of Eden and the very presence of God. From Genesis 4 to 11 we see the global spread of sin, with the climax in the building of the tower of Babel as an act of rebellion against God. It is against this backdrop that we need to understand the election of Abraham to be a blessing to the nations. It is always God who takes the first steps to reconcile his people to himself.

God also made it clear that his covenant had some conditions attached. In Genesis 18:19 the Lord says, "For I have chosen him, so that he will direct his children and his household after him to keep the way of the Lord by doing what is right and just, so that the Lord will bring about for Abraham what he has promised him." The ethical and missional role of Israel is made explicit in this verse. God chooses Abraham in order that he will direct his children and all his descendants to keep to the way of the Lord, by doing what is right and just, so that the Lord will make him a blessing to the nations. Literally, God does not say "I have chosen him" but rather "I have known him" (יְדַעְתִּיו), a word which indicates intimate knowledge rather than just mere head knowledge. This choice is *election*. Keeping of the way of the Lord by doing what is right and just is *ethics*; and fulfilling the responsibility to be a blessing to the nations is *mission*. Election, ethics and mission are directly connected to each other.

The purpose of the calling was so that a God-fearing community would be formed who would reflect the character of God.

Israel

The election of Abraham continues with the reaffirmation of the covenant promise to Isaac (Gen 26:2–3) and to Jacob (Gen 35:10–12). However, by the time we come to the end of the book of Genesis we see Jacob and his descendants arriving in Egypt in a time of famine. God made miraculous provisions for them through Joseph, but Joseph is soon forgotten as another Pharaoh takes charge and the Israelites are enslaved. They are treated cruelly and groan under their slavery. They cry to Yahweh and he remembers his covenant with Abraham, Isaac and Jacob and moved into action. He calls Moses to challenge Pharaoh and to lead his people out of Egypt to the promised land:

> God also said to Moses, "I am the LORD. I appeared to Abraham, to Isaac and to Jacob as God Almighty, but by my name the LORD I did not make myself fully known to them. I also established my covenant with them to give them the land of Canaan, where they resided as foreigners. Moreover, I have heard the groaning of the Israelites, whom the Egyptians are enslaving, and I have remembered my covenant.
>
> "Therefore, say to the Israelites: 'I am the LORD, and I will bring you out from under the yoke of the Egyptians. I will free you from being slaves to them, and I will redeem you with an outstretched arm and with mighty acts of judgment. I will take you as my own people, and I will be your God. Then you will know that I am the LORD your God, who brought you out from under the yoke of the Egyptians. And I will bring you to the land I swore with uplifted hand to give to Abraham, to Isaac and to Jacob. I will give it to you as a possession. I am the LORD.'" (Exod 6:2–9)

Yahweh uses Moses to demonstrate his power by enabling him to perform miracles and bring plagues on Egypt. He delivers the Israelites with his mighty acts, and then at Mount Sinai he gives them the commandments and makes a new covenant with them. The commands are given after he has acted in deliverance and they are asked to obey them as an act of gratitude.

Before the Ten Commandments are given, Yahweh makes it very clear that he was the one who brought them out of Egypt, out of the land of slavery (Exod 20:2). God identifies himself and his redeeming activity before the law is given. Right from the start, then, Israel's keeping of God's law was meant to be a response to what God had already done. This is the foundation of ethics and the key principle running through the moral teaching of the whole Bible. The same order is seen in the New Testament: "Love each other as I have loved you" (John 15:12); "We love because he first loved us" (1 John 4:19).

God's universal interest

Yahweh reminds the Israelites that obedience to him and keeping his covenant were key to their becoming Yahweh's own people: "Now therefore, if you will obey my voice and keep my covenant, you shall be my treasured possession out of all the peoples. Indeed, the whole earth is mine, but you shall be for me a priestly kingdom and a holy nation" (Exod 19: 5–6).

Yahweh makes it clear that all the nations are under his control but that Israel has been chosen for a particular purpose. Israel was a nation among the nations, yet Israel was called to be distinct and different from the other nations. Its historical origin was unique due to God's calling of Abraham, his deliverance of them from slavery in Egypt, the covenant he made with them at Sinai and his gift of the land. Yet all that God did in and for Israel was for the benefit of humanity as a whole.

Ethics

In order for Israel to be a blessing to the nations, they had to be ethically distinct. The context of Genesis 18:19, in which God said "For I have chosen him, so that he will direct his children and his household after him to keep the way of the LORD by doing what is right and just, so that the LORD will bring about for Abraham what he has promised him." is the Lord's conversation with Abraham as the angels set out to destroy Sodom because of the outcry (Heb. *zayaqah*) of those it was oppressing. By contrast, Abraham and his descendants are called to practice righteousness (Heb. *sedaqah*) and justice (Heb. *mishpat*). The very purpose of the call of Abraham and his descendants was that they would uphold an ethical agenda in the midst of a world full of Sodoms.[2] The children were to be instructed in the "way of the Lord," which meant teaching them the law of the Lord and training them to observe his commands (Exod

---

2. Christopher J. H. Wright, *Old Testament Ethics for the People of God* (Leicester: IVP, 2004), 50.

12:25–27; Deut 6:1–3, 6–7, 20–25). They were to be a people who would imitate the character of the Yahweh by committing themselves to practising righteousness and justice in their individual and corporate lives. Chris Wright points out that "these are unquestionably social-ethical values, with economic and political implications."[3]

The calling of Abraham and his descendants was not to take them out of their environment and have them abdicate their socio-political responsibility; rather, it was so that they would be governed by righteousness and justice in their corporate life. This was going to be the means by which they would show themselves to be distinct and reflect the Lord's character in the midst of all the other nations. This is also the call of Christians as we see in Jesus's prayer for his disciples and followers in John's gospel:

> My prayer is not that you take them out of the world but that you protect them from the evil one. They are not of the world, even as I am not of it. Sanctify them by the truth; your word is truth. As you sent me into the world, I have sent them into the world. For them I sanctify myself, that they too may be truly sanctified.
>
> My prayer is not for them alone. I pray also for those who will believe in me through their message, that all of them may be one, Father, just as you are in me and I am in you. May they also be in us so that the world may believe that you have sent me. (John 17:20–21)

I would like to look closely at the three phrases that are used to describe what is expected of the descendants of Abraham in Genesis 18:19. The first is "to keep the way of the LORD." The word "keep" in Hebrew is *shamar*, which is also used to mean "guard" or "protect." It implies that keeping the way of the Lord requires active effort to be obedient to the commands of God. It involves being like the psalmist, who says, "I have hidden your word in my heart that I might not sin against you" (Ps 119:11). In Psalm 1 we are shown the two ways open to every human being – the way of the wicked and the way of the righteous. The righteous person delights in the law of the Lord and meditates on it day and night, allowing God's word to form his or her character. The final outcome of both ways is also clearly explained in Psalm 1; the way of the wicked leads to death and the way of the righteous to life. The way of the Lord is the path marked out for Abraham's descendants and for us by God's command.

---

3. Ibid., 221.

The second phrase in Genesis 18:19 requires them to "do what is right and just." We need to understand clearly what righteousness (Heb. *sedaqah*) and justice (Heb. *mishpat*) mean as these terms were frequently used together and had a clear meaning that was understood by the people of Israel.[4] In the Hebrew Bible the word pair occur five times in the order *sedeqah* and *mishpat* (Gen 18:19; Job 37:23; Ps 33:5; Prov 21:3; Isa 58:2), and twenty-four times in the reverse order *mishpat* and *sedaqah* (1 Kgs 10:9; 1 Chr 18:14; Isa 33:5; Jer 9:23; Ezek 18:5; Amos 5:7, 24; 6:12, etc.). The triplet *emet*, *sedaqah* and *mishpat* occurs in Jeremiah 4:2.[5]

Sedaqah or righteousness is about the right order of things. It describes things as they ought to be from God's perspective. There is a certain right order that God has established in all of creation and also in relationships. To be righteous is to maintain those standards, whether in an individual life or in society or in relationship to God. The Lord revealed to Israel how they were to relate to him and to each other. The law served the purpose of helping the people of God to live in conformity to the will of God. The person who was devoted to the service of God in worship and life was called righteous (Mal 3:18). Thus, righteousness is a state of integrity in relation to God and others, expressing itself in one's speech and actions. Just as the Lord is righteous in his creative, sustaining, and salvific acts, so people are expected to act and speak in ways that exhibit and advance righteousness (Hos 10:12).

Sedeqah has various shades of meaning: It can refer to loyalty to the community in conduct and in honesty (Gen 30:33; 1 Kgs 3:6); it can refer to the justice of a human judge or a king, which includes the elimination of anything that threatens peace and good order (Gen 18:19; 2 Sam 8:15; 1 Kgs 10:9; Isa 5:7); it can refer to the justness of the divine judge who takes action in order to set things right (Isa 5:16; 6:31; Jer 9:23); it can also refer to legitimacy or a legal right or entitlement (2 Sam 19:29; Jer 33:15). So when we try to explain what righteousness means we need to use words like "loyalty," "reliability," "trustworthiness," or "the way things ought to be." It is like a pair of scales when the two pans are equal indicating that the weight is exactly right. It describes somebody who keeps promises. It implies that the person is reliable

---

4. The Dead Sea Scrolls community saw them as upholding *emet*, *sedaqah* and *mishpat*. The same phrasing occurs in 1QS I:5 l *l'soth*, *emet*, and *sedaqah* and *mishpat*, and also in 1QS V:3–4 wl*'soth*, *emet yakhad w'nwah wsedaqah wmishpat* as part of the rule which sets out for the functioning of the community.

5. The common word-pair *mishpat* and *sedaqah* is not found in Micah 6:8, where *mishpat* occurs alone.

and can be trusted. There is a certain constancy, loyalty and trustworthiness about that person.

Sedeq therefore entails maintaining stability, steadiness, and constancy despite changing times and situations. The semantic opposite of *sedeq* is *mirmah*, which means lies, deceit, and deception. So *sedeq* represents truth. Truth is not an abstract value – as implied in Pilate's question, "What is truth?" but something that is concrete and expressed in the context of relationships through faithfulness and reliability.

The other word that is used is *mishpat* or justice, which can be used in the context of a judicial decision or judgement, a dispute or a case, a legal claim, a measure/plan and a law. *Mishpat* is the act of setting right things that have gone wrong. The word acknowledges the reality that loyalty and stability are not always maintained in a fallen world. Here the dynamic aspect of the Old Testament concept of justice comes into play. *Mishpat*, the judicial decision, aims at reversing developments that have led to hardship and people being marginalized. In Akkadian the term is *misharu*. It literally means "making straight," "making something even," "making things fluid and bringing movement into things that had come to a standstill." This is the dynamic aspect of *mishpat*.

Where *sedeqah* is durative and static, *mishpat* is the dynamic. It restores things to what they ought to be. Many of the kings of ancient West Asia inaugurated their reigns with a proclamation of the cancellation of debts, liberation of slaves, and the return of land taken as payment of debt to the original owners. It gave people a second chance to join the mainstream of life. It also restored the balance in society when the gap between the rich and the poor had become dangerously wide. The jubilee year instituted in Leviticus 25 was a similar edict which restored people to their inheritance. Similarly, in Isaiah 61 we have a proclamation of justice: "The Lord has sent me to bring good news to the oppressed, to bind up the broken-hearted, to proclaim liberty to the captives, and release to the prisoners, to proclaim the year of the Lord's favour." Although in some contexts *mishpat* was used in a forensic sense, there is strong evidence that it originally referred to the restoration of a situation or environment that promoted equity and harmony (*shalom*) in a community.[6]

Mishpat is the rescue of those who had fallen through the social net and their reintegration into the society so that they can again participate in

---

6. T. L. J. Mafico, "Just, Justice," *The Anchor Yale Bible Dictionary* 3: 1127–1128.

communal life. This aspect of justice is constantly endorsed by the prophets (Jer 22:3).

The two concepts of *sedeq* and *mishpat* account for the comprehensive concept of justice in the Old Testament. *Sedeq* is the art of maintaining loyalty and reliability throughout the ever-changing flow of life. *Mishpat* is the art of restoring people to give them a new chance if they have fallen out of the mainstream of life.

Mission

We now come to the final phrase of Genesis 18:19: "so that the LORD will bring about for Abraham what he has promised him." The promise to Abraham and his descendants was that they would be a blessing to the nations if they lived the spiritual-ethical life God had called them to in the midst of the nations. Through the behaviour of Israel, the neighbouring nations would get to know who Yahweh is.

We need to examine three key texts, Genesis 18, Exodus 19, and Deuteronomy 4, to see how ethics and mission are directly related.

Genesis 18:19 clearly shows that the ethical agenda is connected to Abraham's election and God's mission. Abraham and his descendants were to "keep the way of the Lord." What does this phrase mean? Abraham was meant to be a teacher who would teach his descendants to walk in Yahweh's ways and do justice and righteousness as opposed to the ways of the other gods or of other nations or their own way or the way of the sinners.[7] This is particularly in the context of Sodom which seems to be the model of the way of the world.

Walking in the way of the Lord could mean that the people of Israel were to carefully observe how God acted with them and follow in his footsteps. God was to be their guide and example and they would follow him. It could also mean that they were to closely follow the instructions God had given in order to reach their destination. In this the key factor is obedience. The laws they were given reflected the character of God and were based on it. If they were obedient to the law, then they would be reflecting the character of God, and so would be a blessing to the nations around them.

As we saw above, the paired words "righteousness and justice" are concrete nouns in the Hebrew. They refer to actual things you do, not abstract ideas

---

7. Christopher J. H. Wright, *The Mission of God: Unlocking the Bible's Grand Narrative* (Leicester: IVP, 2006), 363.

or concepts that you think about. Abraham is called to exercise these virtues, in contrast to the wickedness being practised in Sodom that led to an outcry against it by the oppressed (Gen 18:20; see also Ezek 16:49–50). God moves into action as he is moved by the suffering of the oppressed and acts against the oppressor. Likewise, Abraham is to follow God's model and care for the oppressed. Following Abraham, Israel was to do likewise.

Birch and Rasmussen state that the collective moral reasoning of Israel went like this:

> If the majestic and elusive presence called Yahweh redeemed us, the poor, and knew our sufferings, the sufferings of slaves, so too must we show compassion and redeem the victim and the excluded. If mighty Yahweh visited us as strangers in the land of Egypt and extended saving hospitality to us, we in turn must not oppress strangers but take them in and give them refuge. Indeed, we must love the neighbor, including the stranger as ourselves. If mighty Yahweh identified with us, the powerless and the dispossessed, so too should we as the community of Yahweh. Radical love and caring justice are not optional acts of voluntary piety; they are at the heart of what it means for us to be a people of this God.[8]

Yet in the evangelical world today, righteousness is seldom mentioned. We hear talk about morality, spirituality and piety, but seldom about righteousness. Yet, as Sproul says,

> the goal of our redemption is not piety or spirituality but righteousness. Spirituality in the New Testament sense is a means to the end of righteousness. Being spiritual means that we are exercising the spiritual graces given by God to mould us after the image of His Son. The disciplines of prayer, Bible study, church fellowship, witnessing, and the like are not ends in themselves, but are designed to assist us in living righteously. We are stunted in our growth if we assume that the end of the Christian life is spirituality.[9]

The second passage we need to look at is Exodus 19:4–6:

---

8. Bruce Birch and Larry Rasmussen, *Bible and Ethics in the Christian Life* (Minneapolis: Augsburg, 1988), 28.

9. R. C. Sproul, *Can I Know God's Will?*, Crucial Questions Series 4 (Lake Mary, FL: Reformation Trust, 2009), 14.

"You yourselves have seen what I did to Egypt, and how I carried you on eagles' wings and brought you to myself. Now if you obey me fully and keep my covenant, then out of all nations you will be my treasured possession. Although the whole earth is mine, you will be for me a kingdom of priests and a holy nation." These are the words you are to speak to the Israelites.

We note here that Yahweh first narrates all that he has done for the people of Israel, particularly how he saved them from oppression. It is after this act of redemption that the law is given and they are told to obey it. God always takes the initiative in redeeming us and then expects us to respond in obedience as an act of gratitude for all that he has done for us. The order is the same in the New Testament. God first acts for us – Christ died for us while we were still sinners (Rom 5:8) – and then expects us to respond in obedience. Yahweh goes on to promise the outcome of their obedience: they would be a "treasured possession . . . a kingdom of priests and a holy nation." I would like us to look at these three expressions.

A treasured possession

The phrase "treasured possession" comes from the Hebrew word *segullah*, which refers to somebody's personal property that is very dear to them. It conveys a sense of belonging. When God talks about Israel as a treasured possession, it shows that Israel belongs to God. The picture is like that of a woman clasping her newborn baby in her arms, close to her heart. The word communicates the idea that the property or possession is something very personal and close to the heart of the owner. Israel fully belonged to God. In other words, they were accountable to him for whatever they did. He was responsible for them, to take care of them and to protect them. But all this was conditional on their obedience to his commands. You and I are also God's *segullah*/treasured possession, provided we are obedient to him.

Kingdom of priests

A second term used to define Israel's identity is that it is "a kingdom of priests" – *mamlekheth kohenim*. A priest's primary role was to represent God to the people and bring the people to God. But what does it mean to call a whole nation priestly? A priest in Old Testament thought and practice stood between God and the people, a mediator in both directions. He was someone who stood in the gap. He represented God to the people, both in his person and example (cf. Lev 21:22), and especially in his role as a teacher (Deut 33:10; Hos 4:6; Mal 2:4–7). Through the priests, the word and will of God were to be made known to the people. Now if Israel as a nation were to be priests, the implication is that they would represent God to humankind in a similar way. God's way would be made manifest in their life as a nation.

It would be as they lived out the quality of national and social life demanded by the law, with its great themes of freedom, justice, love and compassion, that they would function as God's holy priesthood, as a nation, among the nations, for the nations.

In Romans 15:16 Paul addresses the Romans saying that he had written to them boldly "because of the grace given me by God to be a minister of Christ Jesus to the Gentiles in the priestly service of the gospel of God, so that the offering of the Gentiles may be acceptable, sanctified by the Holy Spirit." What is Paul's priestly ministry and what sacrifice does he offer? Paul sees his role as being like that of an Old Testament priest especially in relation to temple sacrifices. He considers his work a priestly ministry because he is able to offer his Gentile converts as a living sacrifice to God.

A holy nation

The third phrase used to define Israel's identity was that they were to be a holy nation – *goi kadosh*. The word "holy" meant they were to be distinct and different from the people around them. They were historically unique because of the way that Yahweh had delivered them from bondage out of Egypt. They were also to be distinct in their religious behaviour. They were not to have any other gods or idols. There were to be no compromises with the religious practices of the nations around them. Moreover, religious distinctiveness alone was not sufficient, because the outwardly orthodox worship of the Lord could flourish alongside the most blatant oppression and injustice. This led the prophets to use vehemently indignant language (Isa 1:13–17). The Israelites were also expected to lead ethical lives so that others would see Yahweh's character reflected in them. Socially too they were to be distinct, though Israel fails at this and asks for a king so that they will be like the other nations (1 Sam 8:19–22).

The third text is taken from Deuteronomy 4:32–34:

> Ask now about the former days, long before your time, from the
> day God created human beings on the earth; ask from one end

of the heavens to the other. Has anything so great as this ever happened, or has anything like it ever been heard of? Has any other people heard the voice of God speaking out of fire, as you have, and lived? Has any god ever tried to take for himself one nation out of another nation, by testings, by signs and wonders, by war, by a mighty hand and an outstretched arm, or by great and awesome deeds, like all the things the LORD your God did for you in Egypt before your very eyes?

Yahweh reminded the people of Israel that they were a unique nation who had seen him in all his power and glory. The exodus with its plagues, the death of the firstborn, the parting of the sea, and the death of the Egyptian soldiers was an event the people of Israel had witnessed firsthand. No other nation had the same kind of experiences as the people of Israel had when they were formed as a nation. At Mount Sinai when the commandments were given, they heard the voice of God speaking out of the fire and yet nothing happened to them. Their intimacy and closeness with Yahweh and his mighty power were unique. It was after he had liberated them from bondage to the Egyptians that they were given the law. They were to keep the law as an act of gratitude for what Yahweh had done for them.

Israel failed to fulfil her calling as God's chosen vessel for the sake of the nations. She broke the covenant on numerous occasions and went after other gods, forgetting all that Yahweh had done for her. In the end, we see that Jesus fulfils the role of Israel as God's servant. He leads a life that is pleasing in God's sight without sin.

After the coming of Christ and his work on the cross, his disciples are expected to carry on with the work of being a blessing to the nations. The church, which now fulfils the role of Israel, is expected to be the light to the nations and a blessing to them.

Election, Ethics and Mission within the Indian Church

Distinct "within" or distinct "without"?

How does the church in India understand election, ethics and mission? Many Christians in India seem to feel that they have been called by God as a special people and are therefore superior to others. This attitude is rampant among the clergy, who assume that they have been selected by God because they deserve it. The very idea of having been chosen for the sake of others is completely lost. Clergy and lay people tend to think more of what they can get out of their special status than what they can give to others. The idea of being servants and serving one another in love appears to be totally forgotten. The church looks inward rather than looking outward and seeking to meet the needs of the people around us.

If God has placed us in a geographical location as a diocese or as a church, we are called to be a blessing to the people who live around us. Yet too often we are more focused on the members on our roll than on the members of the society around us for whom we have been primarily called. This calls for deep introspection by the church. We must ask serious questions about whether we are fulfilling the mission of God by being a blessing to the nations. How would the church look if it was to be distinct "without" that is, within the world rather than within its own community?

If the Indian church is to be distinct without, then it has to engage corporately in the issues facing the nation today. Some of the key problems that India faces are the caste system, poverty, corruption, the vast gulf between the rich and the poor, terrorism, and communal tensions. But if we are to speak against the caste system, then we have to make sure that the caste system does not have a role to play within the church. The church has to be seen as a multi-ethnic, multi-racial community rather than one divided along on caste lines. Unfortunately, many of our churches themselves are divided on these lines and there are even specific churches for specific castes. This shows that instead of the church being distinct, it has merged with the world. We have also failed to show our unity in coming together and being a blessing to our nation. Our many denominational differences have hindered us from being distinct in the eyes of the world.

Compassion, reliability, constancy and loyalty

The Indian church has also failed to understand that ethics is a necessity for mission to take place. We can only be a blessing to others when we too walk in the way of the Lord by doing what is just and right and exhibiting the character of Jesus. True compassion needs to be exhibited in the church towards the needs of the world. We are called to reach out to the poor, the marginalized and the oppressed and stand with them for justice. We are called to be a reliable and trustworthy community in the midst of a nation where there is rampant corruption and moral degradation. Moreover, poverty is growing and the divide between the rich and the poor seems to be widening. In all this the Indian church is called to be a prophetic voice.

However, the problem within the Indian church is its lack of ethics, both among the clergy and the laity. The desire for power and positions seem to be the motivating factor rather than a desire to serve others in love in order to be a blessing. As we noted earlier, Birch and Rasmussen say that "radical love and caring justice are not optional acts of voluntary piety" but are at the heart of what it means to be the followers of Jesus Christ. We cannot reflect the character of God if the church in India, both as individuals and as a corporate body, does not practise justice and righteousness.

Finally, the church in India can only be a blessing to the people of India and the nations around us as we begin to hold the three concepts of election, ethics and mission together. As the members of the Indian church begin to understand that they have been elected for the sake of others, then we will indeed be a blessing to our nation. When there is loyalty and stability within the church community, then we will be like the salt of the earth and the light of the world. When there is truth and integrity within our community, then we will indeed be agents of change in a corrupt society. When we are filled with the compassion of Christ then we will truly engage with the poor and the oppressed.

Chris Wright's writings challenging us to hold election, ethics and mission together provide a valuable guide to the church as we seek to fulfil our mission and calling in India.

12

Challenging Poverty in Egypt

Andrea Z. Stephanous

Andrea Zaki Stephanous *has a BTh from Cairo Evangelical Seminary, an MA in Theological Studies from Eastern University, Pennsylvania, and a PhD from the University of Manchester. He is general director of the Coptic Evangelical Organization for Social Services (CEOSS), president of the Protestant Churches of Egypt, and president of the Fellowship of Middle East Evangelical Churches. Dr Zaki teaches at the Evangelical Theological Seminary in Cairo, and is the author of* Jesus and Historical Criticism: The Story of the Conflict between Salvation and Social Change *and* Copts and Revolution. *His other book,* Political Islam, Citizenship and Minorities: The Future of Arab Christians in the Middle East, *has been published in Arabic, English and German. He has also written numerous articles for Arab and English news media and Christian magazines.*

This article is a tribute to the thoughtfulness and curiosity that Chris Wright has helped me develop through our friendship over the past twenty years. As a fellow academic, author, and clergyman, I have been fortunate to be able to work with and learn from Chris on many different fronts – through his books, personal interaction, and the work of Langham and Lausanne.

Chris's pioneering theological thought and writing has taken the Christian faith beyond its literal limitations. We have translated and published many of his books in Egypt. They have been important resources for hundreds of pastors across the Middle East.

Chris has given us the gift of his time through many conferences with church leaders, pastors, and teachers who are active in the Christian faith arena of the Middle East. Discussions and thought-provoking studies with Chris have enlightened and broadened the perspective of Arab Christian theology. It is an honour to count Chris as a friend and colleague.

Introduction

The question of the relative priority of evangelism and social action has challenged Christian churches in Egypt for over five decades. The question became a focus when people started asking questions like, "Which is a better use of time and resources: providing temporary relief to the poor and suffering, or focusing on the salvation of souls?" This led to another question, "Is salvation for this life or the next?"

There were many attempts to deal with this issue. Some started from the biblical concept of salvation and social action. Others began with an analysis of the present historical situation of oppression and built an approach based on situational analysis and biblical concepts that support this analysis. My aim here is to begin with theological reflection on the concept of the kingdom of God, which I see as the theological foundation for the debate.

There have, of course, been numerous interpretations of the kingdom of God. These interpretations can be divided into eschatological and non-eschatological interpretations. Non-eschatological interpretations hold to a social concept of the kingdom: "The kingdom of God is the organization of humanity through action inspired by love."[1] Proponents of the social gospel argue that the kingdom was to come on earth in history. "Jesus never transferred the kingdom hope from earth to heaven. The kingdom is so much of this earth that Jesus expected to return to earth from heaven in order to set it up."[2] According to this view, the kingdom of God is always present. It is humanity organized according to the will of God. It is a nobler social order and it implies the progressive reign of love in human affairs.

In the eschatological interpretation, the kingdom of God is regarded as coming in the future. Those who hold this view, argue that interpreting the kingdom as a present spiritual reality involves importing an element that was not in Jesus's mind. His message was a consistent and continuous eschatology. The kingdom was entirely a future apocalyptic reality that would come by a miraculous intrusion of God into history to terminate human history and inaugurate the kingdom.[3] Rudolf Bultmann, for example, argued that Jesus viewed the kingdom of God as an entirely futuristic world-transforming

---

1. Albert Ritschl, *The Christian Doctrine of Justification and Reconciliation* (New York: Scribner, 1900), 12.

2. Walter Rauschenbush, *Christianizing the Social Order* (Cairo: Macmillan, 1912), 49–66.

3. George Eldon Ladd, *Crucial Questions about the Kingdom of God* (Manila: Eerdmans, 1952), 29–32.

event. The kingdom is present in the recurrent "now" of decision that people can experience in the demand for radical obedience as they encounter their neighbours.[4]

Evangelicals would argue that the kingdom of God is the redemptive reign of God, who is dynamically active to establish his rule among people. This kingdom, which will become manifest through an apocalyptic act at the end of the age, has already come into human history in the person and mission of Jesus, who came to overcome evil, deliver humans from its power, and bring them into the blessings of God's reign. The kingdom of God thus involves both fulfilment within history and consummation at the end of history.[5] Thus the kingdom of God is both present and future. In other words, in the dynamic concept of the kingdom of God, we are testing the age to come in our age. While the kingdom is a present reality, it does not belong exclusively to this age in terms of values and principles. It also belongs to that age which is to come.

The basic summary of the kingdom is found in Mark 1:14–15. "After John was put in prison, Jesus went into Galilee, proclaiming the good news of God. The time has come, he said. The kingdom of God has come near. Repent and believe the good news." But what is the good news of the kingdom? Sider argues that this good news recalls the prophets' messianic hope:

> In the midst of oppression, idolatry and captivity, the prophets looked to the future messianic time. In that day, in the power of the Spirit, the Messiah would bring transformed relationships with God, neighbor and earth. There would be a new society genuinely living according to God's righteous laws finally inscribed on people's hearts and wills.[6]

When he proclaimed that the kingdom of God "has come near," Jesus was declaring that he had invaded human history and our hearts to give us an idea of the age to come. In this context, the kingdom of God is fulfilled through the liberation of the oppressed, the feeding of the hungry, the loving of the unloved, and through sinners accepting Jesus as Saviour and lord.

Chris Wright brings out the duality of this kingdom and of God's mission when he writes as follows about the testimony of the prophet Jeremiah:

---

4. Ibid., 30–32.

5. George Eldon Ladd, *The Presence of the Future* (Manila: Eerdmans, 1974), 218.

6. Ronald Sider, *Good News and Good Works: A Theology for the Whole Gospel* (Grand Rapids: Baker, 1999), 54.

The religious and political leadership included professional prophets among their number. But their only contribution, in the face of the catastrophe that Jeremiah foresaw, was to stand resolutely between the people and the only action that would have prevented that catastrophe – namely genuine repentance, demonstrated by religious and social change. The complacency of the leaders only served to compound the crisis and make it all the more inevitable.[7]

The reference to both "religious and social change" demonstrates and supports the duality of God's mission.

Egyptian Context

The church in Egypt has historically held to an eschatological interpretation of the kingdom, leading it to focus on evangelism and have a negative view of social action. There are several reasons for this emphasis: (1) The church has been fighting to survive and has therefore not been able to participate in social change; (2) Theologically the church viewed evangelism as its sole mission and regarded social action as rooted in liberalism; (3) The church held to an understanding of the gospel as an invitation to eternal life, rather than a call to social change.

The work of Father Matta Al-Miskīn reflects this attitude. He regards attempts by the church to concern itself with earthly matters in the name of Jesus as unwise. To attempt to strengthen church power and obtain group rights in this world is to return to the Jewish dream of the messianic kingdom. When the church turns its back on the greed of this world, it will remember that its master said, "My kingdom is not of this world" (John 18:36). Thus for Al-Miskīn, the sole mission of the church is to proclaim repentance: The subject of Christianity is the sinful human being, its objective is the kingdom of God, and its means is the proclamation of repentance.[8] Al-Miskīn believes that Christian love is not rooted in ethical or social concerns but springs from a desire to serve the poor as an outcome of faith in Christ. The church does

---

7. Christopher J. H. Wright, *The Message of Jeremiah: Grace in the End* (Nottingham: IVP, 2014), 98.

8. Matta Al-Miskīn, *Maqālāt bayn al-Siyāsa wa-al-Dīn* (Articles between Religion and Politics) (Cairo: Dār Majalat Marqus, 1977), 121–116.

not serve society; rather it serves the faith and serves Jesus through serving the poor.

Al-Miskīn suggests that the church should know that Caesar's money must be kept for Caesar, and the things of God must be kept for God. Caesar continues as the example of earthly authority; God is the example of the authority of the Spirit. One cannot serve both at the same time.[9] Al-Miskīn criticizes any emphasis on social services as an exasperating and repetitive process, which serves only to remind the poor that they are poor in contrast to the wealth of the rich.

The theological paradigm shift in Egypt came through Samuel Habib.[10] He used the parable of the ten lepers to support his argument that Jesus had two missions. The first was the mission of evangelism and the second was the mission to help people to become more fully human, as they were created to be. God created all people equal, but sin has led to the rise of social injustice; feudal lords and masters became oppressors and servants and slaves became the oppressed. Women became enslaved to men and injustice mounted through the ages.

In the New Testament, there are situations where Jesus preached and others where he healed without preaching. From this, Habib concludes that Jesus had two independent missions, one for evangelism and the other for social change. Both missions are the responsibility of the church. They coexist along parallel lines, each complementing the other.

Habib did not rest with this as a theoretical position. He put his theology into action by founding the Coptic Evangelical Organization for Social Services (CEOSS), a Christian development organization with headquarters in Cairo, Egypt that currently serves approximately two million people annually.

CEOSS and Models of Development

In the rest of this paper, I will discuss how CEOSS and other Christian and Muslim NGOs, are working to promote development, bring social change and relieve the plight of the poor. I will do this by outlining three models of development and use these to show how the mission of CEOSS has developed over the past seventy years.

---

9. Ibid., 20–33.

10. Samuel Habib is the founder of the Coptic Evangelical Organization for Social Services (CEOSS) and the former President of the Protestant Churches of Egypt. The thoughts provided here are a synthesis of his published works and unpublished sermons.

Social service delivery

The earliest model of development and poverty relief focused on the direct *delivery of social services* such as education, health care, agriculture and economic development to the rural and urban poor. Such efforts have a long history, exemplified – particularly since the middle part of the nineteenth century – by the establishment of a series of charitable organizations (for example, the Islamic Charitable Organization and the Coptic al-Taufiq organization). The first women's organizations, founded before the beginning of the twentieth century, were also characterized by their charitable concerns. Most such organizations relied on charitable donations and traditional religious almsgiving, with a direct material relationship between donor and recipient. It was within such a framework that CEOSS originally began as a publishing house and literacy programme in 1950.

Initially, this model involved giving things to the poor. But with time, the model has become increasingly participatory. Community members are now encouraged to participate in the identification of needs and in planning and implementing solutions. Volunteer leaders from the communities are trained to conduct a variety of the programmes. Participation of individuals at the grass roots is now considered a vital component of social development. The goal is to broaden the choices available to the poor by offering them new abilities and skills that enable them to become self-reliant.

This focus on empowerment is not merely a modern twist on development, but rather addresses the reasons for the phenomenon of poverty, represented by deficient levels of income, lack of education and opportunity for work, and other concomitants of what is known as the culture of poverty.

It is keeping with this perspective that CEOSS has added programmes such as economic development, micro- and small business enterprises, agricultural and environmental development, preventative and remedial health care, rehabilitation of the disabled, housing, appropriate technologies, and education.

Building capacity

In recent years, the role of non-profit organizations involved in community development and social services has increased. They have had to take a more active role to improve the overall impact of development interventions by the government and the private sector to improve the quality of life of the poor segments of Egyptian society. This increased involvement, however, has not always been accompanied by improvement in performance. Substantial numbers of NGOs were started by well-intentioned individuals with limited experience in the voluntary sector and in development. At the same time, there has been a shift in the emphasis in the donor community towards performance with an emphasis on effectiveness, cost efficiency, impact, and accountability. These trends have important implications for the constituencies and stakeholders served and influenced by such NGOs.

Here CEOSS has stepped in to help. Its years of experience and its varied programmes have given CEOSS an in-depth knowledge of comprehensive participatory community development. So CEOSS has shifted its emphasis from direct involvement at the grass roots level to an intermediary role of providing support to local NGOs. As part of this strategy, CEOSS, through its development unit, addresses the issue of NGO capacity building in some of the most disadvantaged areas of the country.

Additional beneficiaries of this capacity building programme are the constituencies of the targeted NGOs: the marginalized and poorest groups in deprived rural and urban communities in the Minia and Beni Suef governorates, and urban squatter areas of the Qalubia and Cairo governorates. They include female-headed households (households headed by women comprise 16.7 percent of families in Egypt), children without access to schools, girls with limited opportunities in education and healthcare, jobless young people, the disabled, and property-less seasonal farmers in communities or societies lacking basic services and facilities and without organizational structures to channel their needs. Special attention is given to women, youth, and the disabled, as they are often on the lowest rung in terms of social status and are subject to discrimination.

CEOSS has applied NGO capacity building to expand its work to eliminate hazardous forms of child labour. A weak economy has created a system that requires children to work to support their families and themselves. In 2016, through the Children at Risk programme, CEOSS has benefitted 56,293 working children, street children, and family members of these children.

The main aim of the CEOSS small and micro enterprise (SME) sector is to improve the economic and living conditions of small and micro enterprise owners and poor entrepreneurs. This will enable them to develop business projects that will help to increase their income, and provide work opportunities for those who are unemployed.

Poor women are a major target of the CEOSS' SME unit. One innovative strategy involves the use of group solidarity in lieu of collateral-providing collaborative support, trust, and human resources to encourage new businesses and to ensure loan repayment. The group lending methodology takes advantage of the Egyptian cultural sense of community and solidarity, making it an ideal way to bridge the mission of CEOSS with the actual practice and the lived realities of Egyptians.

CEOSS understands that women play a vital role in the growth of new markets, communities' overall economic levels, and in the livelihoods of their families. By providing women with capital and economic power, microfinance programmes can both empower women and provide new avenues for children and families to thrive. In 2016, the SME unit distributed 80,556 loans. 70 percent of loan recipients were women, and recipients have maintained a 99.9 percent repayment rate.

Individual loans, a second strategy, are available to those who have an income but wish to expand existing businesses by increasing their inventory, workplace, or tools for increased production. Since 2000, the CEOSS SME unit has distributed 787,835 loans with a value of over 1.3 billion Egyptian pounds (about 55 million British pounds). In 2004, the SME Institute distributed 12,209,800 Egyptian pounds to 4,046 individuals. Loan recipients improved the standard of living of their families. In addition, they positively affected the lives of employees they hired in their enlarged businesses.

In addition to the efforts in small and medium enterprises, CEOSS has embraced local activism models through the adoption of a territorial approach to local development. The territorial approach decentralizes the local development process. This decentralization empowers local partners, community-based organizations, and programme participants to have greater control over their communities and the development process. These initiatives also adhere to the human rights based approach to development.

We have seen that the territorial approach to local development and the human rights based approach work yield greater success when applied together than could be achieved with either of these strategies alone. This is exemplified in our work with rural communities and small farms through our agri-business programme.

The goal of capacity building is to re-engineer the current structure of society to promote social development. Of course, the service delivery model also promotes change. But this change takes place only at the local level. New ideas are promoted within an existing social structure. The primary aim is to increase national income, improve the standard of living by increasing production, and improve social control.

Capacity building, however, aims to create civil society organizations that enhance democracy and create leaders who are proponents of pluralism and diversity. The emergence of new types of leaders at different levels of civil society leads to the restructuring of social elites and creation of competitors. By addressing social, economic, political and cultural issues, capacity building leads to the restructuring of NGOs and to revision of their agendas. In this way, capacity building of civil society organization is a tool for social change.

Of course, "social restructuring" can mean different things. It may be understood as referring to reduced family size, or to urbanisation and the associated change in modes of economic production. It can indicate functional changes in the social contexts of society. It may include changes in the structure of society itself, in social relationships, in social function and in individuals.

Because social restructuring is a comprehensive process, it does not happen overnight but takes time. Over time, however, it can produce changes in social relationships and in cultural dimensions such as values and beliefs. It will affect ecological, economic, political and cultural change, which will influence family and political structures. There will be transformation of structures, systems, relationships and functions. These changes are a continuing process based on causes and results[11] and will manifest themselves in (1) Institutional change – including political changes (e.g. from dictatorship to democracy) and economic change (e.g. from a centralized economy to a free market). (2) Changes in the positions of individuals within society. (3) Changes in the attitudes and skills of individuals, which result in a restructuring of the context in which they exercise power.[12]

Advocacy and networking

A third model of development is *advocacy and networking* for social restructuring. The goal is to strengthen the role of civil society and promote the agenda of civil society organizations in efficient and effective ways. Advocacy in areas of coexistence, equality, justice, human rights and citizenship forces the state to put these issues on its agenda. Advocacy promotes social change from the bottom up. Networking maximises the efforts of civil society organizations at national and international levels.

---

11. Zayied Ahmed, *Social Change* (Cairo: Al Anglo Al Missriah Library, 1992), 11–14.

12. S. C. Docc, *Social Change,* trans. Abd El Hady El Gohary (Cairo: Nahdat El Shark, 1984), 11–14.

CEOSS has worked in recent years to become more involved in advocacy and public diplomacy, domestically and internationally. Our Dialogue Unit, particularly the Forum for Intercultural Dialogue (FID), has spearheaded these efforts. There has been a focus on sharing our experience of the internal political and socio-economic situation with people outside Egypt. FID has also worked with the government and media outlets to advocate for the human rights of all Egyptians.

In addition to dialogue, CEOSS has worked to encourage advocacy and public diplomacy in other areas of our work. Most notably, advocacy has become an integral element of the work of our development unit, as well as a focus of the writing and distribution done through our publishing house, Dar El-Thaqafa. This multifaceted approach to social activism, development, and advocacy allows CEOSS to serve poor and marginalized individuals in a variety of contexts.

Conclusion

The mission of CEOSS represents the other half of the mission of God. Its goal is to promote the sanctity, equity and harmony of life. It seeks to nurture moral and spiritual awareness, enhance a sense of belonging, promote respect for diversity, combat injustice, address conflict, and advance social justice for individuals and communities.

This mission of CEOSS is implemented according to major goals, which include improving the basic conditions of life in impoverished communities and empowering communities and individuals with sustainable development.

Evangelicals in the Middle East must embrace the two missions of Jesus and continue to innovate to fulfil both of these missions. The history of evangelism has built a strong base for the mission Jesus outlines through his preaching and teaching, and has shown that Middle Eastern Christians can effectively spread the good news. However, when it comes to the second mission, there has been a historical lack of effort. Yet by using the tools associated with effective community-based development and empowerment, Christians can continue to bring life to those for whom poverty means death – whether death due to hunger and sickness, or due to the repressive methods used by those who see their privileged positions being threatened by any efforts to liberate the oppressed, or cultural death as their community is ground down.[13]

This is not to suggest that either of these missions should be prioritized over the other, or that they must always work in tandem. There are cases in which social activism can serve alone, cases in which evangelism can serve alone, and cases in which the two missions can work effectively side by side. It is not a question of priority; rather it is a question of context, transparency, and desire to serve the kingdom.

References

Ahmed, Zayied. *Social Change*. Cairo: Al Anglo Al Missriah Library, 1992.

Al-Miskīn, Matta. *Maqālāt bayn al-Siyāsa wa-al-Dīn* (Articles between Religion and Politics). Cairo: Dār Majalat Marqus, 1977.

Docc, S. C. *Social Change*. Translated by Abd El Hady El Gohary. Cairo: Nahdat El Shark, 1984.

Gutierrez, Gustavo. *We Drink from Our Own Wells: The Spiritual Journey of a People*. Maryknoll, NY: Orbis Books and Dove Communications, 1992.

Habib, Samwel. Unpublished Works.

Ladd, George Eldon. *Crucial Questions about the Kingdom of God*. Manila: Eerdmans, 1952.

———. *The Presence of the Future*. Manila: Eerdmans, 1974.

Rauschenbush, Walter. *Christianity the Social Order*. Cairo: Macmillan, 1912.

Ritschl, Albert. *The Christian Doctrine of Justification and Reconciliation*. New York: Scribner, 1900.

Shukr, Abdel Ghafar. "*Local Islamic Organizations and Democratic Development in Egypt*." In *al-Munadhamat al-Ahlia al-Arabia* (Local Organizations in Arab Countries). Edited by Nabil Abdel Fattah et al. Cairo: al-Ahram Center for Political and Strategic Studies.

Sider, Ronald. *Good News and Good Works: A Theology for the Whole Gospel*. Grand Rapids: Baker, 1999.

Wright, Christopher J. H. *The Message of Jeremiah: Grace in the End*. Nottingham: IVP, 2014.

---

13. Gustavo Gutierrez, *We Drink from Our Own Wells: The Spiritual Journey of a People* (Maryknoll, NY: Orbis Books and Dove Communications, 1992), 10–11.

13

The Place of Lament Psalms in God's Mission

Dwi Handayani

Dwi Handayani, *a Langham Scholar, is a graduate of Asia Graduate Theological Seminary, Manila. She has taught at the Bandung Theological Seminary, Indonesia, since 2005 and is also a trainer in the Langham Preaching programme. Her published writing includes* "Spiritual Formation for Today's Indonesian Churches through the Psalms of Lament," International Journal for Religious Freedom; *"Lament Psalms and the Persecuted Churches in Asia,"* in Light for Our Path: The Authority, Inspiration, Meaning and Mission of Scripture (ATA); *and the chapter (co-authored)* "A Doxological Framework for Interpreting Discrimination, Persecution and Martyrdom" in Freedom of Belief and Christian Mission *(Regnum Edinburgh Centenary Series).*

A few years ago many Christians in Indonesia were talking about a book that had changed their whole paradigm of mission: *The Mission of God's People* by Christopher J. H. Wright. Out of curiosity I ordered a copy, and that book changed the way I look at the Bible.

For years I had been taught that the mission of God was solely concerned with saving the soul and that those who were concerned with social issues, justice and liberation were in danger of drifting away from the true gospel. Therefore I had struggled to relate my social activities and my theology. Chris Wright's book helped me to see the holistic nature of mission. On the very first page, he talks about God's sending and he connects the word "sending" with justice and liberation:

> Joseph was sent (unwittingly at first) to be in a position to save
> lives in famine (Gen 45:7). Moses was sent (unwillingly at first)

to deliver people from oppression and exploitation (Exod 3:10). Elijah was sent to influence the course of international politics (1 Kgs 19:15–18). Jeremiah was sent to proclaim God's word (e.g. Jer 1:7). Jesus claimed the words of Isaiah that he was sent to preach the good news, to proclaim freedom, to give the sight to the blind, and to offer release from oppression (Luke 4:16–19; cf. Isa 61:1).[1]

As I read those sentences, a light went on for me, and I began to see the connection between God's mission and concern for justice in the whole Bible. With time, I have begun to see that concern even in the imprecatory psalms of lament.

God's Mission and the Cry for Justice

For many years I had thought that the mission of God was only to redeem sinners from the curse of hell and give them a new destiny in heaven. However, when we read the book of Exodus, we see that God's journey with the Israelites began when an oppressed people cried to God for help. The Israelites cried out against the violence and injustice they were enduring, and God heard their cries and responded to them.[2]

> During those many days the king of Egypt died, and the people of Israel groaned because of their slavery and cried out for help. Their cry for rescue from slavery came up to God. And God heard their groaning, and God remembered his covenant with Abraham, with Isaac, and with Jacob. (Exod 2:23–24)

> Then the LORD said, "I have surely seen the affliction of my people who are in Egypt and have heard their cry because of their taskmasters. I know their sufferings." . . . And now, behold, the cry of the people of Israel has come to me, and I have also seen the oppression with which the Egyptians oppress them. (Exod 3:7, 9)

In the wilderness God reminded the Israelites to do justice to the poor and to strangers because he is attentive to their cries:

---

1. Christopher J. H. Wright, *The Mission of God's People: A Biblical Theology of the Church's Mission* (Grand Rapids: Zondervan, 2010), 23.

2. Even earlier, God had responded to the cry of Abel's blood (Gen 4:9) and the cries that came to him about the crimes of Sodom and Gomorrah (Gen 18:20–21).

You shall not mistreat any widow or fatherless child. If you do mistreat them, and they cry out to me, I will surely hear their cry. (Exod 22:22–23)

We see this again in the book of Judges as God responds to the cries of his people by raising up judges to deliverer his people from the oppression they were enduring at the hands of their enemies (Judg 3:9, 15; 4:3; 6:6–8; 10:10–12; see also 1 Sam 9:16, Job 34:28).

As I reflected on verses like these, I began to realize that the church should be crying out for justice. It is an important part of our mission. God longs to hear our prayers against violence and injustice. We need to step up in the court of the Lord and bring our case before him. We need to be bold to ask God to execute his justice on earth.

We should not do this only when we are the one's suffering injustice; we should also take a stand on behalf of others. This was what the Old Testament prophets did. They stood up against injustice on behalf of the people of God, sometimes even questioning God's justice.

Moses, for example, stood before God and boldly questioned his actions in regard to Israelites. As their hardship in Egypt increased, "Moses turned to the LORD and said, 'O Lord, why have you done evil to this people? Why did you ever send me?'" (Exod 5:22). On Mount Sinai, he challenged God's decision to punish the people: "O LORD, why does your wrath burn hot against your people, whom you have brought out of the land of Egypt with great power and with a mighty hand?" (Exod 32:11). Amos too stood and pleaded for God's mercy on behalf of the people (Amos 7:2–3, 5–6).

Jeremiah's complaint to God about justice is even more personal than the complaints of Moses and Amos. It could be summarized as "Why do the wicked prosper and the righteous suffer?" (Jer 12:1–6). Wright said, "Jeremiah might have joined those protest marches with their antiphonal demands: 'What do we want?' 'Justice!' 'When do we want it?' 'Now!'"[3]

Habakkuk also complained when God seemed to ignore the sin of his people in Judah, "O LORD, how long shall I cry for help, and you will not hear, or cry to you 'Violence!' and you will not save?" (Hab 1:2). However, when God revealed his plan to punish Judah, Habakkuk complained because God was about to use wicked Gentiles to punish his own people. "You who are purer of eyes than to see evil and cannot look at wrong, why do you idly

---

3. Christopher J. H. Wright, *The Message of Jeremiah* (Downers Grove: InterVarsity Press, 2014), 149.

look at traitors and remain silent when the wicked swallows up the man more righteous than he?" (Hab 1:13).[4]

Lament Psalms as Cries for Justice

Justice is the central theme of lament psalms. In all of them, the suffering psalmists call on God to execute justice by punishing the wicked and defending the righteous. Like the people of Israel and the prophets, they cry to God for help. They speak justice, they sing justice, they shout justice, and they cry for justice. "Justice is on every page of the Psalter."[5]

There are four things we should not forget about these laments: a) the writers proclaim the Lord as the judge of the earth, b) they remind him of his earlier judgements, c) they pray for unjust situations to be reversed, and d) they utter these prayers within the context of a covenantal relationship.

Proclamation of the Lord as judge of the Earth

Although many lament psalms are personal complaints, they are very much God-centred.[6] The word "God" is everywhere. He is addressed as the one who judges the world with his righteousness (e.g. Pss 9:8; 94:2), who punishes the unjust with terrors (e.g. Pss 2, 9, 97, 99), destroys them (e.g. Pss 5:6; 9:5), puts them in shame and dishonour (e.g. Pss 6:10; 35:26), breaks their teeth and strikes their cheeks (Ps 3:7).[7] However, this judge of the earth, the only hope of the psalmists, is silent and seems to withdraw himself from the unjust situation in which they, like Jeremiah and Habakkuk, find themselves. Thus they question God.

The first question they ask is "Why?"[8] Why is the righteous judge ignoring evil, and being distant and silent when violence and injustice are everywhere? (e.g. Pss 10:1; 44:23). The psalmists even go so far as to accuse God of being

---

4. Marci Ogrosky, *God's Cranky Prophets: Jonah and Habakkuk* (Bloomington: WestBow Press, 2014), xii.

5. Paul Westermeyer, *Let Justice Sing: Hymnody and Justice* (Collegeville: Liturgical Press, 1998), 30.

6. Christopher K. Lensch, "Prayers of Praise and of Imprecation in the Psalms," *WRS Journal* 7, no. 2 (2000): 17.

7. Ibid.

8. Craig C. Broyles, *The Conflict of Faith and Experience in the Psalms: A Form-Critical and Theological Study* (London: A & C Black, 1989), 63.

their real enemy. He has forsaken and forgotten them in times of trouble (e.g. 22:1; 42:9; 43:2; 74:1; 88:14).

The second question they ask is "How long?" They trust that the Lord will eventually act, but complain that they have to wait so long to see God's justice prevail. They confront God with the fact that he has let them suffer for a long time (Pss 6:3; 13:2; 90:13). He seems far away and has forgotten about the suffering of his people (Pss 13:1; 35:17). He lets the wicked prosper and injustice win (Pss 13:2; 82:2; 94:3). He even lets the wicked mock him (Ps 74:10). To the psalmists, the only explanation for God's failure to act must be that he is angry with his people (Pss 79:5; 80:4).

To emphasize how long they have been waiting for relief, the psalmists often use the word "forever": "Oh, God why do you cast us off forever?" (Ps 74:1); "Will the Lord spurn forever" (Ps 77:7); "How long, O Lord? Will you be angry forever?" (Ps 79:5); "How long, O Lord? Will you hide yourself forever?" (Ps 89:46).[9]

Yet despite the length of time the psalmists have been enduring injustice and the apparent absence of God, they never doubt the existence of God. All the questions they raise up are attempts to provoke God to get involved and establish justice on earth. Even in their difficult situation the psalmists affirm the character of God as the God of justice. "Who is like you, Lord? You rescue the poor from those too strong for them, the poor and needy from those who rob them." (35:10); "Your righteousness God, reaches to the heavens, you who have done great things. Who is like you, God?" (71:19).

In their lament and imprecation, the psalmists are longing for God to reveal himself as the only true and powerful God who judges the earth. But in their cry for judgement, there is also an element of mission as, for example, in Psalm 59:

> Consume them in wrath;
> consume them till they are no more,
> that they may know that God rules over Jacob
> to the ends of the earth. *Selah.* (Ps 59:13)
>
> Pour out your anger on the nations
> that do not know you,
> and on the kingdoms
> that do not call upon your name! (79:6)

---

9. Ibid.

> Let them be put to shame and dismayed forever;
> let them perish in disgrace,
>
> that they may know that you alone,
> whose name is the LORD,
> are the Most High over all the earth. (83:17–18)

The psalmist's desire is that when their oppressors are punished by God, they will acknowledge him as the Most High.

The psalmists also promise that they themselves will be agents of mission. Many lament psalms end with praise, thanksgiving and promises to declare God's name (e.g. Pss 22:22; 71:17–18; 109:26–27) and encourage others to proclaim God's deeds. They also remind God of the risk to their mission if God does not answer their prayers:

> For in death there is no remembrance of you;
> in Sheol who will give you praise? (6:5)
>
> What profit is there in my death,
> if I go down to the pit?
> Will the dust praise you?
> Will it tell of your faithfulness? (30:9)

Reminders of what God did in the past

"The reference to God's earlier saving deeds" is a motif in the lament psalms "which should move God to intervene in the present desperate situation" (e.g. Pss 44:1–3; 83:9–11).[10] The psalmists argue, "you have done it in the past, why do you not do it again now?"

In lament psalms, God's earlier saving deeds are all connected to the issue of justice. In Psalm 44, the psalmist recalls Israel's history when God gave them the land and destroyed their enemies. The psalmist does not reference any particular event, but speaks in general terms that remind us that the Israelites always cried out to God when they were enduring oppression and in danger of losing their land.

In Psalm 83:9–11 the psalmist refers back to the events of Judges 4–8, when the Israelites were oppressed by the Midianites and God raised Deborah, Barak

---

10. Claus Westermann, *Praise and Lament in the Psalms* (Louisville: Westminster John Knox, 1987), 55.

and Gideon to deliver them.[11] At that time, "the people of Israel cried out to the LORD for help, for he [Sisera] had nine hundred chariots of iron and he oppressed the people of Israel cruelly for twenty years" (Judg 4:3). The same prayer is heard in Judges 6:7–8a, "When the people of Israel cried out to the LORD on account of the Midianites, the Lord sent a prophet to the people of Israel." Almost all the saving acts of God in history started when the people of Israel cried out for help to the God of justice.

These references to God's deeds in the past indicate that the psalmists value the importance of history. They view their history from the perspective of God's saving acts. They are confident that it was God who delivered their ancestors from the bondage of slavery and oppression.

The church has sometimes failed to connect our history with God's actions in the past. We need to learn from the psalmists how to view our history from God's perspective, so that we can boldly cry out to him to help us in our present situation.

Prayers that God will reverse situations

In their prayers against injustice, the psalmists show their confidence that God is on the side of the poor and the afflicted. Sometimes the psalmists identify themselves as among the poor (Pss 40:17; 69:29; 70:5; 109:22)[12] and sometimes they do not. It is thus quite possible that the psalmists do not always pray about their own situations but also pray on behalf of others or the whole community against injustice and violence.

In the lament psalms, justice is defined as God's defence and restoration of the poor, the needy, and the afflicted (Ps 9:18; 10:18; 12:5; 35:10; 82:3–4). This inevitably involves punishment of their enemies. Therefore the psalmists also pray for the destruction of those enemies. They seek God's justice rather than personal vengeance.

The psalmists are very clear about the situation they are facing: they are confident of their innocence and the wickedness of their enemies. They know the distinction between the wicked and the righteous and are confident that God is on their side.[13] Sometimes in their prayers they describe in detail the

---

11. John Goldingay, *Psalms Volume 2: Psalms 42–89*, Baker Commentary on the Old Testament Wisdom and Psalms (Grand Rapids: Baker, 2007), 82–83.

12. Steven J. L. Croft, *The Identity of the Individual in the Psalms* (London: Bloomsbury, 1987), 50.

13. John Mark Hicks, "How to Preach a Curse" (DLU Homiletic Seminar, May 1997), 13–14.

sins of the enemies, including being bloodthirsty (Ps 5:6), hotly pursuing the poor (Ps 10:2), murdering the innocent (Ps 10:8), loving violence (Ps 11:5), plundering the poor (Ps 12:5), crushing the people of God (Ps 94:5), slaying the widow and the stranger, and murdering orphans (Ps 94:6).

The psalmists sometimes use very strong language when they curse their enemies:

> May his days be few;
> may another take his office!
> May his children be fatherless
> and his wife a widow!
> May his children wander about and beg,
> seeking food far from the ruins they inhabit!
> May the creditor seize all that he has;
> may strangers plunder the fruits of his toil!
> Let there be none to extend kindness to him,
> nor any to pity his fatherless children! (Ps 109: 8–12)

However we have to read this psalm as more than just a curse; it is an expression of anger at injustice. With strong emotion the psalmist appeals to the just God. The psalmists refuse to play safe or remain silent. They are boldly challenging God with tough questions, questioning his justice and asking him to establish it by restoring the innocent and punishing the enemies.

Prayers in the context of covenantal relationship

The reason the psalmists can show such boldness in approaching God is that their relationship with him is rooted in the covenant. That covenantal relationship is "consistently driven between mercy and justice."[14]

The expression of this covenantal relationship appears when the psalmists address God as "my God" (e.g. Pss 3:7; 5:2; 13:3; 7:1, 3; 22:1, 2, 10; 31:14; 35:23, 24).[15] J. Carl Laney suggests that the covenantal basis for the curses in the imprecatory psalms is the Abrahamic covenant, which includes blessing for the righteous and cursing for the unrighteous.[16]

---

14. Jennifer A. Herrick, *Does God Change? Reconciling the Immutable God with the God of Love* (Boca Raton, FL: Universal, 2003), 17.

15. Mathew V. Thekkekara, *The Psalms of the First Covenant People of God* (Bloomington: iUniverse, 2013), 145.

16. J. Carl Laney, "A Fresh Look at the Imprecatory Psalms," *Bibliotheca Sacra* 138 (1981): 41–42.

In the imprecatory psalms the psalmist affirms his loyalty to God's covenant and his uprightness in terms of this covenant. He is confident of his innocence and invites God to test his heart (Ps 139:23–24).[17] Commenting on Psalm 7, Richard J. Clifford affirms that the curse in the psalm is the covenant curse against covenant breakers.[18] Therefore the curses in the imprecatory lament psalms are an appeal to God to fulfil his covenant.

The psalmists sometimes suggest that God is the one who is breaking the covenant (e.g. Ps 44).[19] Therefore they boldly enter the divine court, appealing for justice with the conviction that the God of the covenant takes injustice seriously and will not let covenant breakers escape his judgement.

Reflection for the Church

The church lives in the midst of an unjust society. Thus we too are called to protest not only injustices against Christians but against all injustice. We need to look beyond our own interests and cry to God for justice for all. We need to stand with others who are fighting for justice. We need to proclaim that our God is the God who is concerned with justice, and that he executes judgement on the earth.

In Indonesia, we encounter discriminations and racism, even institutionalized racism. The media testify to the corruption of the justice system and the government. Many live in extreme poverty that sometimes leads to slavery. We are struggling for peace, justice, and liberation. We need God to defend us, to stand by us and to fight with us.

Throughout history, the people of God have had to live with the tension of living in unjust societies while crying out to the God of justice, who has revealed himself as the God of the poor, the needy and the oppressed. This God became flesh to complete his act of redemption, and he himself lamented to God in the word of Psalm 22: "My God, my God, why have you forsaken me?" Rebekah Eklund says, "Jesus joins in the lamentation of all humanity and suffers in solidarity with us."[20]

---

17. Hicks, "How to Preach a Curse," 14.

18. Richard J. Clifford, *Psalms 1–72,* Abingdon Old Testament Commentaries (Nashville: Abingdon, 2002), 131.

19. Geoffrey Grogan, *Psalms* (Grand Rapids: Eerdmans, 2008), 285.

20. Rebekah Eklund, *Jesus Wept: The Significance of Jesus' Laments in the New Testament* (London: Bloomsbury, 2015), 52.

As the church of Jesus Christ, we need to learn how to use the laments and imprecations in the Psalms as prayers against injustice. The following modernized adaptations from the psalms are offered as a suggestion for how we might do so today.[21]

Psalm 3: A Prayer of the Persecuted Church

Lord, how they increase who trouble the church!
Many are they who rise up against your people.
Many are they who say, "Their Lord will not help them!" Selah
But You, O Lord are our protector, our glory and will lift us up.
We cried to the Lord with our voice, and he heard us from his holy
*　　hill. Selah*
We are calm and at peace for the Lord sustains us.
We will not be afraid of those who destroyed and burnt our church,
who banned us from worship.
Arise O Lord, save us, O our Lord!
Destroy our enemies, scatter them, and expose all their sin and
*　　shame.*
Salvation belongs to the Lord,
Your blessing is upon your people.

Psalm 12: A Prayer against Corrupt Government

Help Lord for we see only few godly people in the government!
For the honest and righteous persons are fired from their offices.
The others speak idly to one another;
With flattering lips and double heart they speak.
May the Lord cut all flattering lips,
And the tongue that speaks proud things,
Who have said, "We will use our position to rob the people,
we will increase their taxes and make ourselves rich."
"For the oppression of the poor, and the sighing of the needy,
now I will arise," says the Lord;

---

21. I adapted this model from Zephania Kameeta, *Why, O Lord? Psalms and Sermons from Namibia* (World Council of Churches, 1986), 24–59.

"I will protect the poor from the greedy and I will provide all their
needs."
The words of the Lord are pure words,
Like silver tried in furnace of earth, purified seven times.
You shall protect Indonesia, O Lord.
You shall preserve it from generation to generation,
The corrupt officials prowl on every side,
When the wickedness is spread among the people.

Psalm 35: A Prayer against Corrupt Judicial Systems

Sue them, O Lord, those who want to sue the righteous;
Fight against those who fight against your people!
Take your robe of justice and rise for our help!
Use your pen and hammer against the ungodly people in the court.
Say to your people, "I am your deliverance!"
Let them be put to shame and dishonour
who bribe the judges and the prosecutors.
Let them be turned back and confounded
Who devise evil and hate the righteous people in the court.
Let them be like chaff before the wind,
With the angel of the Lord driving them on!
Let their way be dark and slippery,
With the angel of the Lord pursuing them!
For without cause they set a trap for the godly
Without cause they bring us to the court for judgement
Let ruin come upon them unawares!
And let their own trap ensnare them;
Let them fall into their own wicked plan.
Then my soul shall rejoice in the Lord
Exulting in his deliverance.
All my bones shall say, "O Lord, who is like you,
You who deliver the weak from evil courts,
The poor and the needy from those who rob them."
False witnesses come forward;
they question me on things I know nothing about.
They put me in a corner with false evidence
and leave me like an orphan.

Yet I never do any harm to them
And I always have been a good citizen.
I paid taxes, I obeyed the law,
I went about mourning for my country
as though for my friend or brother.
I bowed my head in grief
as though weeping for my mother.
But when I stumbled, they gathered in delight;
Assailants gathered against me without my knowledge.
They slandered me without ceasing.
Like the ungodly they maliciously mocked;
they gnashed their teeth at me.
How long, Lord, will you look on?
Rescue me from their ravages,
my precious life from these lions.
I will give you thanks in the great assembly;
among the throngs I will praise you.
Do not let those gloat over me
who are my enemies without cause;
do not let those who hate me without reason
maliciously wink the eye.
They do not speak peaceably,
but devise false accusations
against those who live quietly in the land.
They sneer at me and say, "Aha! Aha!
With our own eyes we have seen it."
Lord, you have seen this; do not be silent.
Do not be far from me, Lord.
Awake, and rise to my defence!
Contend for me, my God and Lord.
Vindicate me in your righteousness, Lord my God;
do not let them gloat over me.
Do not let them think, "Aha, just what we wanted!"
or say, "We have swallowed her up."
May all who gloat over my distress
be put to shame and confusion;
may all who exalt themselves over me
be clothed with shame and disgrace.

May those who delight in my vindication
shout for joy and gladness;
may they always say, "The Lord be exalted,
who delights in the well-being of his servant."
My tongue will proclaim your righteousness,
your praises all day long.

References

Broyles, Craig C. *The Conflict of Faith and Experience in the Psalms: A Form-Critical and Theological Study*. London: A & C Black, 1989.

Clifford, Richard J. *Psalms 1–72*. Abingdon Old Testament Commentaries. Nashville: Abingdon, 2002.

Croft, Steven J. L. *The Identity of the Individual in the Psalms*. London: Bloomsbury, 1987.

Eklund, Rebekah. *Jesus Wept: The Significance of Jesus' Laments in the New Testament*. London: Bloomsbury, 2015.

Goldingay, John. *Psalms Volume 2: Psalms 42–89*. Baker Commentary on the Old Testament Wisdom and Psalms. Grand Rapids: Baker, 2007.

Grogan, Geoffrey. *Psalms*. Grand Rapids: Eerdmans, 2008.

Herrick, Jennifer A. *Does God Change? Reconciling the Immutable God with the God of Love*. Boca Raton, FL: Universal, 2003.

Hicks, John Mark. "How to Preach a Curse." DLU Homiletic Seminar, May 1997.

Kameeta, Zephania. *Why, O Lord? Psalms and Sermons from Namibia*. World Council of Churches, 1986.

Laney, J. Carl "A Fresh Look at the Imprecatory Psalms." *Bibliotheca Sacra* 138 (1981): 41–42.

Lensch, Christopher K. "Prayers of Praise and of Imprecation in the Psalms." *WRS Journal* 7, no. 2 (2000): 17.

Ogrosky, Marci. *God's Cranky Prophets: Jonah and Habakkuk*. Bloomington: WestBow Press, 2014.

Thekkekara, Mathew V. *The Psalms of the First Covenant People of God*. Bloomington: iUniverse, 2013.

Westermeyer, Paul. *Let Justice Sing: Hymnody and Justice*. Collegeville: Liturgical Press, 1998.

Westermann, Claus. *Praise and Lament in the Psalms*. Louisville: Westminster John Knox, 1987.

Wright, Christopher J. H. *The Mission of God's People: A Biblical Theology of the Church's Mission*. Grand Rapids: Zondervan, 2010.

———. *The Message of Jeremiah*. Downers Grove: InterVarsity Press, 2014.

14

Marginalizing God in the Book of Judges

Athena E. Gorospe

Athena E. Gorospe *is an associate professor at Asian Theological Seminary, Manila, Philippines, where she teaches biblical studies and theology. With the help of a scholarship from Langham USA, she obtained her PhD in Theology with an Old Testament concentration from Fuller Theological Seminary. She was a member of the Theology Working Group of the Lausanne Movement when Chris Wright was chair.*

The concept of the *missio Dei* is that mission springs from who God is and not from what the church does. A right relationship with God and the worship of God is the source of mission. The Cape Town Commitment of the Lausanne Movement emphasizes this by beginning not with mission strategies, or even with contemporary challenges, but with the God we love, or rather the God who loves us.[1] As David Bosch writes, the purpose of the missionary activities of the church "can therefore not simply be the planting of churches or the saving of souls; rather it has to be service to the *missio Dei*, representing God in and over against the world, pointing to God."[2]

In the same way, Christopher Wright affirms that "mission is not ours; mission is God's."[3] Mission springs from God's desire to be known as the true

---

1. Lausanne Movement "Cape Town Commitment," Part 1.1, www.lausanne.org/content/ctc/ctcommitment#preamble.

2. David Bosch, *Transforming Mission: Paradigm Shifts in Theology and Mission* (Maryknoll: Orbis, 2009), 400.

3. Christopher Wright, *The Mission of God: Unlocking the Bible's Grand Narrative* (Downers Grove: InterVarsity Press, 2006), 62.

God – incomparable in power, faithfulness, and mercy; who rules over heaven and earth in righteousness and justice; and who is unique – Yahweh is God and there is no other.[4] In mission we invite others to know this God in the person of Jesus Christ.[5] Thus, it is "the task of biblical mission" to "lead people back to acknowledge the only true and living God."[6] This leads to a confrontation with idolatry because the latter "dethrones God and enthrones creation."[7]

The Old Testament portrays ancient Israel as the channel through which the true God can be known. However, Israel often failed in its missional task because it succumbed to the idolatry of the surrounding nations. In the book of Judges, this is seen in how Israel "did evil in the eyes of the Lord" (2:11; 3:7, 12; 4:1; 6:1; 10:6; 13:1). This phrase, which stands at the beginning of the cyclical framework of Judges,[8] identifies this evil as idolatry, as can be seen in the exposition after its first occurrence in 2:11–13b.[9]

> And the people of Israel did evil in the eyes of the Lord (v. 11a)
> A They served the Baals (v. 11b)
>> B They abandoned Yahweh the God of their fathers (v. 12a1),
>>> the one who brought them out of the land of Egypt (v. 12a2)
>>> C They followed after strange gods (v. 12b1)
>>>> which came from the gods of the peoples around them (v. 12b2)
>>> C' They bowed down to them (v. 12c1)
>>>> and provoked Yahweh to anger (v. 12c2)
>> B' They abandoned Yahweh (v. 13a)
> A' They served Baal and the Astartes (v. 13b)[10]

Here, idolatry is described as abandoning Yahweh and following strange gods. While Israel has not dropped Yahweh from its list of deities, the space and attention it gives to other gods and to individual and tribal self-interest have pushed Yahweh from the centre of life into the periphery. Hence, as

---

4. Ibid., 75–83.

5. Ibid., 105–35.

6. Ibid., 171.

7. Ibid., 164.

8. Judges is structured around a programmatic, cyclical theological framework of sin, oppression, deliverance, and rest, which is introduced in 2:11–21 and whose elements are repeated in full or partial form in the central portion of the book (3:10–16:31).

9. For this structure, see Athena E. Gorospe with Charles Ringma, *Judges*, Asia Bible Commentary (Carlisle, UK: Langham Global Library, 2016), 29, modified from Barry G. Webb, *The Book of Judges*, NICOT (Grand Rapids: Eerdmans, 2012), 141.

10. Note that here and elsewhere in this chapter, the author has provided her own translations, rather than relying on one published version.

the narrative progresses, God is portrayed in a more ambivalent light,[11] becoming increasingly withdrawn and silent.[12] This leads to the theme of the marginalization of God.

We associate marginalization with people but not with God because God always has access to resources and power. In the book of Judges, references are made to groups and individuals who are marginalized, the foremost of which are the women.[13] Nevertheless, we are not speaking here of marginalization in relation to ultimate power, nor are we speaking of marginalization in relation to discourse, since there is plenty of God-talk in the book of Judges. Rather, marginalization in this article has to do with how Israel's judges regarded the role of Yahweh vis-à-vis their own role in the deliverance of the nation. My contention is that God becomes increasingly marginalized in the life of Israel and in the mission of the later judges. This will be shown in the stories of Gideon and Jephthah.[14]

Marginalizing God in the Gideon Cycle

Sharing credit with Yahweh

The structure of the Gideon narrative, based on the theme of power, can be described as a movement from disempowerment to empowerment to the misuse of power.

Disempowerment

Although as the youngest child Gideon is marginal in relation to his family, his family seems to be wealthier than others in their community and his father is shown to have considerable influence.[15] Nevertheless, as an Israelite living under the oppressive control of Midian, Gideon belongs to a marginalized

---

11. Cheryl Exum, "The Centre Cannot Hold: Thematic and Textual Instabilities in Judges," *CBQ* 52 (1990): 411.

12. Exum, "The Centre Cannot Hold," 418, 422, 424, 426.

13. See, for example, Esther Fuchs, "Marginality, Ambiguity, Silencing: The Story of Jephthah's Daughter," in *A Feminist Companion to Judges,* ed. Athalya Brenner (Sheffield: Sheffield Academic Press, 1993), 116–130. Aside from Deborah, Achsah, Jael, Delilah, and Samson's mother, who are initiators and exercise active roles, there are many women who remain nameless and whose fates are determined by the men around them – Jephthah's daughter, the Levite's concubine, and the women of Jabesh-Gilead.

14. Parts of the following material on Gideon and Jephthah appear in Gorospe and Ringma, *Judges.*

15. Daniel Block, *Judges, Ruth,* NAC (Nashville: Broadman & Holman, 1999), 258.

group. The Midianite occupation has "greatly impoverished" Israel, as is described in detail in Judges 6:2–6. The Hebrew verb for "impoverished," דלל 6:6)a), means not only to become economically poor but also "to become insignificant," "powerless," and to be "brought into a lowly state."[16] The economic exploitation brings about a form of powerlessness that arises not only from a lack of material resources but also from being cut off from the capacity to produce these resources, since the Midianites do not wait for tribute to be brought to them but ransack and pillage the land (6:3–5).

Empowerment

God's work of deliverance begins by empowering Gideon. By empowerment I mean the processes by which people are moved from a position of apathy, passivity, and hopelessness to a place of action and initiative, leading to a change in their situation and that of their communities.[17] This happens as people are able to appreciate their own strengths and capabilities, and to discern God's presence among them.

Many commentators view Gideon's reaction to God's call negatively.[18] However, one needs to understand Gideon's doubt, scepticism, despondency, and feelings of abandonment from the perspective of oppressed peoples. The constant threat to one's livelihood, the focus on daily subsistence and survival, and the lack of opportunities can spawn not only distrust and cynicism but also apathy, a sense of betrayal, and a lack of hope.[19] Thus, what Gideon needs is encouragement and not rebuke.

Through God's empowerment in terms of affirming speech, confidence-building measures, and the work of the Spirit, Gideon is able to accomplish his mission.[20]

---

16. See definitions for דַּל and דלל, *HALOT* 1 (study ed.), 221–22, 223; *BDB*, 195.

17. For a discussion of empowerment as an approach to community development, see John Williamson, *Practical Community Empowerment: Concepts, Organizational Issues, and the Process* (Akron, PA: Mennonite Central Committee, 2000) and Joel Maribao, *Strategies for Empowerment: A Filipino-Christian Perspective* (Manila: Logos Publications, 1996).

18. Block, *Judges*, 260–261. Cf. Lilian Klein, *The Triumph of Irony in the Book of Judges* (Sheffield: Almond Press, 1988), 53–56; Ellie Assis, *Self-Interest or Communal Interest: An Ideology of Leadership in the Gideon, Abimelech, and Jephthah Narratives (Judg 6–12)* (Leiden: Brill, 2005), 30–41; Jacobus Marais, *Representation in Old Testament Narrative Texts* (Leiden: Brill, 1998), 108–109.

19. See Athena E. Gorospe, "A Biblical Model of Empowerment: The Story of Gideon," in *Church and Poverty in Asia,* ed. Lee Wanak (Mandaluyong City: OMF Literature, 2008), 58–59.

20. Gorospe, "Model of Empowerment," 54–72.

Misunderstanding the source of power

However, when Gideon becomes empowered and accomplishes his mission, he takes shared credit, magnifying his own contributions while diminishing the role of Yahweh in the work of deliverance. Gideon also becomes more autocratic and violent, acting out a personal agenda and his desire for people to remember what he has done. Human intervention is magnified while God is marginalized.

Dorsey sees the turning point in the Gideon story in Judges 7:15–22, the episode when Yahweh gives the victory. Whereas before this episode "Yahweh was in charge, and all went well," after this episode "Yahweh no longer seems to be involved and all goes badly."[21] Indeed, an analysis of the narrator's account beginning in Judges 7:23 shows the absence of any references to Yahweh. All the references come from Gideon's lips (8:7, 19, 23). The last attribution made by the narrator to Yahweh is in Judges 7:22, which affirms unmistakably that it is God who granted the victory. Yet a disquieting feature of Gideon's call to arms diminishes the role that God played in the whole process: "A sword for Yahweh and for Gideon" (7:18; 7:20)[22] seems to put the spotlight on both God and Gideon.[23] In the call to arms of Ehud and Deborah, only God's name is mentioned (3:28; 4:6–7, 9).[24] Moreover, Gideon's call emphasizes the human instrument by which victory is achieved – the sword – rather than focusing on the power of God.[25]

---

21. David Dorsey, "Judges," *The Literary Structure of the Old Testament: A Commentary on Genesis to Malachi* (Grand Rapids: Baker, 1999), 110. Dorsey divides the narrative into three symmetrical units with the account of the victory at the middle (7:15–22). The first unit, the beginning of oppression (6:1–10) is matched by the end of oppression (8:28–32). The second unit, Gideon's divine call and destruction of idolatry at Ophrah (6:11–40), is matched by Gideon's call by the Israelites and his lapse into idolatry at Ophrah (8:22–27). The third unit, troops gather for the battle (7:1–14), corresponds to the troops disperse after the battle (7:23–8:21). Even though the chiasmus is imperfect and the division of the verses is arbitrary (e.g. he alternatively sees the central unit as 7:9–32), there is a clear turning point in the story. On the other hand, Webb divides the narrative into two movements, with the second movement beginning in Judges 8:4, when Gideon and his men crossed the Jordan, but he also sees a different Gideon emerging in the second movement. See Barry Webb, *The Book of Judges: An Integrated Reading* (Sheffield: JSOT Press, 1987), 147; cf. Klein, *Triumph of Irony*, 61.

22. Clint McCann, *Judges*, Interpretation (Louisville: Westminster John Knox, 2002), 65.

23. L. Juliana Claassens, "The Character of God in Judges 6–8: The Gideon Narrative as Theological and Moral Resource," *HBT* 22 (2001): 61; Dennis T. Olson, "Judges," in *The New Interpreter's Bible*, vol. 2 (Nashville: Abingdon, 1998), 803; Marais, *Representation in Narrative Texts*, 112; Assis, *Self-Interest or Communal Interest*, 77.

24. Assis, *Self-Interest or Communal Interest*, 76.

25. Marais, *Representation in Narrative Texts*, 112.

As the narrative progresses, Gideon comes more and more to the fore while Yahweh recedes into the background. The formulas for divine assistance ("The LORD gave . . . into their hands," "The LORD was with . . . ," "The LORD caused confusion. . . .") are no longer present, except on Gideon's lips (8:7).[26] Moreover, there is the predominant use of the first person singular pronoun in Gideon's speech: "I am pursuing" (8:5), "I will thresh" (8:7), "I will pull down" (8:9).[27] Yahweh becomes increasingly marginalized as Gideon magnifies his own contributions to the work of deliverance, while minimizing Yahweh's role and power.

Driven by victory, Gideon begins to act in a more autocratic way. Moreover, the battle takes on the character of a vendetta due to a personal affront.[28] With Gideon's increasingly despotic actions, it is not surprising that the people ask him to rule over them (8:22), attributing to him rather than to Yahweh the victory over the Midianites. Although the verb *mashal* "to rule" rather than *malak* "to be king" is used, something similar to a monarchy is what the people had in mind, as can be seen in the request for dynastic succession. Even though Gideon refuses to be ruler (8:23), he does not disabuse Israel of the notion that he is responsible for the victory.[29] This is exactly what God warns Gideon about: "lest Israel take the glory for itself, in disregard of me, saying, 'My own power has delivered me'" (7:2). Moreover, Gideon's refusal does not stop him from acting like a king, as many commentators have noted.[30]

Gideon's making of an ephod[31] seems an aberration after his earlier decisive dismantling of Baal's altar and the symbols of the Canaanite cult (6:25–27). This action should not simply be interpreted as a substitute for Canaanite idolatry. A

---

26. Claassens, "Character of God," 64; Olson, "Judges," 807.

27. Claassens, "Character of God," 62–63; McCann, *Judges*, 68–69.

28. Tammi Schneider, *Judges*, Berit Olam (Collegeville: Liturgical Press, 2000), 123–24; Assis, *Self-Interest or Communal Interest*, 92–94; Webb, *Book of Judges*, 261.

29. Block, *Judges*, 299; Claassens, "Character of God," 65.

30. Gideon's prior and subsequent actions evoke many of the privileges exercised by ancient Near Eastern kings. He harshly treated those who opposed him (8:4–9, 13–17), he appropriated for himself the royal symbols of power worn by the Midianite kings (8:21, 26), he asked for a share of the spoils of battle and accumulated a treasure fit for a king (8:24–26), he established a religious oracular site often maintained by kings (8:27), he kept a harem (8:30), he named one of his sons Abimelech ("my father is king") (8:31), and he did not seem to have sufficiently challenged the notion of dynastic succession since his sons still ruled after him (9:2). Arthur Cundall and Leon Morris, *Judges and Ruth: An Introduction and Commentary*, TOTC (Leicester: IVP, 1968), 121; Block, *Judges*, 299–301.

31. The ephod in the Gideon story seems to be distinct from the elaborate garment worn by the priest (cf. Exod 28:3–14, 31–35). It is made of gold and very heavy and may have been a portable oracular device to ascertain the will of God (cf. 1 Sam 23:6–11). For discussion, see

more likely scenario is that Gideon wants to remind people of the great victory that Yahweh accomplished for Israel. But in doing so, he is also reminding people that he was the main instrument of the victory. First, Gideon does not ask for a share of the spoils of battle on Yahweh's behalf; rather, the people give in gratefulness to him because they think he is the one who delivered them. Second, Gideon places the ephod in his own town, which further serves to reinforce Israel's perception of his central role in the deliverance.[32]

The ephod then functions as a memorial to what Gideon has accomplished and what the Israelites themselves have contributed.[33] In this way, it "became a snare to Gideon and his household" (8:27). A *moqesh* "snare" is a trap that catches prey by surprise because they unknowingly walk into it. If the creation of the ephod were just a return to Canaanite worship, it would not have had the nature of a trap. The ephod becomes a trap in the sense that its institution is supposed to promote Yahweh worship, but it resulted only in the marginalization of Yahweh and the glorification of Gideon. Thus the language of prostitution is used (8:27: cf. 2:17), since Israel's actions constitute a turning away from Yahweh and substitution of a pseudo-worship that actually minimizes the role of Yahweh.

Gideon starts out as a marginalized figure in the book of Judges and God empowers him to play a central role. But in the end, this previously marginalized figure marginalizes God.

We think of idolatry as involving the worship of gods represented by physical or nature images, but fundamental to idolatry is the elevating of the works of human hands and regarding them as equal to or even above the living God.[34] Chris Wright believes that "therein lies the root of all other forms of idolatry: we deify our own capacities, and thereby make gods of ourselves and our choices and all their implications."[35]

Hence, empowerment can lead to idolatry if we begin to attribute our power to our own virtues, strengths, or position. Thus, we may subtly claim the credit for what God has accomplished. Moreover, a messianic complex may creep

---

Jason S. Bray, *Sacred Dan: Religious Tradition and Cultic Practice in Judges 17–18* (New York: T & T Clark, 2006), 112–115.

32. Assis (in *Self-Interest or Communal Interest*, 106–107) thinks that the ephod was a victory monument for Gideon.

33. Wolfgang Bluedorn, *Yahweh versus Baalism: A Theological Reading of the Gideon-Abimelech Narrative* (Sheffield: Sheffield Academic Press, 2001), 174.

34. Wright, *Mission of God*, 147–61.

35. Ibid., 164.

in, so that we may unconsciously think that deliverance and transformation is up to us, without discerning that God is already working ahead of us, and we are just invited to participate in God's mission.

Marginalizing God in the Jephthah Cycle

Using God and using people

Like Gideon, Jephthah starts out as a marginalized person. Even though he is a mighty warrior (11:1a), he is also the son of a prostitute (11:1b). Thus, Jephthah is of ambiguous and mixed heritage: "an outsider without inheritance rights and . . . extolled as a hero."[36] When grown-up he is driven out of his father's household by his brothers. Having been deprived of home and inheritance and experiencing deep rejection, he lives outside Israel and gathers around him a group of other marginal figures – mercenaries who go out raiding with him (11:3).[37] But with the people of Gilead under threat from the Ammonites, Jephthah is given the chance to play a more central role.

The story is made up of five episodes, and at the centre of each is a dialogue between two characters, whether the character is an individual or a group.[38] The characters of each episode, except the last, are involved in some form of negotiation or confrontation. A spirit of utilitarianism pervades each episode, so that even Yahweh is treated as an object to be manipulated and used.

Utilitarian confession

Episode one acts as a prologue that connects this story with the other judges' stories, featuring a dialogue between Yahweh and Israel (10:6–16). The narrative starts with the cyclical theological framework that introduces the stories: "The people of Israel again did evil in the eyes of the Lord" (10:6), but this time the

---

36. Victor Matthews, *Judges and Ruth,* New Cambridge Bible Commentary (Cambridge: Cambridge University Press, 2004), 117.

37. The phrase *anashim reqim* ("outlaws," NRSV; "adventurers," NIV; "worthless fellows," ESV) does not seem to refer to immoral men (C. F. Burney, *The Book of Judges with Introduction and Notes and Notes of the Hebrew Text of the Book of Kings with an Introduction and Appendix* [New York: KTAV Publishing, 1970], 308; cf. Robert Boling, *Judges,* Anchor Bible [Garden City: Doubleday, 1975], 171; Webb, *Judges: Integrated Reading,* 223, n. 20, but rather to those who, like Jephthah, have been pushed out or have opted out of the predominant structures of Israelite society. Thus, they make their living by fighting or killing for a wage, or by raiding outlying villages, which corresponds to today's mercenary soldiers (see Judg 9:4; 1 Sam 22:2; 2 Chr 13:7).

38. Robert Polzin, *Moses and the Deuteronomist: A Literary Study of the Deuteronomistic History* (New York: Seabury, 1980), 177.

gods that Israel worshipped are enumerated. After the second element in which the Lord hands them over to a foreign power with its accompanying oppression (10:7–9), the third element, "the people of Israel cried to the LORD" (10:10) is introduced, but this time the cry is accompanied by a confession of sin (10:10).

Israel's confession of sin starts with a formulaic phrase: "We have sinned." The confession seems to indicate that the people have realized their own culpability and have repented, leading to a break in the repetitive cycle of sin–oppression–deliverance–rest. Hence, God's response to Israel's confession is surprising. Rather than words of forgiveness, God gives an indictment speech (10:11–14) that ends in refusal to save them – "Therefore, I will no longer continue to deliver you. Go and cry out to the gods you have chosen. Let them save you in the time of your distress" (10:14).

The Israelites reiterate their confession of sin, and it seems that their repentance is genuine. First of all, the confession of sin is followed by an acceptance of responsibility and consequences: "We have sinned; do to us what seems good in your sight" (10:15a). Second, it is followed by acts of repentance: "And they removed the foreign gods from their midst and served the LORD" (10:16a). However, there is a hint that Israel's confession of sin and their act of putting away their foreign gods are just ways of finding immediate relief from their suffering. The confession of sin adds a line, which reveals this attitude: "We have sinned . . . Only rescue us today" (10:15b). As Polzin comments, "What comes through quite forcefully in this dialogue are both Israel's rather self-serving conversion as an apparent attempt once more to use Yahweh to insure their peace and tranquillity, and Yahweh's argument that a slighted and rejected God will be used no longer."[39]

The last line in this episode (10:16b) introduces a textual ambiguity that reflects something of the growing ambivalence of Yahweh towards Israel, as the following translations show:

NRSV: he could no longer bear to see Israel suffer.
NIV: he could bear Israel's misery no longer.
Boling:[40] the plight of Israel became intolerable to him.
ESV: he became impatient over the misery of Israel.
Polzin:[41] he grew annoyed (or impatient) with the troubled efforts
    of Israel.

---

39. Ibid., 178.
40. Boling, *Judges*, 190.
41. Polzin, *Moses and the Deuteronomist*, 177.

The reason for the ambiguity lies in the expression *qetsar nephesh*. *Qetsar* can mean "to be shortened, reduced, or diminished,"[42] but when paired with *nephesh* (soul) or *ruah* (spirit), it takes on the meaning of "to be impatient."[43] For example, the phrase is used to describe Samson's exasperation at the constant nagging of Delilah (16:16).[44] Thus, the translation "to be impatient" is warranted.[45] Nevertheless, there is sufficient ambiguity in the phrase for the translation "he could no longer bear," to be possible, since the impatience may have something to do with God wanting to alleviate Israel's miserable situation.

One further nuance of *qetsar nephesh* that is ignored in the different translations is, "his soul is diminished." McCann makes the point that the literal meaning of the phrase is God's "life is shortened," in the sense that God's quality of life is diminished. Drawing from the work of Terence Fretheim,[46] McCann interprets this diminishment in terms of God suffering not only *with* his people but *because* of his people.[47] However, the diminishment may also have something to do with God's ability being reduced or rendered ineffective to act on Israel's behalf.[48] Beginning with the Jephthah story, God seems to have fallen into silence and has left them to their own devices, rarely intervening even in times of personal tragedy, Israel's fragmentation and people's moral confusion. This does not mean that God's actual power has become less, but that Israel's adoption of other gods has pushed Yahweh to the periphery so that God is rendered "powerless" to do something about their situation. Something akin to this is expounded by Bowman[49] who, as he considers the characterization of God in Judges, shows that "the exercise of divine power is limited by the exercise of human freedom, the exercise of which frequently misuses and abuses human potential."[50]

---

42. *HALOT*, III, 1126.

43. See Num 21:4; Judg 16:16; Zech 11:8; Mic 2:7; Job 21:4.

44. Cf. Webb, *Judges: Integrated Reading*, 46–47.

45. Cf. Webb, *Judges: Integrated Reading*, 47–48; McCann, *Judges*, 79; David Janzen, "Why the Deuteronomist Told about the Sacrifice of Jephthah's Daughter," *JSOT* 29, no. 2 (2005): 347.

46. Terence Fretheim, *The Suffering of God: An Old Testament Perspective* (Philadelphia: Fortress, 1984).

47. McCann, *Judges*, 79.

48. Webb, *Book of Judges*, 306, connects the idea of God being powerless in four verses (Num 11:23; Isa 50:2; 59:1; Mic 2:7), but does not see this meaning in Judg 10:16.

49. Robert Bowman, "Narrative Criticism of Judges: Human Purpose in Conflict with Divine Presence," in *Judges and Methods: New Approaches in Biblical Studies*, ed. Gale A. Yee, 2nd ed. (Minneapolis: Fortress, 2007), 36–41.

50. Ibid., 41.

Utilitarian negotiations

The next episode (10:17–11:11) shows Jephthah and the elders in negotiations in which the name of Yahweh is used several times. Jephthah uses God's name to manoeuvre his way so that the elders will appoint him head over Gilead (11:9); the elders use God's name as witness so that they can get Jephthah to save them from the Ammonites (11:10); and Jephthah and the elders sealed their pact "before the LORD" (11:11). Despite the frequent use of God's name, the Lord appears detached from all the wheeling and dealing, with no recorded speech or action from the narrator affirming God's involvement.[51]

Moreover, the negotiations between the elders of Gilead and Jephthah reflect the dialogue between God and Israel in the prologue.[52] Just as Israel's confession to Yahweh was motivated by the exigency of their situation, so the Gileadite elders' initiative to invite Jephthah back (11:4–11) was a utilitarian move on their part because they needed a champion to deliver them from the Ammonites.[53] The elders of Gilead wanted to use Jephthah, in the same way that Israel wanted to use Yahweh for their own purposes.

Only twice does the narrator report Yahweh's involvement in the actions of the characters. The spirit of the Lord[54] (11:29) came upon Jephthah while he was mustering the troops, signalling the granting of the victory, and in the actual battle the victory formula is repeated: "the LORD gave them [the Ammonites] into his hands" (11:32).

The presence of the spirit in empowering Jephthah shows an ambiguity in God's involvement similar to the ambiguity shown in 10:16, where the wording seems to indicate a deity who feels both compassion and impatience at his suffering/stubborn people. On one hand, God is remote and uninvolved in the selection of Jephthah as leader of Israel; on the other hand, he makes available the resources of his spirit in ensuring that Jephthah is victorious against the oppressors of Israel. So even as Jephthah and the elders of Israel marginalize Yahweh and use his name only to legitimize their schemes, and God himself

---

51. Regarding this, Boling (*Judges*, 198) comments, "Yahweh had now been relegated to the position of confirming the elders own selection of the highest leadership." Cf. Phyllis Trible, *Texts of Terror: Literary Feminist Readings of Biblical Narratives* (Philadelphia: Fortress, 1984), 95.

52. Polzin, *Moses and the Deuteronomist*, 178.

53. Cheryl Exum, "On Judges 11," in *A Feminist Companion to Judges*, ed. Athalya Brenner (Sheffield: Sheffield Academic Press, 1993), 132–33, notes the subtle negotiations that took place.

54. The action of the spirit of Yahweh figures prominently in the book of Judges, endowing an individual with strength just before an encounter or a skirmish with the foreign oppressors of Israel (6:34; 11:29; 13:25; 14:6, 19; 15:14). Thus, it is connected with the judge's task of deliverance rather than with the expression of a moral quality.

does not intervene or say anything amidst all the devious negotiations conducted in his name, Yahweh is prepared to join at the crucial stage where the defeat of the Ammonites through the spirit-empowered leadership of Jephthah would result in a temporary reprieve for Israel.

Utilitarian vow

The same hard-nosed bargaining employed by Jephthah with the elders is seen in his negotiations with the Ammonite king in the third episode (11:12–28) and in his vow to God in episode four (11:29–40). The vow seems to be rooted in Jephthah's need to be victorious, or else lose his leadership position and be relegated to his previous status: rejected by the community and stripped of his status and power.[55]

Jephthah's vow (11:30–31) follows the structure of many vows in the Old Testament. It begins with a condition: "If you . . . ," a plea for divine action. It is then followed by a promise, "then I will . . . ," which stipulates the worshipper's response when God acts on the petitioner's plea.[56] A vow arises from a situation of distress, and what is vowed is often a sacrifice including burnt offerings.[57]

In terms of the form, the petition for victory in battle[58] and the promise of a burnt offering, there is nothing unusual about Jephthah's vow. What is different, however, is, first of all, the timing of the vow. Jephthah makes his vow when the spirit of the Lord has already come upon him, so that he already has the empowerment needed for victory. Thus, he is not in a situation of dire need, as are other petitioners who make a vow.[59]

Webb shows that the vow is an intervening episode that interrupts the narrative flow of Jephthah's military campaign against the Ammonites.[60] The fourfold repetition of the word 'abar ("to cross over" or "pass on") links the route of Jephthah's inevitable march to victory (11:29, 32). Thus, the vow is extraneous since it is not integral to the victory march. It is Jephthah's endowment with the spirit that directly leads to his victory over the Ammonites

---

55. Webb, *Book of Judges*, 328–329; E. John Hamlin, *Judges: At Risk in the Promised Land*, ITC (Grand Rapids: Eerdmans, 1990), 117–118; Trible, *Texts of Terror*, 96.

56. See Tony Cartledge, *Vows in the Hebrew Bible and the Ancient Near East* (Sheffield: JSOT, 1992): 16–17.

57. Cartledge, *Vows in the Hebrew Bible*, 13, 29.

58. Cf. Num 21:2.

59. Cf. Cartledge, *Vows in the Hebrew Bible*, 178.

60. Webb, *Judges: Integrated Reading*, 62–63; *Book of Judges*, 330.

(11:29).[61] Thus, the vow is not the cause of the victory and the action of the spirit of Yahweh is not the source of the vow.

The second difference between Jephthah's vow and other vows in the Old Testament is the content of Jephthah's promise. While animal sacrifices in the form of a burnt offering are common in what is pledged in a vow,[62] what is unusual is the ambiguity in what Jephthah intends to offer – whether a human being or an animal.[63] The rendition of the different translations as either *whatever* or *whoever*[64] (11:31) leaves open the question of whether Jephthah primarily means an animal or a human being, or whether he has his daughter in mind as he utters the vow.[65]

Jephthah's language might have been deliberately ambiguous. On one hand, the narrator might have made the reference imprecise (whether animal or human being) in order to heighten suspense and maximize the emotional impact of the daughter herself coming out to meet her father, and finding to the latter's consternation that it is his only offspring that he has unwittingly committed to sacrifice. On the other hand, the ambiguity in the reference might have been deliberate on the part of Jephthah as "a cunning attempt to promise one thing while hoping for a lesser outcome."[66]

Among the Canaanite nations surrounding Israel, it was thought that the sacrifice of a son or daughter would gain the favour of the gods and thus guarantee victory in battle. That is why the covenant in Deuteronomy warns Israel against imitating the nations around them that offer their children as sacrifices to their gods (Deut 12:29–31).[67] Despite the ambiguity in the reference, the suggestion remains that Jephthah thinks that he can buy Yahweh's

---

61. Webb, *Judges: Integrated Reading*, 63.

62. Cartledge, *Vows in the Hebrew Bible*, 29, n. 1. Cf. Lev 22:18.

63. The Masoretic Text reads literally, "*the one that comes out that comes out* from the doors of my house to meet me" (11:31; italics mine).

64. Most versions have smoothed out the translation, following the Septuagint which drops the first part "the one that comes out," regarding it as a dittography; thus, "whatever comes out" (NIV, ESV, NASB, NJPS) or "whoever comes out" (NRSV).

65. David Marcus argues that Jephthah has in mind a human being rather than an animal because the phrases used in the vow are only applied to human beings and never to animals (*Jephthah and His Vow* [Lubbock, TX: Texas Tech Press, 1986], 13–14. On the other hand, Boling thinks that Jephthah has animals in mind, arguing that the structure of Iron Age houses, which integrated livestock pens in the lower storey (Boling, *Judges*, 208), means that animals can wander out of their pens when people arrive.

66. Cartledge, *Vows in the Hebrew Bible*, 179.

67. Janzen, "Why the Deuteronomist," 344. This is also one of the practices condemned by the Deuteronomist (2 Kgs 16:3; 17:17; 21:6).

favour by approximating the value of a human sacrifice. In this, his thinking has become like the Canaanite nations around Israel, a theme that resonates with the whole book of Judges.[68]

Jephthah's way of coping with the experience of marginalization and rejection is by becoming opportunistic, skilled in negotiations, and utilitarian in his approach to life. The tragedy is that in his attempt to get out of his marginal status, he in turn marginalizes God. According to Chris Wright, idolatry "is the attempt to limit, reduce and control God by refusing his authority, constraining or manipulating his power to act, having him available to serve our interests," so that "God, who should be worshipped, becomes an object to be used."[69] When we become utilitarian in our approach to God and to others, it is a short step to idolatry.

Conclusion

In the Gideon and Jephthah stories, we see previously marginalized figures marginalizing God once they try to overcome their marginalization by their use of power. Thus, God's marginalization comes about as the human characters desire to have more power or use God's power for their own ends. Towards the end of the book of Judges, the utilitarian nature of Israel's relationship to God, as introduced in the Jephthah narrative, comes more to the forefront, as God is not only marginalized but also domesticated. God is thus treated as someone whose primary function is to serve personal, familial, and tribal needs.[70]

Part of our missional task today, according to Chris Wright, is to participate in God's mission by "exposing the idols that continue to blur the distinction" between the Creator God and the creation.[71] In contemporary life, these may include the things that entice us, the things that we fear, or the things that we need,[72] to the point that they become the central force of our lives, pushing God to the periphery. The only antidote to these idolatries is to worship the true and living God.

---

68. Block, *Judges*, 58, sees the theme of the whole book as the Canaanization of Israel. Cf. Janzen. "Why the Deuteronomist," 341.

69. Wright, *Mission of God*, 164, 165.

70. For more on this, see Gorospe and Ringma, *Judges*, 211–240.

71. Wright, *Mission of God*, 165, 187.

72. Ibid., 166–171.

References

Assis, Ellie. *Self-Interest or Communal Interest: An Ideology of Leadership in the Gideon, Abimelech, and Jephthah Narratives (Judg 6–12)*. Leiden: Brill, 2005.

Block, Daniel. *Judges, Ruth*. NAC. Nashville: Broadman & Holman, 1999.

Bluedorn, Wolfgang. *Yahweh versus Baalism: A Theological Reading of the Gideon-Abimelech Narrative*. Sheffield: Sheffield Academic Press, 2001.

Boling, Robert. *Judges*. Anchor Bible. Garden City: Doubleday, 1975.

Bosch, David. *Transforming Mission: Paradigm Shifts in Theology and Mission*. Maryknoll: Orbis, 2009.

Bowman, Robert. "Narrative Criticism of Judges: Human Purpose in Conflict with Divine Presence." In *Judges and Methods: New Approaches in Biblical Studies*, edited Gale A. Yee, 2nd ed. Minneapolis: Fortress, 2007.

Bray, Jason S. *Sacred Dan: Religious Tradition and Cultic Practice in Judges 17–18*. New York: T & T Clark, 2006.

Burney, C. F. *The Book of Judges with Introduction and Notes and Notes of the Hebrew Text of the Book of Kings with an Introduction and Appendix*. New York: KTAV Publishing, 1970.

Cartledge, Tony. *Vows in the Hebrew Bible and the Ancient Near East*. Sheffield: JSOT Press, 1992.

Claassens, L. Juliana. "The Character of God in Judges 6–8: The Gideon Narrative as Theological and Moral Resource." *HBT* 22 (2001): 61.

Cundall, Arthur, and Leon Morris. *Judges and Ruth: An Introduction and Commentary*. TOTC. Leicester: IVP, 1968.

Dorsey, David. "Judges." In *The Literary Structure of the Old Testament: A Commentary on Genesis to Malachi*. Grand Rapids: Baker, 1999.

Exum, Cheryl. "On Judges 11." In *A Feminist Companion to Judges*, edited by Athalya Brenner, 132–133. Sheffield: Sheffield Academic Press, 1993.

———. "The Centre Cannot Hold: Thematic and Textual Instabilities in Judges." *CBQ* 52 (1990): 411–426.

Fretheim, Terence. *The Suffering of God: An Old Testament Perspective*. Philadelphia: Fortress, 1984.

Fuchs, Esther. "Marginality, Ambiguity, Silencing: The Story of Jephthah's Daughter." In *A Feminist Companion to Judges,* edited by Athalya Brenner, 116–130. Sheffield: Sheffield Academic Press, 1993.

Gorospe, Athena E. "A Biblical Model of Empowerment: The Story of Gideon." In *Church and Poverty in Asia,* edited by Lee Wanak, 58–59. Mandaluyong City: OMF Literature, 2008.

Gorospe, Athena E., with Charles Ringma. *Judges*. Asia Bible Commentary. Carlisle, UK: Langham Global Library, 2016.

Hamlin, E. John. *Judges: At Risk in the Promised Land*. ITC. Grand Rapids: Eerdmans, 1990.

Janzen, David. "Why the Deuteronomist Told about the Sacrifice of Jephthah's Daughter." *JSOT* 29, no. 2 (2005): 347.

Klein, Lilian. *The Triumph of Irony in the Book of Judges*. Sheffield: Almond Press, 1988.

Marais, Jacobus. *Representation in Old Testament Narrative Texts*. Leiden: Brill, 1998.

Marcus, David. *Jephthah and His Vow*. Lubbock, TX: Texas Tech Press, 1986.

Maribao, Joel. *Strategies for Empowerment: A Filipino-Christian Perspective*. Manila: Logos Publications, 1996.

Matthews, Victor. *Judges and Ruth*. New Cambridge Bible Commentary. Cambridge: Cambridge University Press, 2004.

McCann, Clint. *Judges*. Interpretation. Louisville: Westminster John Knox, 2002.

Olson, Dennis T. "Judges." In *The New Interpreter's Bible*, vol. 2. Nashville: Abingdon, 1998.

Polzin, Robert. *Moses and the Deuteronomist: A Literary Study of the Deuteronomistic History*. New York: Seabury, 1980.

Schneider, Tammi. *Judges*. Berit Olam. Collegeville: Liturgical Press, 2000.

Trible, Phyllis. *Texts of Terror: Literary Feminist Readings of Biblical Narratives*. Philadelphia: Fortress, 1984.

Webb, Barry G. *The Book of Judges*. NICOT. Grand Rapids: Eerdmans, 2012.

———. *The Book of Judges: An Integrated Reading*. Sheffield: JSOT Press, 1987.

Williamson, John. *Practical Community Empowerment: Concepts, Organizational Issues, and the Process*. Akron, PA: Mennonite Central Committee, 2000.

Wright, Christopher J. H. *The Mission of God: Unlocking the Bible's Grand Narrative*. Downers Grove: InterVarsity Press, 2006.

15

Images of Food in Genesis: Feasts, Family Feuds and Famine

Gail Atiencia

Gail Atiencia *has served as a missionary in Colombia with the Latin America Mission since 1976. Initially seconded to IFES, she and her husband have, since 2001, supported the formation of Bible expositors through escuelitas in Colombia and have worked with Langham Preaching in various countries in Latin America. She has also served as coordinator of simultaneous interpretation teams at international gatherings of IFES and the Lausanne Movement. Gail holds a BA and an MBA from the University of British Colombia, a Diploma in Christian Studies from Regent College, Vancouver, and has taken numerous courses in adult education.*

Dr Christopher Wright has significantly influenced the way I perceive God, the cosmic scope of his mission and how the flow of the story told on the pages of the Bible – the Old Testament in particular – leads to and culminates in the person of Jesus Christ. To use his own words in the preface to the *Mission of God's People*, "all the great sections of the canon of Scripture, all the great episodes of the Bible story, all the great doctrines of the biblical faith, cohere around the Bible's central character – the living God and his grand plan and purpose for the whole of creation. The mission of God is what unifies the Bible from creation to new creation." Wright affirms that this plan and purpose in Scripture have two "great acts" and that "The Old Testament tells the story which Jesus completes."[1] In light of the scope of Dr Wright's influence, I feel humbled and privileged – if not somewhat overwhelmed – before the task of writing a piece for this festschrift that honours him and his contribution to the people of God around the world.

This article represents a very small part of a project to trace *food* as a unifying thread in the Bible, to help readers gain a coherent overview of the story begun in the Old Testament and continued in the New. Dr Wright, in virtually all his writings, goes out of his way to show how such a vision – stretching between *creation* and *new creation* – is absolutely necessary in order to comprehend not only our sacred text, but who God is, who we are, the catastrophic presence of evil and the final destiny of humankind.

Why food? The reasons have to do with both the world we live in and the content of Scripture. Our world has practically deified food. *Foodies* – people who are devoted to knowledge about food and the experience of eating and drinking – pursue their passion religiously, chefs and restaurants obsessively vie for Michelin Stars, cable networks offer entire channels dedicated to cooks and cooking, while multinationals lobby and manipulate to gain monopolies on seeds and outlandish levels of control over global food production. We are enticed by supermarket coupons, offers of fast-food, home-delivery, nutritional supplements, vitamins, gourmet food for our pets, organic labels, creative vegan and vegetarian options, the "endless possibilities" of molecular gastronomy,[2] etc. In wealthier nations, families and industries throw away unused food, while in less privileged areas there is no unused food to throw away and increasing numbers of infants are dying from malnutrition.[3] Controversy continues over whether genetically modified foods represent the perfect solution to the global food shortage or constitute a crime against humanity.[4]

---

1. Christopher J. H. Wright, *Knowing Jesus through the Old Testament* (Downers Grove: InterVarsity Press, 1992), 2.

2. "Molecular gastronomy blends physics and chemistry to transform the tastes and textures of food." Accessed 6 January 2017: http://www. molecularrecipes. com/molecular-gastronomy/.

3. Eighty-seven infant malnutrition deaths have been reported in one single province in Colombia so far this year: "Muerenen la Guajira otros 4 niños de malnutrición," *El Tiempo*, 16 December 2016. (Ironically *The Economist* has just declared Colombia "Our Country of the Year," accessed 22 December 2016, http://www. economist. com/news/leaders/21712136-which-country-improved-most-2016-our-country-year.)

4. Contrast, for example, David Schubert and Steven Drucker, "How 121 Nobel Laureates Were Misled into Promoting GM Foods," *GM Watch Review* 375, November 2016, with Ivo Vegter, "110 Nobel Laureates Warn Greenpeace of 'Crime against Humanity' on GMOs," *Daily Maverick* (South Africa), 2 August 2016.

This article does not in any way purport to resolve such complex issues. However, with food being a hot topic and a vital issue in our world, its significant role in the Bible makes it worthy of our focused attention.

Another reason for exploring food in Scripture has to do with the content of the Bible itself. To be theologically significant, I believe, any biblical theme should qualify on at least three levels: framing, frequency, and Christology. Food meets all these criteria.

First, food frames biblical revelation, being present at both the beginning and the end. Christopher Wright affirms the theological importance of the fact that the biblical story begins with "creation" and culminates in "new creation." The creation narratives in Genesis are permeated with food. The *tree of life* – "delightful to the eye and good for food" (Gen 2:9) – stands tall in the centre of the gastronomical buffet provided by God in the Garden of Eden. In the *new creation*, the *tree of life* reappears for abundant urban and global provision: "bearing twelve crops of fruit, yielding its fruit every month. And the leaves of the tree are for the healing of the nations" (Rev 22:2).

Second, in terms of frequency, the sheer number of biblical references to food and eating speaks for itself: more than 3,400. Many occur in key scenes or turning points in the history of salvation, such as the fall, the famine that drives Jacob's family to Egypt, the Passover meal before the Exodus, the provision of manna in the desert, the "clean" vs. "unclean" eating options in the Levitical law code, the promise of abundant food if Israel observes the covenant, *Wisdom* as a banquet hostess, starvation and siege as elements of God's justice, Jesus's temptation to turn stones into bread, his insistence on "eating with tax collectors and sinners," the command to Peter to eat the unclean contents of the celestial sheet lowered from heaven, Paul's response to the dilemma of ingesting meat offered to idols, to name a few.

Third, a valid theological motif must also lead to Christ. The Gospels leave no doubt about this, as Jesus declares, "I am the bread of life" (John 6:35, 48). Food and eating are highlighted in the Gospels some 420 times, in actions, parables and Jesus's startlingly controversial metaphors like, "Whoever eats my flesh and drinks my blood has eternal life" (John 6:54).

This article, for reasons of space will be limited to Genesis. I propose to explore how food scenes shed light on the character of the actors in the story, including God.

Food "in the beginning . . ."

Genesis begins with the majestic, cosmic sweep of creation and leads into the delectable intimacy of Eden's garden where God, man and woman, and the animals feed and commune.

The first image of food reflects the genius and generosity of the Creator – genius hidden in the very smallness of a seed from which a sufficient, ongoing and self-perpetuating supply of nutrition will meet global needs. On day three of creation, the voice of *Elohim* endows the earth with the capacity to produce food:

> And God said, "Let the land produce vegetation: *seed*-bearing plants and trees on the land that bear fruit with *seed* in it, according to their various kinds." And it was so. The land produced vegetation: plants bearing *seed* according to their kinds and trees bearing fruit with *seed* in it according to their kinds. And God saw that it was good. (Gen 1:11, 12, emphasis added)

The conditions necessary for photosynthesis to sustain these tender food-producing plants is ensured on day four (Gen 1:14–19), followed by the creation of the vast zoological array of living creatures who will eat them, including human beings, male and female, who are the uniquely endowed image-bearers of God. Food is God's first gift, excellent in essence and global in scope; it culminates the "work" of creation:

> Then God said, "I *give* you every seed-bearing plant on the face of the *whole earth* and every tree that has fruit with seed in it. They will be yours for food. And to . . . everything that has the breath of life in it [birds and animals], I *give* every green plant for food. God saw all that he had made and it was very good." (Gen 1:29–31, emphasis added)

There is beautiful irony in the fact that from the miniature dimension of seeds will come enough food to sustain the whole earth. The genius of the seed ensures the ongoing,[5] abundant, unstoppable, natural reproduction of life-giving nourishment in an essentially vegetarian habitat. In a world where carnivores – including many of us – "naturally" kill to eat, this affirmation of primeval vegetarian sustenance for both humans and animals invites us to contemplate a world where death has not yet been let loose. This food image

---

5. The emphasis on self-perpetuating supply is achieved with six references to seeds in the space of three verses: 1:11, 12, 29.

powerfully embedded in the text bears witness to the fact that in the beginning no living creature on earth needed to die in order for another to live. In this sense, vegetarians and vegans may be onto something.

In Genesis 1, the image of food as a universal, sufficient gift of God fits with the cosmic breadth of the text. Humans are blessed and told to multiply, fill the earth and responsibly rule over other forms of life (1:28), imaging the person and work of God as Creator and food-giver. The text raises questions concerning the pretensions of certain multinational companies to "patent" the very seed given in Genesis as a sacred *gift* for the whole earth.

The lens then zooms in on Genesis 2, where a specific man ("*adam*" – אָדָם in Hebrew) is formed from earth ("*adamah*"- אֲדָמָה), and placed in a garden enclosure with food trees, two of which are named: the tree of life and the tree of the knowledge of good and evil. The woman is formed because aloneness is "not good." She is formed by God from the raw material of the *adam* and sculptured into help[6] for one who needs help. The food images continue to evoke abundant supply and sustainability through rivers and rain, but two elements are added: delight and decision. The trees are both visually stunning (2:9a) and morally charged (2:15): "And the LORD God commanded the man, 'You are free to eat from any tree in the garden, but you must not eat from the tree of the knowledge of good and evil for when you eat of it, dying you will die'"[7] (2:16, 17).

The Lord God hangs the destiny of humanity on a decision to *eat* or not to *eat* from one tree. As Thomas Mann observes: "eating and food pervade chapters 2–3, constituting the fulcrum on which humanity's relationship turns from intimacy to alienation."[8] But, why *eating*? Were the issue simply obedience to God's command, an option like washing or climbing would have accomplished the same thing. He could have said, "You are free to wash in any of the rivers flowing through the garden, but you must not wash in the river of the knowledge of good and evil." Or, "You are free to climb any of the mountains on the edge of the garden, but you must not climb the mountain

---

6. Genesis 2:18. The Hebrew word for "help" (עֵזֶר – ezer) is used almost exclusively in the Old Testament with reference to God. Rather than implying any kind of subordination, it underlines the appropriate nature and efficacy of help provided for one who needs it.

7. The phrase translated "you shall surely die" in the NIV may be read as "dying you shall die" in the original Hebrew text (Terry Mortenson, "Genesis 2:17 'You Shall Surely Die,'" accessed 15 November 2016, https://answersingenesis. org/death-before-sin/genesis-2-17-you-shall-surely-die/).

8. Thomas Mann, "Not by Word Alone: Food in the Hebrew Bible," *Interpretation* 67, no. 4 (2013): 351–362.

of the knowledge of good and evil." Whereas wet bodies dry very soon and sore climbing muscles recover quickly, something much more profound happens with eating: the substance eaten is transformed into the eater.[9] Apple becomes me, taco becomes you, caribou becomes wolf. The image is startlingly graphic – eating of this particular tree means the "knowledge of good and evil" is internalized and has become *part of* the man and the woman. But a tragic drama begins because they do not have the capacity to handle it *apart from* God. By eating, the first couple opts for moral autonomy[10] and the DNA of their descendants will include the inevitable inclination towards evil. The rest of the biblical account will deal with the unfolding consequences of this tragedy and with God's complex and integral plan to resolve it in history and bring forth his new creation.

Food images dominate the story in these two chapters and are intensely personal as a dialogue focused on eating unfolds between God and his creatures[11] and the serpent and the woman.[12] The consequences of having eaten the forbidden fruit are personal and yet global. Access to food is radically affected. The *adam*, estranged from God, wife and earth, instead of plucking lunch off the nearest tree will now struggle against thorns and thistles and eat by the "sweat of his brow" (3:19). At the macro level, the ground is "cursed" and food henceforth will be gained only by "painful toil" (3:17). God also declares the beginning of a long "enmity" between the serpent's "seed"[13] and the "seed" of the woman, "He will crush your head and you will strike his heel"

---

9. For a detailed analysis of the philosophical and physiological implications of this see Leon R. Kass, *The Hungry Soul: Eating and the Perfecting of Our Nature* (Chicago: University of Chicago Press, 1999), 25–31.

10. "What is forbidden to man is the power to decide for himself what is in his best interest and what is not." Victor P. Hamilton, *The Book of Genesis: Chapters 1–17* (Grand Rapids: Eerdmans, 2010), 166.

11. Between God and his creatures: [God] "You are free to *eat. . .* you must not *eat. . .* for when you *eat. . .* Have you *eaten* of from the tree I commanded you not to *eat* from?" (2:16, 17; 3:11) [Man] "The woman . . . gave me . . . and I *ate* it." (3:12) [Woman] "The serpent deceived me and I *ate*." (3:13) [God] "Because you listened to your wife and *ate* from the tree . . . Cursed is the ground because of you, through painful toil you will *eat* of it . . . it will produce thorns and thistles and you will *eat* the plants of the field. By the sweat of your brow you will *eat* your food." (3:17, 18, 19, emphasis added.)

12. Between the serpent and the woman: [Serpent] "Did God really say, 'You must not *eat* from any tree'?" (3:1) [Woman] "We may *eat* fruit from the trees . . . but God did say, 'You must not *eat* of the fruit from the tree that is in the middle of the garden . . . or you will die.'" (3:2) [Serpent] "You will not surely die, for God knows that when you *eat* of it . . . you will be like God." (3:4, emphasis added.)

13. The Hebrew word for *seed* in 3:15 (זֶרַע – *zera*) is the same word used for food creation in Genesis 1:11, 12, 29.

(3:15). Some commentators[14] find here a reference to the fatal deathblow dealt to Satan[15] by Christ.

Genesis continues through chapter 11 in what Wright describes as,

> an extensive introduction to the dilemma of the whole human race. Genesis 1–11 is entirely occupied with humanity as a whole, the world of all nations, and with the apparently insoluble problem of their corporate evil.[16]

Although actual references to food are quite sparse in this section, the narrator describes a renewed covenant with humanity where "never again will there be a flood to destroy the earth," (Gen 9:11) and God expands the gift of food to include meat: "Everything that lives and moves will be food for you. Just as I gave you the green plants, I now give you everything" (Gen 9:3). In a world where sin and death abound, eating will reflect such a scenario – some living creatures *die* in order for others to live.

Food in the Patriarch-Matriarch Stories

Having created his exuberant food-producing world and made his presence felt against the deepening depravity of the nations, God announces his far-reaching, seed-bearing multinational project to a childless, seventy-five-year-old migrant married to a sterile old woman: "I will make you into a great nation and I will bless you . . . and all the peoples on earth will be blessed through you" (Gen 12:2, 3). The same Word that created the universe will now direct the lives of the patriarchs; the rest of Genesis is the story of Abraham–Isaac (Gen 12–24), Isaac–Jacob (Gen 25–36) and Jacob–Joseph (Gen 37–50). Embedded in each of these major sections are very telling food events.

---

14. Hamilton lists Schaffer, Leupold, Vos, Kidner, Alders and Stigers among those who interpret 3:15 messianically and offers a cautiously exegetical analysis of the messianic possibilities of this verse. Hamilton, *Book of Genesis*, 197–200.

15. Although the serpent is referred to only as "the serpent" in this narrative, Revelation 12:9 (cf. 20:2), describes judgement upon "the great dragon . . . that serpent of old, called the Devil and Satan, who deceives the whole world." Esteban Voth affirms that Genesis 3 increasingly hints that the serpent is more than a serpent and represents or symbolizes a force that is antagonistic to God's purposes. Esteban Voth, *Génesis: Primera Parte* (Miami: Editorial Caribe, 1999), 92.

16. Wright, *Knowing Jesus*, 36.

Abraham: Fresh Bread and Sizzling Tenderloin (Genesis 18:1–18)

Twenty-five years after the first promise of a son, the Lord appears in human form[17] to Abraham in a scene often passed over by commentators, perhaps because at first glance it seems not to advance the story. But the details of the actual menu and the hurried flurry with which Abraham sets a sumptuous meal before the deity invite attention. In addition to revealing a new aspect of the character of Abraham, as host, the meal scene in this strangely domestic text accomplishes two other things: the inclusion of the woman whose "seed" will bruise the head of the snake and a significant change in the relationship between Abraham and the Lord.

Hospitality invites strangers into intimate domesticity. The deity arrives with dirty feet, sweaty from walking in the heat of the day and needing to be refreshed. Abraham is almost self-effacing when he bows to the ground to present himself as "*your servant*" (Gen 18:3) offering a "*little water*" (18:4) for foot-washing and a mere "*morsel of bread*"[18] (18:5). He then proceeds with all the urgency good hospitality requires, to lay before them a feast of mouth-watering abundance: hot bread *kneaded* and made with *22 litres* (!) *of fine flour*, fresh meat from a *selected, choice* and *tender calf* served with *curds and milk*. Abraham reveals his generous character, receiving strangers and abundantly providing for their needs even before he knows for sure who they are. His food hospitality goes beyond the physical; he gives sustenance for the *heart* (18:5), the inner region of understanding and decision making.[19] (He is hosting the Host of the universe and the Lord seems to delight in receiving Abraham's hospitality.[20])

---

17. The narrator tells the reader (v. 1) the "Lᴏʀᴅ" appeared to Abraham who, when he looks up only sees "three men" (18:2). Waltke clarifies, "this is actually the Lord and two angels . . . One man is none other than the Lord, as 18:2–3 and especially 10, 13–15 make explicit. However the Lord and his heavenly assembly in their incarnation appear in human form." Bruce Waltke, *Genesis: A Commentary* (Grand Rapids: Zondervan, 2001), 266, 267.

18. A literal translation of the phrase rendered "something to eat" in v. 5 of the NIV would be "a morsel of bread." Accessed 6 January 2017, https://www.blueletterbible.org/kjv/gen/18/5/s_18005.

19. לֵב leb, the word used here for "heart," when used figuratively often refers to feelings, the will and even the intellect (Strong's Hebrew Lexicon on Blueletterbible.org). See also Psalm 104:14, 15 (NABRE) where God "brings (s) forth food from the earth . . . oil to make their faces shine and bread to sustain the human *heart*" (emphasis added).

20. Waltke observes that immediately following this scene, the narrator creates a "multi-level contrast" between Abraham as "model host" and Lot who "fails as a host." *Genesis: A Commentary*, 266–267, 273.

The menu of the day also reveals God's character as inclusive. The narrator's focus on Sarah begins when Abraham involves her in the bread-making. While eating, the visitors ask, "Where is your wife Sarah?"[21] The question ensures she will hear the divine announcement ostensibly addressed to Abraham but directed specifically to her, "about this time next year, Sarah your wife will have a son" (18:10). Sarah – old, worn out, and well into menopause – laughs silently to herself but is caught red-handed: "Why did Sarah laugh? Is anything too hard for the LORD? I will return at the appointed time next year and Sarah will have a son" (18:14). The scene closes on a tender note, with Sarah fearfully denying she laughed and the Lord leaving aside the indirect communication with Abraham to speak directly to her, "Yes you did laugh" (18:15). Sarah's inclusion is further emphasized in the birth announcement of their son, *Laughter* (Isaac).

> Now the LORD was gracious to *Sarah* as he had said, and the LORD did for *Sarah* what he had promised. *Sarah* became pregnant and bore a son to Abraham in his old age at the very time God had promised . . . *Sarah* said, 'God has brought *me* laughter and everyone who hears about this will laugh with *me*.' (Gen 21:1, 2, 6, emphasis added)

The meal also effects a shift in the relationship between Abraham and the Lord. Domesticity has flavoured the story up to now but the text will not allow us to *domesticate* God. His tent mission accomplished, YHWH dons his judge's robes – he is about to pronounce a death sentence on two depraved cities, both of which are sexually violent (Gen 19:5–9) and "arrogant, overfed and unconcerned, oppressing the poor and needy" (Ezek 16:49). The cosy domestic scene changes to the road as the visitors finish eating; its closeness to the meal suggests that food has shifted the relationship between Abraham and the Lord to a new level. The movement is from conversation at table to declaration of judgement on the macrostructure of injustice in the city states of Sodom and Gomorrah (18:20). The meal serves as the prelude to a demonstration of God's character as judge of the earth.

---

21. The Lord uses her recently changed name (17:15). A change of name signals a change of the identity and destiny of a person. According to Herbert Lockyer, "Sarah came from Ur of the Chaldees, Babylonia, and her former name Sarai ('princely') identifies her as coming from an honored family . . . With the change of name from Sarai to Sarah ('princess') comes the promise of ancestorship of many nations: 'I will bless her and she shall become nations.'" "Alphabetical Exposition of Named Bible Women," https://www. biblegateway. com/resources/ all-women-bible/toc.

Food scenes are not neutral in their effect, as Francesco Mangiapane indicates in an article on culinary cinema: "people having a meal together around a table involves eating as a basic transformational act."[22] The Lord and Abraham are both different after the meal. Having feasted on Abraham's delicacies, the Lord now seems reticent about keeping secrets from his host; "Shall I hide from Abraham what I am about to do?" (18:17). Abraham too is changed; accustomed to speaking to God only about his offspring (or lack thereof), at times falling face-down in his presence (17:3, 17; 18:3), he assumes a new stance in the wake of having fed and hosted the Lord: "Abraham remained standing before the LORD. Then Abraham approached him and said, "Will you sweep away the righteous with the wicked?" (Gen 18:22, 23).

He begins to bargain fiercely but humbly,[23] beseeching YHWH to spare from destruction the *many wicked* in the city, for the *sake of a few*. He knows the Lord well enough by now to sense the awesome power of this just judge to utterly destroy or to let the presence of a righteous few activate his mercy and move him to save even the lives of a multitude of evildoers – a foreshadowing of the day when a single Righteous One will save the world.

Jacob: Red Lentil Stew and Goat Goulash

The section of Genesis that deals with Jacob traces God's stubborn insistence on making himself present for nation-blessing in the ever-so-ordinary and humanly flawed lives of Abraham and Sarah's descendants. At the same time we are not allowed to forget how the insidious tendency towards death contaminates the very heart of the family. Where love, life and harmony should be most natural – between brothers – fratricide lurks. Cain murdered Abel after both offered a food sacrifice to the Lord (Gen 4); now in a powerfully emotional meal scene Esau vows, "I will kill my brother, Jacob" (27:41).

There are in fact two Jacob–Esau incidents involving food. Bread with mouth-watering lentil stew and tender goat goulash are the weapons conniving Jacob uses to usurp Esau's blessings (27:25). In this Ancient Near Eastern context, the division of a father's inheritance is calculated according to "the number of sons and the firstborn always had a right to two of these

---

22. "Feasting with the Outlander: Semiotics of Culinary Cinema," *International Association for Semiotic Studies: Proceedings of the World Congress of IASS* (2014), accessed 30 November 2016, http://www. iass-ais.org/proceedings2014/view_lesson. php?id=107.

23. "I am nothing but dust and ashes . . . May the Lord not be angry" (Gen 18:27, 30).

portions . . . If there are only two sons, the firstborn inherits everything."[24] Thus, as the firstborn of the twins, Esau has the privilege of the birthright and total inheritance in the line of Abraham.

Our very first glimpse of adult Jacob is a cooking scene – Esau returns from hunting empty-handed and famished, to the overpowering aroma from Jacob's kitchen and demands food. Jacob's price for the meal is outrageous: Esau's birthright. Sold!

In contemporary terms, we could compare the transaction to an older sister coming home from work hungry and selling her engagement ring – including the right to marry her fiancé – to her younger sister for a fresh homemade pie. The narrator uses a simple but delectable bowl of red lentil stew, to pit two clashing world views against each other: "deferred prosperity versus immediate satisfaction."[25] "Esau ate and drank and got up and left" (25:34), as if what he has lost is trivial. What Jacob has done is despicable, but ironically even in deceit he shows himself to be desirous of the future promised by God to Abraham. Jacob values the birthright and acting to take possession of it puts him in the line of promise. The meal scene contrasts the character of the two brothers.

Years later in a lengthy suspense-filled incident, Isaac – old, totally blind and facing death – asks Esau to prepare a sumptuous meal of freshly-hunted venison so he can pronounce the firstborn blessing on him. Once again Jacob supplants him. Disguised as Esau, he serves his father an equally delectable goat goulash, quickly prepared by his mother from their domestic goat herd. The blessing Isaac thinks he is giving Esau reveals his awareness that the Abrahamic line will not pass through his "favourite" firstborn in that he omits any mention of descendants, limiting "Esau's" future to abundant food, wine, power and protection (27: 28, 29). This becomes even clearer when, just before Jacob flees from his brother's murderous intentions, Isaac calls for him and "by faith"[26] bestows upon him in unequivocal terms the Abrahamic blessing:[27]

> Take a wife for yourself there from among the daughters of Laban
> your mother's brother. May God Almighty bless you and make
> you fruitful and a community of peoples. May he give you and

---

24. Waltke, *Genesis: A Commentary*, 363.

25. Ibid.

26. See Hebrews 11:20.

27. This concept of what Isaac thought is developed at length by Rabbi Jonathan Sacks in a fascinating article, "Was Jacob right to take the blessings?" accessed 5 December 2016, http://www.chabad.org/parshah/article_cdo/aid/2757118/jewish/Was-Jacob-Right-To-Take-the-Blessings.html.

your descendants the blessing given to Abraham, so that you may take possession of the land where you now live as an alien, the land God gave to Abraham. (28:2–4)

A strange food image at the close of the Jacob–Esau saga suggests a deep change in Jacob's character following a face-to-face encounter with God – an all-night wrestling match – in which he is left with a permanently dislocated hip and a new name, Israel.[28] The mysterious transformative power of the encounter affected the dietary customs of the nation he would father: "and he was limping because of his hip; therefore to this day the Israelites do not eat the tendon attached to the socket of the hip" (32:31, 32). Jacob would never be the same.

These three food images illuminate Jacob's character, evident from birth as "grasper of the heel" or the deceiver, but also highlight the faithfulness of God who chooses whom he will, not allowing human flaw, error or deceit to thwart his promise to Abraham.[29]

Joseph: Grain Sheaves, Scrawny Cows, and Lunch at Home

In the thirteen chapters (37–50) that comprise the Jacob–Joseph story, food and eating are mentioned some 150 times. The gastronomic images, as is appropriate to the Genesis stage of biblical revelation, shift from the domestic level to the larger level as the narrative prepares for the book of Exodus where the family of promise will indeed become a nation. The food images continue to shed light on the character of God as well as the human actors currently on stage.

Brotherly hate continues as a sub-theme in Genesis. The dramatic tale opens with a dream about sheaves of grain – a basic food staple. An obnoxious, adolescent Joseph gives his brothers, who already despise him, the juicy details of his nocturnal vision: "suddenly my sheaf rose and stood upright, while your sheaves gathered around mine and bowed down to it" (37:7). Hardly a recipe for harmony: "his brothers hated him all the more" (37: 8) and soon hatched a plan to kill him (37:18).

The plot to murder Joseph and throw his body into a cistern is conceived when Jacob sends him to search for his brothers, who have wandered farther

---

28. Israel means *he struggles with God*.

29. For reasons of space, we have concentrated on Jacob's character, but the food scenes also illuminate the characters of Isaac, Rebecca and Esau.

than usual tending their flocks. They seize the hated dreamer, strip him of his elegant multi-coloured-favourite-son cloak, and heave him (alive) into an empty cistern before having lunch.

> As they sat down to eat their meal, they looked up and saw a caravan of Ishmaelites . . . on their way . . . to Egypt. Judah said to his brothers, "What will we gain if we kill our brother . . . ? Let's sell him to the Ishmaelites and not lay our hands on him; after all, he is our brother, our own flesh and blood." His brothers agreed. (37:26, 27)

This eating picture serves to point us to the character of Judah – this is important because, although none of the family is aware of it, Judah's line will continue, protected and highlighted, for more than a thousand years to culminate in the promised blessing of the nations in Jesus.

Flowing from this same food scene is an entire chapter focused on Judah, a kind of interruption with no apparent connection to the long story where Joseph is so preponderant that the reader could easily assume that the Abrahamic promise will be fulfilled through him. Joseph *is* the agent God uses to ensure that the chosen family will "live and not die" (42:2, 7; 43:8; 50:20), but the bigger story is leading towards the redemptive coming of the "lion of the tribe Judah" (Rev 5:5). Thus, this apparent interruption, covering several decades, is highly intentional: it shows how the potential danger of the extinction of Judah's line is averted when Tamar, his Canaanite daughter-in-law, disguises herself as a prostitute in order to become pregnant through Judah, who denies her right to levirate marriage with his son. Judah and Perez, the resulting son, appear along with Tamar in the genealogy of Matthew. Dr Christopher Wright underlines the importance of Matthew's genealogy in showing how the whole sweep of Old Testament history finds it fulfilment in the person of Jesus, whose birth is inseparable from the entire line of what has gone before.[30]

The brothers' meal has served to highlight Judah's character as one who sides with life over death.[31] It also points to his place in the larger story. God once again shows his character to be inclusive of both Gentiles and women in carrying out his redemptive plan.

---

30. Wright, *Knowing Jesus*, 1–8.

31. This long chapter shows us other character traits in Judah: he keeps his promise to pay Tamar with a young goat (food again . . .), his humility in publicly admitting that she "is more righteous than I" and his sexual integrity in that he "did not sleep with her again."

Two more food scenes are on the menu in Genesis: First, Pharaoh's double-barrelled dream about seven scrawny cows and seven scorched heads of grain that devour seven fat cows and seven robust heads of grain; secondly the full-course lunch Joseph provides to his unsuspecting, terrified brothers.

With Pharaoh's dream, for the first time since the covenant with Noah, the food image shifts to the macro level. The cows and heads of grain herald seven years of unprecedented national abundance followed by widespread famine.[32] God permits Joseph to understand the dream and warn Pharaoh, who converts him in one day from jailbird to Minister of Agriculture and Food Provision – second-in-command in all of Egypt.[33] The image points to the sovereignty of God over all the nations and the centrality of his person as food provider; it also highlights Joseph's character, in Pharaoh's own words, as "one in whom is the spirit of God."[34]

The second image, lunch *chez* Joseph, appropriately returns us to the family level; it takes place on the brothers' second trip to Egypt in search of food.[35] Joseph, still unrecognized by his eleven brothers, uses the eating occasion as an excuse to plant his silver cup in Benjamin's grain sack, pursue them, accuse his blood-brother of having stolen it, and sentence him to perpetual Egyptian slavery. Joseph's obnoxious streak is not entirely gone. This post-meal scene returns us to Judah who pleads before this disguised "foreign authority" to be allowed to take the punishment for Benjamin, "Let your servant remain here as my lord's slave in place of the boy . . . How can I go back to my father if the boy is not with me? . . . His brother is dead and he is the only one of his mother's sons left, and his father loves him" (44:33, 34, 20).

---

32. The text emphasizes the global extent of the famine, "There was famine in *every country* but throughout the land of Egypt there was food . . . the famine was severe in the land of Egypt. *Every nation* came to Joseph in Egypt to buy grain, for the famine was severe in *every land*" (Gen 41:54, 57, emphasis added).

33. Joseph has spent years in Egypt, where his experiences have ranged from sexual harassment while administering a wealthy household to unjust imprisonment. While he was still hurting from family wounds, confined to a dungeon (41:14) and powerless in the face of systemic injustice, we are told no less than six times that "the LORD was with Joseph" giving him "success in everything he did" (39:2, 3, 5, 21–23). Appearances to the contrary, he has not been abandoned by God.

34. Genesis 41:37: alternate translation: "*the spirit of the gods.*"

35. The narrator of Genesis uses creative literary devices to enhance the unity of the book, including repetitive events in successive generations. Three famines occur; the first two displace Abraham (12:10) and Isaac (26:1) bringing them before foreign rulers; the third brings Jacob's sons to Egypt where they *bow down with their faces to the ground* before Joseph (42:6) taking him for a *foreign ruler*; his adolescent dream (37:7; 42:8) comes true.

Joseph can take it no longer, dismisses the Egyptians and makes himself known to his brothers, "weeping so loudly that even Pharaoh's household heard" (45:2). The greatness of his character reveals itself when he declares to his stunned brothers,

> I am your brother Joseph, the one you sold into Egypt. And now do not be distressed and . . . angry with yourselves for selling me here, because it was to save lives that God sent me ahead of you . . . to preserve for you a remnant on earth and to save your lives by a great deliverance . . . Now hurry back to my father and say to him . . . Come down to me . . . you shall live in the land of Goshen and be near me – you, your children and grandchildren . . . because five years of famine are still to come. (45:4–11)

Through the moving words and actions of Joseph and Judah, this extended meal scene foreshadows the "great deliverance" to be effected by a descendant of Judah who although innocent will also offer himself in place of others. Here with the reconciliation of Joseph and his brothers and the displacement of their seventy family members to Egypt, the story can now move on to Exodus – the next historical phase in God's plan to bless all the peoples of the earth during which Israel will pass "from the crucible of slavery to the constitution of freedom as a people under the sovereignty of God."[36]

Conclusion

Genesis is the book of the Bible where food and eating are most plentiful – some 300 references. Created by God and given as his first gift to humankind, food, which is "very good" and life-giving in its essence, points beyond itself. Food images reveal character, signal moral dilemmas and changes in relationships. The images are embedded in a story that is going somewhere, moving its participants, including us, towards the culmination of history in the wedding feast of the Lamb in the new Jerusalem, under the shadow of the tree of life, whose fruit ripens each month and whose leaves are for the healing of the nations.

---

36. David Hulme, "The Law, the Prophets and the Writings, Part 7, Judah, Joseph and Jacob," accessed 8 December 2016, https://www. vision. org/visionmedia/religion-and-spirituality-old-testament-studies/71192. aspx, where he quotes Rabbi Jonathan Sacks.

Christopher Wright in all his writing never lets us forget where the story is going and encourages us to pause and consider in each image and each mini-narrative the larger picture and the centrality of Jesus Christ, the Bread of Life.

References

Amos, Claire. *The Book of Genesis*. Werrington, UK: Epworth, 2004.

Atkinson, David. *The Message of Genesis 1–11*. Downers Grove: InterVarsity Press, 1990.

Ayres, Jennifer R. *Good Food*. Waco, TX: Baylor University Press, 2013.

Bauckham, Richard. "Humans, Animals and the Environment in Genesis 1–3." In *Genesis and Christian Theology*, edited by Nathan MacDonald, Mark Elliott, and Grant Macaskill, 175–189. Grand Rapids: Eerdmans, 2012.

Beyer, Krisha D. "Hunger and Abundance in the Old Testament: A Contribution to a Biblical Theology of Food." Master's thesis, Regent College, 2009.

Borgman, Paul. *Genesis: The Story We Haven't Heard*. Downers Grove: InterVarsity Press, 2001.

Brueggemann, Walter. *The Bible Makes Sense*. Winona: St Mary's Press, 1997.

———. "A Biblical Perspective on the Problem of Hunger." *Christian Century* 94 (1977): 1136–1141.

———. *Theology of the Old Testament: Testimony, Dispute, Advocacy*. Minneapolis: Fortress Press, 1997.

Chapman, Stephen B. "Food, Famine, and the Nations: A Canonical Approach to Genesis." In *Genesis and Christian Theology*, edited by Nathan MacDonald, Mark Elliott, and Grant Macaskill, 323–333. Grand Rapids: Eerdmans, 2012.

Fee, Gordon D., and Douglas Stuart. *How to Read the Bible Book by Book: A Guided Tour*. Grand Rapids: Zondervan, 2002.

Guijarro Oporto, Santiago, and Miguel Salvador García, eds. *Comentario al Antiguo Testamento*. Madrid: La Casa de la Biblia. PPC/Sígueme, Verbo Divino, 1997.

Grimm, Veronika E. *From Feasting to Fasting, the Evolution of a Sin: Attitudes to Food in Latin Antiquity*. New York: Routledge, 1996.

Grumet, David. "The Case for Food Rules: A Christian Diet." *Christian Century* 127, no. 7 (2010): 34–37.

Hamilton, Victor P. *The Book of Genesis Chapters 1–17*. Grand Rapids: Eerdmans, 2010.

Hulme, David. "Judah, Joseph and Jacob." In *The Law, the Prophets and the Writings, Part 7*. Accessed 8 December 2016. https://www.vision.org/visionmedia/religion-and-spirituality-old-testament-studies/71192.aspx.

Jacobs, H. E. *Six Thousand Years of Bread: Its Holy and Unholy History*. New York: Lyons, 1944.

Juengst, Sara C. *Breaking Bread: The Spiritual Significance of Food*. Louisville: Westminster John Knox, 1992.

Kass, Leon R. *The Hungry Soul: Eating and the Perfecting of Our Nature*. Chicago: University of Chicago Press, 1999.

Lockyer, Herbert. "Alphabetical Exposition of Named Bible Women." Accessed 29 November 2016. https://www.biblegateway.com/resources/all-women-bible/toc.

MacDonald, Nathan. *Not Bread Alone: The Uses of Food in the Old Testament*. Oxford: Oxford University Press, 2008.

_____. *What Did the Ancient Israelites Eat? Diet in Biblical Times*. Grand Rapids: Eerdmans, 2008.

Mangiapane, Francesco. "Feasting with the Outlander: Semiotics of Culinary Cinema." *International Association for Semiotic Studies: Proceedings of the World Congress of IASS* (2014). Accessed 10 November 2016. http://www.iass-ais.org/proceedings2014/view_lesson.php?id=107.

Mann, Thomas. "Not by Word Alone: Food in the Hebrew Bible." *Interpretation* 67, no. 4 (2013): 351–362, 347.

Matvejevic, Predrag. *Nuestro pan de cada día*. Barcelona: Acantilado, 2013.

Meyers, Carol. "Food and the First Family: A Socio-economic Perspective." *Vetus Testamentum Supplements* 152 (2012): 138–157.

McKibbin, Jean, and Frank McKibbin. *Cookbook of Food from Bible Days*. Monroeville, PA: Whitaker Books, 1965.

Mortenson, Terry. "Genesis 2:17 'You shall surely die.'" Accessed 15 November 2016. https://answersingenesis.org/death-before-sin/genesis-2–17-you-shall-surely-die/.

Patterson, Barbara A. B., and Shirley M Banks. "Christianity and Food: Recent Scholarly Trends." *Religion Compass* 7, no. 10 (2013): 433–443.

Sacks, Rabbi Jonathan. "Was Jacob Right to Take the Blessings?" Accessed 5 December 2016. http://www. chabad. org/ parshah/article_cdo/aid/2757118/jewish/Was-Jacob-Right-to-Take-the-Blessings. html.

Schmemann, Alexander. *For the Life of the World*. New York: St Vladimir's Seminary Press, 1973.

Schubert, David, and Steven Drucker. "How 121 Nobel Laureates Were Misled into Promoting GM Foods." *GM Watch Review* 375 (2016).

Strenghold, Jos. "God's First Temple: Creation." Accessed 8 May 2015. http://strengholt. blogspot. com/2015/03/gods-first-temple-creation. html.

Usme Lopez, Yuli Norbelia. "El Alimento como Símbolo. Apuntes para una alquimia culinaria." *Dialogo Académico: Campos de Estudio y Acción de la Comunicación. Volumen I*. Bogotá, Colombia: Fundación Universitaria IMPAHU, 2011.

Vegter, Ivo. "110 Nobel Laureates Warn Greenpeace of 'Crime against Humanity' on GMOs." *Daily Maverick* (South Africa), 2 August 2016.

Voth, Esteban. *Génesis: Primera Parte*. Comentario Bíblico Hispanoamericano. Miami: Editorial Caribe, 1999.

Walkte, Bruce. *Genesis: A Commentary*. Grand Rapids: Zondervan, 2001.

Watts, Rick. "Making Sense of Genesis 1." Accessed 11 May 2015. http://www. asa3. org/ASA/topics/ Bible-Science/6–02Watts. html.

Wirzba, Norman. *Food and Faith: A Theology of Eating*. Cambridge: Cambridge University Press, 2011.

Wright, Christopher, J. H. *Knowing Jesus through the Old Testament*. Downers Grove: InterVarsity Press, 1992.

———. *The Mission of God's People*. Grand Rapids: Zondervan, 2010.

———. *Sweeter than Honey: Preaching the Old Testament*. Carlisle, UK: Langham Preaching Resources, 2015.

16

The Portrayal of Women in Arabic Proverbial Wisdom

Riad A. Kassis

Riad A. Kassis *is assistant professor of Old Testament Studies at Arab Baptist Theological Seminary and visiting professor at the Near East School of Theology, Beirut, Lebanon. He is the international director of the International Council for Evangelical Theological Education (ICETE) and the international director of the Langham Scholars programme. Riad holds a BA in Economics from the University of Damascus, an MDiv from Alliance Biblical Seminary, Manila, and a PhD in Old Testament from the University of Nottingham, where he was a Langham Scholar. His English publications include* The Book of Proverbs and Arabic Proverbial Works *and* Frustrated with God: A Syrian Theologian's Reflections on Habakkuk. *He has also published Arabic works, whose titles can be translated as* Understanding Solomon's Proverbs and Arabic Proverbs *and* Why We Do Not Read the Book That Christ Read? Towards A Better Understanding of the Old Testament.

Christopher J. H. Wright has significantly contributed to making the Old Testament relevant to the ethical issues facing Christian communities in our modern world. His *Old Testament Ethics for the People of God* is a major contribution to achieving this goal. He has done that in a creative way, following in the steps of the late Dr John R. W. Stott who used to speak often on the importance of "double listening." By this he meant that we are called to listen both to the Word of God, and to today's world, in order to relate the one to the other.

In 2003 Chris Wright and I co-taught a course entitled "Witness and Wisdom: The Old Testament and Christian Mission and Ethics" at Regent

College, Vancouver. It was during that time that I started to develop an intimate friendship with him. It was fascinating for me to see his love for God's mission and God's people, for mission as outlined in the Old Testament. Since then Chris and his wife Liz have become good friends and colleagues in ministry through Langham Partnership. Izdihar, my wife, and I were always impressed by Chris's love and respect for Liz. In fact, he dedicated his book *Living as the People of God: The Relevance of Old Testament Ethics* to Liz "in the spirit of Proverbs 31:10–11, 28–29." Hence I dedicate this article to both Chris and Liz.

In his PhD dissertation at Cambridge University that dealt with the Old Testament economic ethics of land and family, Chris dealt with the topic of women in the Old Testament. While it is often alleged that women were just chattels of men in ancient Israel, he argued strongly in a different direction, particularly as regards wives (as distinct from slave concubines and daughters). So in his book *God's People in God's Land* a whole chapter is devoted to wives. So it is appropriate for me to direct my attention to the topic of how women are portrayed in Arabic proverbial wisdom.

In her study of more than 4,000 proverbs in more than 240 languages and dialects in more than 150 countries, Mineke Schipper (2003: 400) found out that women are viewed negatively in most proverbs. Other studies from Ghana, Europe and Japan support that conclusion.

Although Arabic proverbs tend to confirm Schipper's conclusion, some of them also convey a positive perspective on women. I have chosen to focus on these for two reasons. First, most studies of Arabic proverbial wisdom dwell on the negative perspective of women. Second, this positive perspective is more in line with the biblical book of Proverbs, which I have written about elsewhere.[1] By dealing with Arabic proverbial wisdom I also record again my debt to Langham Partnership for giving me the opportunity and the means to do my PhD studies with a focus on the book of Proverbs and Arabic proverbial wisdom tradition.

"The One Who Knows": On the Treatment of Women

"The one who knows, knows and the one who does not know will say: 'Just for a handful of lentils.'" This is a common Arabic proverbial saying in the Levant. It is said that during the lentil harvest season people used to spend the night

---

1. Riad Kassis, *Understanding Solomon's Proverbs and Arabic Proverbs* (Beirut: Dar Manhal al-Hayat and Arab Baptist Theological Seminary, 2013).

in the field to protect their harvest. One night a man woke up to see another man sexually harassing his wife. He shouted at him and began to chase him. As he ran, the other man grabbed a handful of lentils. When they got to the village, the villagers were surprised to see the one man pursuing the other. They told the aggrieved husband to calm down, because there was no need to be so angry about the theft of a mere handful of lentils! This put the husband in an embarrassing situation: he did not want to bring shame on his wife by admitting that the other man had been harassing her, and so he said: The one who knows (the context), knows (what is really going on), but those who do not know (the context and the reality) say "just for a handful of lentils!"

This proverb reminds us that we often judge on appearances without knowing the context and the facts. Moreover, it also reminds us that the husband was unable to defend the rights of his wife who has been harassed, quite possibly because he feared for his own reputation rather than hers. To keep the community happy, the husband had to hide the truth, the harasser remained free, and the woman had to endure! Should women be treated in such a way?

It is interesting to notice that the majority of Arabic proverbs on woman were coined by or attributed to men. The woman's voice is almost absent in these proverbs. Āṣ-Ṣabbar (1999: 65) argues that the reason for this is that men use proverbs to protect their elevated status in society. On the other hand, Muniah (2008: 36–39) in her field research on Moroccan proverbs on women found that a large number of women happily recite popular proverbs, including those that describe their inferiority to men.

Women in Old Arabic Proverbs

One of the most important collections of ancient Arabic proverbs is that of Āl-Maydāny, which includes more than 6,000 proverbs. Three percent of the proverbs in Āl-Maydāny's collection relate to women. This is a major reference for this study but other collections and commentaries on ancient Arabic proverbs will be consulted as well.

Women depicted negatively

In his study of the Shiite wisdom tradition Āl-Ḥabbāz (2009: 144–146) clearly finds that women have been depicted negatively. However, he argues that the problem does not lie in the text itself but in its interpretation. For example, the saying: "The woman is all evil, but what is worse (than that) is you need her" was understood by Muġnyeh to describe woman as evil, but Faḍllalah finds this saying contradictory to the teachings of Islam. Āl-ʿĀmily understands the saying as a reference not to all women but to a particular woman in a certain context.

In ancient Arabic proverbs, if there is no distinction between the text and its interpretation, the negative portrayal of woman can be seen in three main areas: her purpose in life, her conduct and her social status.

Most ancient Arabic proverbs refer to a woman as a "bride," implying that a woman's purpose in life is to be married and bear children. This orientation may explain why almost 59 percent of ancient Arabic proverbs on woman focus on physical beauty (Bany Yasyeen and Ār-Rababʿah 2001: 30–39, 49). They describe her appearance, body, face, hair, and even her sexual parts (Bany Yasyeen and Ār-Rababʿah 2001: 108; ʿAbd Ār-Raḥman 1998: 42, 52, 128, 154–155, 159, 316).

Abu ʿAly (2001:48) argues that ancient proverbs in pre-Islamic Arabia depicted woman as seeking "a sexual oasis" and that her very nature as a human being heavily relies on her being "fruitful" by reproducing children. "More apt to marry than Um Ḥariğah" (Bany Yasyeen and Ār-Rababʿah, 2001: 30–39, 49) is a proverb that describes a woman who married more than forty men and was regarded as "the mother" of many Arab tribes.

When referring to a woman's conduct it is noteworthy that many ancient Arabic proverbs associate adultery with women (Abu ʿAly 2001: 497–545; ʿAbd Ār-Raḥman 1998: 48, 109, 363).

The most common social status or profession for women is that of a concubine or a slave. There were so many concubines in pre-Islamic Arabia that they formed their own social stratum (Āl-Asad 1988: 18–19). A woman was considered a commodity to be bought and sold, whence the famous saying: "Do not praise a slave maid when you buy her" (Āl-Maydāny 1988: 2, 252; Āl-Zamaḫšary 1977: 2, 254; Abu ʿUbayd 1980: 67; Āl-Bakry 1971: 67). Moreover, there are several proverbs on how to deal with a slave maid. One should not joke with her (ʿAbd Ār-Raḥman 1998: 365) and never share a secret with her (Āl-Maydāny 1988: 2, 313; Āl-Bakry 1971: 56). In fact, not only are slave maids regarded as unworthy of trust but women in general are described as the "devil's traps" (ʿAbad Ār-Raḥman 1998: 442–443). Therefore "any tribe dependent on women will be humiliated" and "obedience to women will eventually lead to regret" (Āl-Munaġġid 1981: 73, 91, 135).

Women depicted positively

In Āl-Maydāny's large collections of ancient Arabic proverbs women are viewed positively in their capacity as mothers. They are praised for their ability to bear children, their deep love and compassion for their children and their willingness to help and sacrifice at all times: "The afflicted will run to his mother" ('Abd Ār-Raḥman 1998: 145). To be motherless is regarded as an enormous loss, which may be why the saying "You have no mother" is regarded as an extreme insult ('Abd Ār-Raḥman 1998: 360; Āl-Munaǧǧid 1981: 115).

Although physical beauty was highly regarded in ancient Arabic proverbs, when it comes to choosing between beauty and moral characteristics one should prefer the latter. Therefore, the sage Āktam bin ṣayfy says: "Do not let beauty overcome pure lineage" (Āl-'Skary 1988: 1, 22). There are also sayings that warn against beauty if it is not united with high ethical standards (Ār-Raḥman 1998: 127).

Women's faithfulness and integrity were praised in sayings like, "More faithful than Ǧameel's mother." This proverb refers to a historical incident where a woman called Ǧameel's mother, who belonged to the Ābu Huryrah tribe, provided a safe haven to Hišham bin Ā-Maǧera.

Another proverb that describes the strength of a woman is: "More powerful than Qirfah." Qirfah, the wife of Malik bin Badir, was famous for having fifty swords in her tent ('Abd Ār-Raḥman 1998: 74–75, 105–106). "More dignified than Āz-Zabbā'" refers to the queen of Palmyra ('Abd Ār-Raḥman 1998: 385). There are other proverbs that depict women as speaking elegantly, giving generously and showing creativity (Āl-Munaǧǧid 1981: 146–147).

Earlier we looked at the negative portrayal of women as slaves and concubines, but there are also other perspectives on the social and professional roles of women. These counter proverbs present women as midwives, rulers, singers, saleswomen and hired weepers. It is also interesting to observe that the second most common role of women after being slave maids is that of a warrior, or at least participating in wars in one form or another (Bany Yasyeen and Ār-Rabab'ah, 2001: 16–30; Ār-Raḥman 1998: 55; Āl-Munaǧǧid 1981: 30, 131–132).

Women in Modern Arabic Proverbs

One of the best comprehensive collections of modern Arabic proverbs related to women is that of Āṭ-Ṭyby's *Encyclopedia of Popular Proverbs on the Arab*

Woman. His collection includes proverbs from the Middle East and North Africa as well as the Arabian Gulf and Peninsula. It should be noted at the outset that while many of the ancient Arabic proverbs we discussed above are not in wide circulation nowadays, modern or popular Arabic proverbs are widely used in many contexts, including education, news, drama, TV programmes, films as well as in daily conversations throughout the Arab world.

Women depicted negatively

Āl-May, a Tunisian author, argues that modern Tunisian proverbs depict a very negative view of women: "These proverbs belong to a corrupt heritage that has to be eliminated and replaced with an enlightened one" (2007: 9–10). He also asserts that the "collective memory has humiliated women and undermined her role except that of a mother" (2007: 85).

Manal Āl-Muġraby, a female Arab researcher, analysed 3,600 Palestinian proverbs and found that 82.5 percent of them insult women, 16.5 percent praise women and 1 percent are neutral (2010). Analysis of Syrian, Saudi, Egyptian and Moroccan modern proverbs yields similar results. Women are considered as lacking mental abilities: "A woman has half a brain" (Lebanese proverb), "a woman has only half a brain, half a religion and half an inheritance" (Syrian proverb, Āl-Ḥaššāš 1988: 131). "A woman has a quarter of a brain that she shares with a donkey" (Moroccan proverb, Muniah 2008: 184). "A chick has a larger brain than a woman" (Bedouin proverb, Bailey 2004: 410). A Syrian proverb even goes further, saying: "Every twenty women have the brain of a stupid chick" (Hindy 2006: 145).

Given these insulting descriptions of women, modern proverbs instructions on how to treat women come as no surprise: "When men are present women should be silent" (Rišraš 1985: 112), "obedience to women leads to the fire of hell" (Moroccan proverb, Āṭ-Ṭyby 2000: 317), "the manly (authentic) man is the one who never consults his wife" (Egyptian proverb, Āṭ-Ṭyby 2000: 21).

Husbands are advised to use violence: "Beating for women is like a fertilizer to your plants" (Āṭ-Ṭyby 2000: 84), "Beat your wife on a daily basis. Even if you do not know why, she will know why" (Āṭ-Ṭyby 2000: 46). However, physical violence is not the only way to discipline one's wife: "Discipline camels by a rod and discipline a woman by marrying another woman" (Bedouin proverb, Bailey 2004: 153). If one wants to root the problem of evil in women, there are religious grounds for that: "Women are inspired by Satan" (Hindy 2006: 142) and even "Satan said 'I direct men but I receive my orders from women'" (Āl-Ḥaššāš 1988: 127).

This view of women contributes to viewing women as burdens: "A daughter is a disaster" (Palestinian proverb), "girls will cause distress until they die" (Arabian Peninsula proverb, Āl-Ḥaššāš 1988: 218), "he who gets daughters will have increased concerns" (Tunisian proverb, Āṭ-Ṭyby 2000: 292), "a daughter is a disgraceful commodity" (Libyan proverb, Āṭ-Ṭyby 2000: 295), "a daughter will bring shame and enemies to your household" (Lebanese proverb, Āṭ-Ṭyby 2000: 57). There are two options when it comes to dealing with a daughter: "A daughter should either be married or dead" (Lebanese proverb, Āṭ-Ṭyby 2000: 60), "Spoil your son and you will be rich; spoil your daughter and will face shame" (Āl-Ḥaššāš 1988: 218). This is why the father of a woman who bears only girls is to be cursed: "Let her father be cursed if she does not beget a son" (Egyptian proverb, Elkhadem 1993: 161).

Women depicted positively

There are, however, some modern Arabic proverbs that depict women as having great influence on their husbands: "The one who feels jealousy towards her husband will control him (literally, trim his feathers so he is unable to fly)" (Elkhadem 1993: 16), "your son will follow your lead and your husband as well" (Elkhadem 1993: 6). Lest men think that women are weak and powerless, a woman is referred to as "a man's sister" who does not fear men (Āṭ-Ṭyby 2000: 44; Elkhadem 1993: 151). And while there are many modern proverbs that warn men against trusting women, there are also some proverbs that warn women against trusting men: "Men cannot be trusted" (Elkhadem 1993: 69; Āṭ-Ṭyby 2000: 36). Women are also able to lead and take initiative: "In April women are in charge;" "Flowers have blossomed and now women will rule" (Āṭ-Ṭyby 2000: 60, 73). These two proverbs refer to the need of men for women at this time of the year. It is when women gain authority and control over them.

Men are also called to respect their wives in front of others: "People will salute the one who respects his wife;" "If a man shows disrespect to his wife, others will humiliate her" (Elkhadem 1993: 28).

The most positive portrayal of woman is in her capacity as a mother: "Paradise is under mothers' feet," "all humanity is a mother," and "a good mother makes a good family" (Āṭ-Ṭyby 2000: 64, 71). A mother is regarded as full of mercy and compassion: "Only God is more merciful than a mother towards her child" (Āṭ-Ṭyby 2000: 114), "if your mother passes away all who love you pass away as well" (Āt̤-Ṭyby 2000: 159). This is why a young man is given the important advice: "As you look for a wife, ask about her mother" (Āt̤-Ṭyby 2000: 46).

Women are praised in modern Arabic proverbs for their ability to take care of their household: "A home with no woman goes backward" (Hindy 2006: 141), "the woman builds up the house" (Bailey 2004: 403). She is also compared with her husband and portrayed as excelling over him in her ability to run the household: "A mother's wing gathers while a father's wing flies away" (Āt̤-Ṭyby 2000: 63), "If the man is a sea, woman is a bridge" (Āt̤-Ṭyby 2000: 12).

Modern Arabic proverbs are similar to ancient Arabic proverbs in describing the beauty of women, with particular reference to her body and eyes. They also compare physical beauty with moral beauty and give priority to the latter: "Get married to a woman, not to her face," "beauty with no morals is like a flower without a scent," "beauty with no brain is like a flower in the mud" (Hindy 2006: 59–77).

Conclusion

In presenting this article to Chris Wright on his seventieth birthday I would like to express my gratitude to him for his passion to bring equality to both men and women in serving God's kingdom and to wish him well for many years to come. I also present this article with the hope that Dr Wright will devote more of his writing to addressing the role of women in the biblical story and its relevance to our global context.

References

Bailey, Clinton. *A Culture of Desert Survival: Bedouin Proverbs from Sinai and the Negev*. New Haven: Yale University Press, 2004.

Elkhadem, Saad. *Life Is Like a Cucumber: Colloquial Egyptian Proverbs, Coarse Sayings, and Popular Expressions*. Fredericton, Canada: York Press, 1993.

Schipper, Mineke. *Never Marry a Woman with Big Feet: Women in Proverbs from around the World*. New Haven: Yale University Press, 2003.

ʿAbad Ār-Raḥman

عبد الرّحمن، عفيف، قاموس الأمثال العربيّة التّراثيّة: عربيّ – عربيّ. بيروت: مكتبة لبنان ناشرون، 1998.

Abu ʿAly

أبو علي، محمّد توفيق، صورة العادات والتّقاليد والقيم الجّاهليّة في كتب الأمثال العربيّة من القرن 6 – 9/12 – 15 م. بيروت: شركة المطبوعات للتّوزيع والنّشر، 2001.

Abu ʿUbayd

أبو عبيد، القاسم بن سلاّم، (توفي 224/838)، كتاب الأمثال. تحقيق عبد المجيد قطامش. من التّراث الإسلامي 7. دمشق/بيروت: دار المأمون للتّراث، 1980.

Al-Asad

الأسد، ناصر الدّين، القيان والغناء في العصر الجاهليّ. بيروت: دار الجيل، الطبعة الثالثة، 1988.

Āl-Bakry

البكري، أبو عبيد، (توفي 487/1094)، فصل المقال في شرح كتاب الأمثال. تحقيق إحسان عبّاس وعبد المجيد عابدين. بيروت: دار الأمانة/ مؤسّسة الرّسالة، 1971.

Āl-Ḥaššāš

الحشّاش، عبد الكريم عيد، الأسرة في المثل الشعبي الفلسطيني والعربي. دمشق: المطبعة العلمية، 1988.

Āl-Ḥabbāz

الخباز، محمد، صورة المرأة في التراث الشيعي: تفكيك لآليات العقل النّصي. بيروت: الانتشار العربي، 2009.

Āl-May

المي، محمد، صورة المرأة في الأمثال العامية التونسية. تونس: الشركة التونسية للنشر وتنمية فنون الرسم، 2007.

Āl-Maydāny

الميداني النيسابوري، أبو الفضل أحمد بن محمّد بن أحمد بن إبراهيم (توفي 518/1124)، مجمَع الأمثال، جزءان. تعليق نعيم زرزور. بيروت: دار الكتب العلميّة، 1988.

Āl-Muġraby

المغربي، منال "صورة المرأة في الأمثال الشعبية"، مقال على شبكة الإنترنت، ٦ فبراير (شباط)، ٢٠١٠. https://echraqq.wordpress.com/2012/06/18/

Āl-Munaǧǧid

المنجّد، صلاح الدّين، أمثال المرأة عند العرب: ما قالته المرأة العربيّة وما قيل فيها. بيروت: دار الكتاب الجديد، 1981.

Āl-ʿSkary

العسكري، أبو هلال الحسن بن عبدالله بن سهل، (توفي حوالي 395/1005)، كتاب جمهرة الأمثال. جزءان. تحقيق أحمد عبد السّلام ومحمّد سعيد بن بسيوني ز غلول. بيروت: دار الكتب العلّميّة، 1988.

Āṣ-Ṣabbar

الصبار، خديجة، المرأة بين الميثولوجيا والحداثة. المغرب: أفريقيا الشرق، 1999.

Āṭ-Ṭyby

الطيبي، عكاشة عبد المنان، موسوعة الأمثال الشعبية في المرأة العربيّة. بيروت: دار اليوسف، 2000.

Āl-Zamaḫšary

الزّمخشري، أبو القاسم محمود بن عمر (توفي 538/1144)، المُستقصى في أمثال العرب. جزءان. بيروت: دار الكتب العلّميّة، 1977.

Bany Yasyeen and Ār-Rababʿah

بني ياسين، رسلان والربابعة، حسن محمد، المرأة العربيّة ودلالاتها في «مجمع الأمثال» للميداني: دراسة نقدية. منشورات جامعة اليرموك: عمادة البحث العلمي والدراسات العليا. إربد: جامعة اليرموك، 2001.

Hindy

هندي، إحسان، الحكم والأمثال الشعبية في العلاقات العائلية والزوجية. مشروع جمع وحفظ التراث الشعبي 2. دمشق: منشورات وزارة الثّقافة، 2006.

Muniah

منية، بل العافية، المرأة في الأمثال المغربيّة. الذار البيضاء: دار توبقال للنشر، 2008.

Rišraš

رشراش، أنيس عبد الخالق، التّربية في الأمثال الشّعبيّة: دراسة تحليليّة ومُقارنة للأمثال الشّعبيّة التّربويّة في 13 بلداً عربيّاً. لبنان: دار الرافد، 1985.

17

Preaching to Impress or to Save: An Exposition of 1 Corinthians 1:17–2:5

Mark Meynell

Mark Meynell *is associate director (Europe & Caribbean) of Langham Preaching, having first become involved with Langham in 2002 while on the faculty (and subsequently acting principal) of Kampala Evangelical School of Theology, Uganda. From 2005 to 2014, he was also on the senior ministry team of All Souls Church, Langham Place, in London. He has written a number of books, most recently* What Angels Long to Read: Reading and Preaching the New Testament, *which is the companion volume to Chris Wright's* Sweeter Than Honey.

Chris Wright is not an impressive preacher. He rarely scintillates with oratorical fireworks, he cannot claim his own TV station; he isn't even a celebrity scholar who dines out on the proceeds of his brilliance.

Nevertheless, it is entirely appropriate to celebrate his seventieth with this volume! For so many of us, he has been a mentor and a model of committed, faithful scholarship that genuinely serves the global church. That is why I think (and hope) that he will not be offended in the slightest by such a negative introductory assessment. He has never aspired to any of those things. Instead, he has far higher goals that flow out of deep theological conviction. This chapter will explore how and why such an attitude is possible.

A Ugandan Village Challenge

Some years ago, a good friend found himself in a tight situation. He was at home in his village, not far outside Kampala, where he had helped to plant a small but growing church. He was confronted by a significant challenge from a disturbing source: the neighbourhood traditional healer. This man was protesting my friend's right to minister in the village, threatening all kinds of spiritual attacks if he didn't withdraw. This did not come as a surprise, however. One of the healer's most regular customers had recently come to Christ and conspicuously burned all her charms.

Since the gauntlet had been thrown down in public, it could not be ignored. People slowly gathered to witness the church-planter's response. The question uppermost in my friend's mind was how this would affect the young church. Would people now join? Or leave? What would happen to his reputation in that tiny community? It was a make or break moment.

Similar spiritual battles occur throughout the world in many different guises. The temptation to attempt to make a strong impression is almost impossible to resist. Who wouldn't seek to make an obvious impact? Isn't that what Elijah did on Mount Carmel, all in the name of seeing God glorified? A major display of divine power, whatever that might entail, would grind the spiritual forces of darkness into submission. It would also attract spiritual waverers.

But I suspect that the Apostle Paul would have resisted this temptation. For one thing, he would have recognized it would not guarantee the desired effect. For example, when the apostles performed works of power in the book of Acts, some people believed the gospel, but others dismissed it. In Lystra, a healing miracle led to serious misunderstandings (Barnabas must be Zeus and Paul his spokesman Hermes) and to potential disaster (Paul was stoned and left for dead) (Acts 14:8–20). On different occasions, Paul was beaten and jailed, just as Peter and others had been. And when Stephen performed signs and preached powerfully, he was murdered, sparking a fresh outbreak of persecution. That was hardly Stephen's intention, of course. But it is arguable that these works of power merely aggravated the situation, provoking the enemies of the gospel to greater determination. Of course, that never stopped the apostles persevering in their great works and preaching. They were not trying to impress people into conversion but simply to be faithful and thus save some. The passage we will be looking at in Corinthians helps us to explain why.

So, what did my church-planting friend do, as he stood in the clearing before the assembled villagers? He began to explain to that healer and the bystanders who Jesus is. In particular, he argued that Jesus's death on the cross brought victory over all enemy powers and forces, and so provides forgiveness for all who believe. This was why he had nothing to fear from the healer, and why he would resolutely continue his ministry.

Some laughed. Others listened. My friend was very honest about it afterwards. He said he felt like a fool. Which is precisely what some of the onlookers thought he was. His response seemed so weak and pathetic. Just to use words. Words about an executed Saviour! A sermon to combat spiritual powers and charms?

But a fool is precisely what Paul expected us to feel like.

1. We Won't Impress with Our Preaching . . . (1 Cor 1:17–25)

Paul was bluntly realistic:

> Christ did not send me to baptize but to preach the gospel – not with words of human wisdom, lest the cross of Christ be emptied of its power. For the message of the cross is foolishness to those who are perishing, but to us who are being saved it is the power of God. (1 Cor 1:17–18)

The reason my friend felt a fool, and was considered a fool, is precisely because of his message. Paul is clear – it does appear foolish. Yet that is no grounds for reticence. What we see depends on the filters that affect our vision. When people come to the message of Jesus and his cross, it is almost as if they are wearing sunglasses – they don't see the cross in its true colours. They see it in only one way – darkened by their lenses. And, according to Paul, the cross actually divides the world into two groups: those who think the cross is folly, stupidity verging on madness, and those who think it is the power of God. The deciding factor is whether a person is perishing or being saved.

Paul offers two reasons for the gospel's folly and weakness. The first is startling.

Because of God's deliberate plan

If there is one thing that God consistently condemns throughout the Bible it is human pride. So, it is no accident that Paul quotes the Old Testament here.

> For it is written: "I will destroy the wisdom of the wise; the intelligence of the intelligent I will frustrate."

> [So Paul asks] Where is the wise man? Where is the scholar?
> Where is the philosopher of this age? Has not God made foolish
> the wisdom of the world? (1 Cor 1:19–20)

Taking his cue from Isaiah 29, Paul states God's purpose of destroying human arrogance once and for all. He will destroy human wisdom because it has too often become the tool of human rebellion. When it comes to finding God, the worldly wise, the brilliant scholars and agora philosophers are no help. In fact, too often they lead people *away* from God. So, God responds: he makes human wisdom look stupid. Why?

> For since in the wisdom of God the world through its wisdom did
> not know him, God was pleased through the foolishness of what
> was preached to save those who believe. (1 Cor 1:21)

Follow the logic. It is precisely *because* human wisdom is unable to help us reach him that God is pleased to use a different method: a message that seems unwise. We know this from experience. We know we cannot think our way to God. If we could, global universities and colleges would be bastions of piety and orthodoxy. Instead, God uses something that seems stupid and unwise in order to save, to bring to himself those who are sufficiently humble to believe their way to God, rather than think their way to God.

There is something very fair, and even democratic, about that. Conversion is not dependent on degrees, let alone doctorates; in fact, literacy is not even a requirement. The only *sine qua non* is humility to trust. This is God's deliberate purpose. Therefore, when we preach the gospel, we are not ultimately dependent on arguments to reach people (important though they often are). We need to lead them to faith – which may well include a gospel defence and unpacking complexity. But we never try to impress them. We seek to lead them to the cross because the cross is the only way to save them. We preach the cross, despite its folly.

Yet, why does the cross seem so absurd?

Because of the world's demanding pride

With an apostolic disregard for political correctness, Paul divides the world into the two major groups he encountered on his missionary journeys – Jews and Greeks. After all he was writing this letter to Corinthian Christians. The world today of course has countless more divisions, on religious, political, ethnic or tribal grounds. Yet these two categories from the Pauline era still illuminate our own generation.

> Jews demand miraculous signs and Greeks look for wisdom. (1 Cor 1:22)

They do it differently, but these two groups share an attitude. Both say to God, "I will not believe and trust you *unless* you satisfy my curiosity; *unless* you satisfy my intellectual demands; *unless* you do what *I* want." Human beings, out of a pride that expects the Creator must meet his creatures' demands, say in effect, "God must obey me before I'll even listen to him." Just who do we think we are?

Jews demand signs

At one point, Pharisees came to Jesus demanding a sign. His response? Blunt refusal. He even said, "a wicked and adulterous generation asks for a sign" (Matt 12:39). Soon after, Jesus deliberately set out for Jerusalem for his execution, a plan that confused even his closest disciples (Matt 16:21). That was hardly an impressive "sign." It certainly was inappropriate for a Messiah. Jewish kings usually took on their responsibilities at their anointing, not their execution. A crucified king? As pointless as an executed president, because an executed president is an ex-president. No wonder the Jewish world demanded signs of power from Jesus, both to assert his authority and inaugurate his rule. Instead, Paul offers them Jesus in his apparently total failure and weakness. No wonder the cross is a trip hazard. It is unacceptable. It is pathetic.

Greeks demand wisdom

Ancient Greece's greatest legacy was its philosophy. The most respected person in Greek society was the thinker. A prevailing prejudice, stemming from Platonic worldviews, was the belief that material reality is evil. The ideal existed on a different plane altogether. Consequently, the purpose of life is to escape the world of the material, to break out, to become truly spiritual.

This squarely places the Christian kerygma on a collision course with Greek thought. God invades the material to become human, to become material, to follow a diametrically opposed trajectory. Why on earth would God do that? Not only that, he comes *in order* to die. Not only that, he comes to earth to die as a contemptible criminal. An ancient Greek with any sense would have laughed at the absurdity. As Paul says in 1:23, the cross is stupidity. It is almost madness.

Both Jews and Greeks fall into the same trap. They expect the Creator to squeeze into their creaturely agendas. But no box can ever contain God. He always exceeds our wildest imaginings.

This is why Paul resists the demands of the world in his ministry. The temptation is always to fit in with the Jews and Greeks. He could give them what they wanted. He could try to be clever – after all, he *was* clever! He could easily impress them with his remarkable intellect. He could call down thunder and lightning in front of them. He could easily have argued from a miracle that even though Jesus was weak on the cross, look at the potential of his power now.

If Paul had done that, however, his audience would have been left with the presumption that we are the centre of the world, that God does whatever we need him to do. That is outrageous. It ought to be the other way around. For in preaching, we do not prove how God does what we want; instead we call people to do what God wants. This is in fact why Langham Partnership, and others around the world, are so committed to expository preaching. For it is in the Scriptures that we learn most clearly what our Creator and Lord expects from us. To expound the Scriptures is the surest way, humanly speaking, of calling people to that. God's concern is never to impress with cleverness or power (which anyone can take or leave). He is not perturbed by scorn or perceptions of weakness.

So Paul perseveres.

. . . but people will still believe and be saved

> to those whom God has called, both Jews and Greeks, Christ the power of God and the wisdom of God. For the foolishness of God is wiser than man's wisdom, and the weakness of God is stronger than human strength. (1 Cor 1:24–25)

When the message of the cross is preached, God does call people – from both Jews and Greeks, from every tribe, language and nation, from the Baganda and Basoga of Uganda, from the Hutu and Tutsi of Rwanda, even from the French and English of Northern Europe. As Paul wrote in Romans 1, it is the message itself that is the power of God to save. Through the preaching of the message, God removes the filters that distort the cross. He enables those he has called to see in the clear light of day that the cross represents remarkable power and wisdom.

Who could ever have conceived of the cross? Only a divine imagination, surely? It is now the wellspring of all Christian joy, confidence and hope. For it is God's own means by which he saved us from his own judgement on our sin – God in Christ dying in my place that I might live in his. That is wisdom; that is power. No Greek philosopher or Jewish Pharisee or traditional healer or Nobel laureate or Booker-winning novelist would ever have dreamt that one up. And it crushes human pride. It takes great humility to admit one's *need* for this cross. Yet, believe it people do, which is why Paul perseveres in preaching the cross in any and every cultural context.

This is crucial for a ministry like Langham Partnership that seeks to equip and train scholars, writers and preachers across the globe. One of the great hallmarks of the ministry, in large part because of both John Stott's personal legacy and Chris Wright's sensitive missiological antennae, is that it takes every unique cultural context very seriously. The focus and style of a scholar or preacher from Bangalore will never be identical with those from Sarajevo or Cochabamba.

Yet one thing is clear from this passage, and it informs the convictions of the work. We preach a crucified and risen Christ – a message that we anticipate will be a cultural trip hazard *wherever* he is preached. It will never initially impress anyone in Kampala, in St Petersburg, or in Bangkok. It will *always* seem unimpressive. That is why my church-planting friend did the courageous but correct thing – he told people about the crucified King, even in the face of a witchdoctor's scorn.

Jews think they can be reached through their eyes – by impressive signs and wonders.

Greeks think they can be reached through their ears – by impressive arguments and ideas.

God will only reach us through the heart – a heart of humble submission to his lordship and authority. Any preaching and any ministry that is motivated by a desire to impress people, whether by appealing to their eyes with signs or to their ears with cleverness, will fail to be faithful to God's call. Our preaching must always bring people face to face with the lordship of our God and the Cross of his Christ, even if people laugh at us when we do so. We do not show God doing what people want. Instead we call people to do what God wants. To believe.

2. We Won't Impress with Our People . . . (1 Cor 1:26–31)

> Brothers, think of what you were when you were called. Not many
> of you were wise by human standards; not many were influential;

not many were of noble birth. But God chose the foolish things of the world to shame the wise; God chose the weak things of the world to shame the strong. He chose the lowly things of this world and the despised things – and the things that are not – to nullify the things that are, so that no-one may boast before him. It is because of him that you are in Christ Jesus, who has become for us wisdom from God – that is, our righteousness, holiness and redemption. Therefore, as it is written: "Let him who boasts boast in the Lord." (1 Cor 1:26–31)

In our celebrity obsessed culture, one of the least valued virtues seems to be modesty. Boasting is the order of the day, with tweets, instagrams and PR events all designed to keep a face visible and a name on people's lips.

One of the weirdest cultural juxtapositions during our four years in Uganda was the arrival of the *Big Brother* reality TV show in Africa. In this show, several strangers are thrown together in a sealed environment for several weeks under the relentless gaze of a network of cameras. For the African pilot, a South African studio brought together individuals from across the continent, including a young Ugandan called Gaetano Kagwa. He lasted for several weeks, eventually finishing fourth. Back home, he became a national hero, despite not having won. He had an easy charm and good looks, and he rose to national prominence simply because he had been on TV. When he flew back to Uganda, the crowds lining the road to greet him were incredible – far larger than those for the Kabaka (king) of the Baganda or President Museveni. I was caught up in the traffic at Kibuye roundabout, and the crowd was easily six people deep on either side of the road. It apparently took his car four hours to reach Kampala from the airport, a journey that normally takes forty minutes. The superficiality of Western pop-culture had well and truly arrived in East Africa.

While in the Big Brother house, he had become quite notorious. Many Ugandan Christians were publicly rebuking him for his apparently loose morals and behaviour. But how many prayed for him to know the Lord? Yet, imagine what would happen, if he was converted. I think I know. His popstar status would almost guarantee that any pastor who attracted him to his or her congregation would parade him around to publicize the church. It would make everyone sit up and notice, giving the kind of publicity that money can't buy.

The temptation to thrust high-profile converts quickly into the public arena is strong. We even boast about them – as if people will be impressed enough to reconsider the gospel. Well they might; it can happen that way. But what would Paul have done? I suspect – and I realize this is speculation – that he would have been more reticent. For those who are opposed to the gospel will not be impressed, whoever gets converted. They will simply assume that Gaetano must have lost his mind. What other explanation could there be? So, they'll ignore him. They won't be impressed at all.

You see, Paul reminds the Corinthian Christians of what they were. Not many were wise, influential or noble. Notice the implications of that. *Some* were. Not many were cabinet ministers, or directors of NGOs, or high-profile entrepreneurs, but a handful might have been. But even if some in the church were noble, wise or influential in human affairs, it did not mean Paul would be impressed. Or that God would be. In fact, it wouldn't matter if there were no "big men" in the church at all. Because Paul understands how God works. In 1:27, God is up to the same tricks as he was before. He is demolishing human pride by choosing "the foolish things of the world to shame the wise and . . . the weak things of the world to shame the strong."

The key concepts from the previous paragraph recur here: wisdom and foolishness, strength and weakness. What the world thinks is wisdom and strength, God despises. He wants to use what the world thinks is stupid and pathetic. This includes people. The Corinthian church had little to boast about in the world. None of us has anything to boast about before God. We are sinful, weak and frail. But this is no problem for God. There is still hope.

. . . but we will still have something to boast about

Before moving to Uganda, I worked in a church in the north of England. I often found myself looking out at the church during the song before getting up to preach. I would look along the rows and see all these people that I knew, some of them very well, many that I loved dearly. Yet I remember thinking what a strange group of people we were. Who would ever have brought us together? We had all kinds of people – some influential yes, but most not – many unemployed, many suffering grief, many struggling with persistent sins, many who just didn't fit in. But they were there.

If I was getting a group of people together to follow God, these certainly weren't the people I would choose. But chosen they were. Who can take the credit for that? Who was responsible for bringing this strange hodgepodge together? Only one person – God. We have little if anything in ourselves to boast about. But he chose us anyway. Not because we are impressive, not because we are clever or powerful or influential, but because he wanted to and he has a plan. No other reason.

Paul seems to be echoing Moses here, from Deuteronomy 7:7–10, and it is fitting in this context because this astonishing proclamation of God's *hesed*, his covenant faithful love, is one which Chris Wright has revelled in during his preaching and ministry.

> The LORD did not set his affection on you and choose you because you were more numerous than other peoples, for you were the fewest of all peoples. But it was because the LORD loved you and kept the oath he swore to your ancestors that he brought you out with a mighty hand and redeemed you from the land of slavery, from the power of Pharaoh king of Egypt. (Deut 7:7–8)

This lies at the very heart of the trajectory of biblical theology. For as Chris has written, the givenness of the land, together with all the other blessings of the old covenant, forever

> preserved the right perspective in Israel's relationship with their God. The LORD could not be regarded in the same way as the gods of other nations – a figurehead for their own nationalism or a merely functional protector of their military or territorial claims. Rather, the reverse: without him they would have been no nation and had no land.[1]

As with the old covenant, so with the new covenant in which the relevance of Israel's story gets broadened out to include the whole of humanity through Christ. Both covenants function as a "declaration of [humanity's] dependency"[2] on God.

God hates human pride. He never wants people to boast about themselves. He wants people to boast about Jesus, our Lord. That entails shaming the "big men and women," the power brokers and kingmakers who think that they understand true power. God knows they don't. He wants them to notice the prostitutes, the drug addicts and the homeless, the corrupt and the criminal and those at the bottom of the pile and say, "Look! God loves even people like that. How unimpressive!"

But to be included in those chosen people? That is a very different matter. "God is interested in *me*, even when nobody else is?" That would surely lead to boasting in the Lord.

---

1. Christopher J. H. Wright, *Old Testament Ethics for the People of God* (Leicester: IVP, 2004), 86.

2. Ibid., 85.

So, let us pray for the Gaetanos of the world to know Christ, as well as for all the leaders and stakeholders in our countries. It is right to pray for the world's presidents and kings. But we must never be deceived into echoing the world's thinking, as if God is only interested in the powerful or influencers or "strategic" converts. He deliberately chooses the weak to shame the powerful. Don't try to impress the world by parading our impressive people – we simply won't be impressive. Instead, only preach about the God who loves without discrimination. As Jeremiah once said, "Let him who boasts boast in the Lord."

3. We Won't Impress with Our Preachers . . . (2:1–5)

Our message looks unimpressive – but we preach anyway, because God's power and wisdom at the cross destroy human pride. People will still believe it and be saved.

The people who are saved look unimpressive – but we boast about the Lord who can save anyone, especially if they are at the bottom of society. God does not discriminate.

Finally, Paul turns his attention to himself. What of those with the temerity to preach in God's name. Just who do we think we are?

> When I came to you, brothers, I did not come with eloquence or superior wisdom as I proclaimed to you the testimony about God. For I resolved to know nothing while I was with you except Jesus Christ and him crucified. I came to you in weakness and fear, and with much trembling. My message and my preaching were not with wise and persuasive words, but with a demonstration of the Spirit's power, so that your faith might not rest on human wisdom, but on God's power. (1 Cor 2:1–5)

There is no doubt that Paul was a genius. Just read Romans. It is highly likely that he was an effective preacher as well. He preached the gospel faithfully, and many were converted. But what was it about him that enabled that?

Unimpressive to look at

This at least is what Paul claims here. It is unlikely he would have had a successful TV career. For a start, he got nervous, and seemed to show it. Perhaps you could see the sweat running down his face while he preached. That is not a great look on the small screen. Perhaps his hands shook as he turned the pages of his Bible. His lack of gravitas was obvious to all, and he was by no means a smooth, celebrity preacher, overflowing with confidence.

But his lack of concern about this is telling. He is not embarrassed and so has no need to hide it. But that was not the only problem.

Unimpressive to listen to

Ancient Greek citizens could listen to great orators for hours. They loved them not only for the showmanship of their performances, but also for their choice of language, for their wit and rhetorical flourishes. They loved having their minds twisted into knots by the world of ideas. Paul simply could not compete. When measured against the benchmark of contemporary itinerant philosophers and market place charlatans, he was woefully inadequate.

> I did not come with eloquence and superior wisdom as I proclaimed the testimony about God. I resolved to know nothing while I was with you except Jesus Christ and him crucified. (1 Cor 2:2)

Paul's intention here has been frequently misunderstood. He is not suggesting an ignorance of all other types of knowledge. He merely insists that seeking to impress his audiences was nowhere close to his greatest priority. He sought not to impress but to testify, to speak truth, to honour God. In short, he aimed for faithfulness to what God has revealed in the crucified Christ, to explain that as clearly as he could, and to ensure that the direct implications of that revelation were not lost on his hearers. This is consistent with what we find throughout the Pauline epistles. For example, see his (no doubt) oft-repeated instruction to Timothy:

> *Faithfulness:* Do your best to present yourself to God as one approved, a worker who does not need to be ashamed and who correctly handles the word of truth. (2 Tim 2:15)

Then notice how he asks his supporters to pray for him:

> *Clarity:* And pray for us, too, that God may open a door for our message, so that we may proclaim the mystery of Christ, for which I am in chains. Pray that I may proclaim it clearly, as I should. (Col 4:3–4)

> *Relevance:* Pray also for me, that whenever I speak, words may be given me so that I will fearlessly make known the mystery of the

gospel, for which I am an ambassador in chains. Pray that I may
declare it fearlessly, as I should. (Eph 6:19–20)

Each of these flows out of the strong conviction that God has acted uniquely
but decisively in human history and on earth, for the purposes of restoring a
fractured cosmos and rescuing a broken humanity. As Paul explains elsewhere,
Christ's paradoxical Good Friday–Easter victory has achieved all this and more.

Yet, for all Paul's intellectual brilliance and missiological creativity, this was
emphatically not his own message. He never tried to take any credit for it. He
was faithfully stubborn – this was his glorious kerygma from which he would
never be shifted. That far outshone anything else. Even when the message
seemed limp and unimpressive. Even when it failed to draw in impressive
converts. Even when preachers like himself were dismissed as fools and idiots.

What made such obstinate perseverance possible?

... but we still have the power to change lives

My message and my preaching were not with wise and persuasive
words. (1 Cor 2:4)

That was no problem for Paul since it never impeded conversions. This is
because of the manner in which God works. Preaching itself came with

a demonstration of the Spirit's power, so that your faith might not
rest on human wisdom, but on God's power. (1 Cor 2:4–5)

It is vital to be sensitive to what Paul means by "power" here. Whatever it
means, it cannot connote worldly, impressive power. That is too obvious and
familiar. This is power that will never look to us like power. This is power not
in an impressive but in a humbling message. Not in impressive converts, but in
a converting God. Not in impressive preachers, but in faithful preachers who
allow themselves to be servant-hearted ambassadors. For the defining measure
of God's power for all the world must be the cross. There, God destroys arrogant
wisdom and strength and brings women and men to their knees. When the
cross is preached, God shows his power to remove the filters that blind people
to the truth about Jesus and his cross. Thereafter, God's power and wisdom
gleam in glorious sunlight.

Once that happens, only one can take the credit, and it is not the
preacher. It's God himself. His is cross-shaped power. It seems weak; it looks
unimpressive. But simultaneously it is the greatest demonstration of divine
power in history. Never be fooled by appearances. And never take the credit

for what is God's alone. If people come to the Lord when we preach, it's never because we impressed them, but because God called them. Our task is to be faithful.

This has great significance for the entire mission of Langham Partnership. All three programmes are committed to serving the church by serving the gospel. In desiring to help men and women receive training to the highest levels, it is never because high academic achievement is an end in itself. The goals of publishing books, attaining doctorates, and equipping public speakers may appear to converge with worldly ambitions, which is why they all have a dangerous allure. Yet this Corinthian correspondence makes it all too clear how God responds to human pride. He always subverts and shakes it. Hence, following the model of John Stott, who himself imitated great divines like Charles Simeon and Charles Spurgeon, Langham Partnership has always resisted such siren calls. The fact that this consistency has continued is in large part due to Chris Wright, a leader who has impeccable scholarly credentials and cross-cultural experience, who has resolutely sought to serve the church. His security in doing that rests squarely on the Lord's great gospel revelation, convincing him and many of us who are inspired by him, to invest in things that appear weak and frail but are, in reality, transformative and eternal.

More specifically, the passage we have looked at is vital for any involved in preaching the Scriptures. The expository method espoused by Langham Preaching seeks to help people around the world grow in their faithfulness to what has been revealed. But this type of ministry faces countless challenges, cultural, theological, and ecclesiological. Preachers will only persevere if they cling to the convictions that Paul outlines in 1 Corinthians. Otherwise, it will seem entirely futile, culturally disconnected, and missiologically ineffective. That is why it has been an inspiration to work under Chris's leadership. We wouldn't want him to be impressive to the world (although, actually, he is in many ways!). Instead, we are simply grateful that he is faithful.

18

Faithful, Clear, Relevant: The Marks of Good Biblical Preaching

Greg R. Scharf

Greg R. Scharf *is professor of homiletics at Trinity Evangelical Divinity School, Deerfield, Illinois, USA. He was a pastor for twenty-five years, serving as curate at All Souls, Langham Place in London; assistant minister at Knox Church, Toronto; and senior pastor of Salem Evangelical Free Church in Fargo, North Dakota, before joining the faculty of Trinity in 1999. A biology graduate of Rice University, he received the MDiv and DMin from Trinity and is an ordained minister of the gospel of the Evangelical Free Church of America. His books include* Prepared to Preach, Relational Preaching, *and* Let the Earth Hear His Voice. *He edited and abridged John Stott's* Between Two Worlds, *now available in several languages as* The Challenge of Preaching.

What makes a biblical sermon a good one? Any answer to that most basic homiletical question that suits only one culture, or one cultural block such as the West, is of limited value, at least when it comes to cross-cultural training in preaching. What I as a North American think constitutes good preaching is almost certainly shaped by what others in my home culture will receive as good preaching. Is that really what I – or anyone else – should be exporting to other cultures as good preaching? I think not. Any acceptable answer to the question of what makes good preaching faces the twin obstacles of cultural transposition on the one hand, and the necessity of simplicity without oversimplification on the other.

The forebears of Langham Preaching, John Stott and Chris Wright, had already faced these concerns by the time I was invited to conduct preaching seminars under Langham's auspices.[1] By then, Jonathan Lamb was leading this face of the movement and it was he whom I first heard use the acronym FCR, standing for "faithful, clear, relevant." I am not sure who first crystalized these essential criteria, but in the Langham movement they have become useful shorthand for what trainers want to see in the sermons of the next generation of preachers and teachers. They are useful criteria because they are biblically defensible and so, by definition, are transcultural. They are useful because they are uncomplicated enough to be transferable. They are useful because they can function as a very simple rubric that is both *applicable* to every culture and *adaptable* to that culture. This means that preachers can use these three essentials to evaluate their own preaching and offer better feedback to others in their preaching clubs.

What I attempt to do in this essay is to marshal some of the biblical underpinnings for each essential, to develop in the case of faithfulness what it entails, and to offer a few strategies that I hope fellow preachers from any culture can employ to improve their preaching. As I have collected and organized my ideas for this happy undertaking, I have been reminded again how few of them are actually *my* ideas and how much I have been influenced and enriched by the scholarship, writing and preaching of Chris Wright. Some of the thoughts here have been triggered by his; many more have been informed and corrected by his writings; virtually all of them enriched by fellowship with him and by his example as a brother in Christ and as a preacher.

I first met Chris and Liz when he was Principal of All Nations Christian College, where I was privileged to teach a couple of courses while on leave from the church I then served. Later, when I had joined the faculty of Trinity Evangelical Divinity School, I served for nine years on the board of what is now the Langham Partnership USA, about five of those years as its chair. In that capacity I heard Chris give many moving reports and watched him lead others towards strategic ways to meet the wonderful objectives of that organization and its global parent organization, the Langham Partnership. Before I met him, I had read some of his early books on Old Testament ethics. Since then I have eagerly read or consulted most of his other major works. Their scope – from detailed, academic treatments and rigorous yet readable commentaries

---

1. I served in this capacity in Poland, Pakistan, Lebanon, Kenya, Uganda, Indonesia, and Trinidad.

to working documents on theological education, to his acclaimed work on mission, to meditations on Psalm 119 – is an impressive achievement in itself. But this range also represents Chris's great strength. Alongside his commitment to serious, detailed, well-documented scholarship is an evident love for the global church and those called to serve within it and on its behalf. Chris Wright does quality scholarship for the good of God's people at both the strategic and tactical levels, writing to serve fellow scholars, Christian leaders, pastors, and everyday Christians as well as those sadly still outside the church. I have been greatly enriched by his writings, and the thoughts collected here are probably more indebted to him than I realize.

As I tackle my objective of defending, explaining, and using these three essentials of biblical preaching, it is important to recall that the order – FCR – is intentional and necessary. Faithfulness has to come first, for reasons we will see. After that, clarity bridges the space from faithfulness to relevance and overlaps with both because a truly faithful sermon will be clear because its source document, the Bible, is clear. It will be clear not in some theoretical sense, but clear to the listeners to whom it is preached. Only then, when it is clear to them, can it be relevant *to them*.

If for any reason a sermon is *not* faithful, then what would have been positive criteria – clarity and relevance – become a menace. An *unfaithful* message communicated clearly and relevantly is worse than no message at all, for it masquerades as a word from the living God when it is not. So, faithfulness is foundational. We begin there.

Faithfulness

The biblical case for faithfulness

The Apostle Paul, writing in 1 Corinthians, simultaneously addressed the divisions in that church and set out his reasons for preaching as he did. He forbade exalting one leader over another. That directive he rooted in his understanding of his and Apollos' role in the church: "This is how one should regard us, as servants of Christ and stewards of the mysteries of God. Moreover, it is required of stewards that they be found faithful" (1 Cor 4:1, 2). The biblical necessity of faithfulness is rooted in the nature of the preacher's role. Preachers, like the apostles, are servants of Christ. We preachers take our orders from him, are accountable to him, and look to him for our authority and ultimately for his approval. Paul sharpens the definition further. Preachers are not just servants in some general sense, but *responsible* servants entrusted with "the mysteries of God" that is, the gospel and the sound doctrine that clusters around it. The word that best describes a responsible servant is *steward*. A steward is a servant who is entrusted with something by a master so that it can be put to the use intended by the master. In this case that "something" is the gospel, and the master's intended use is that it be accurately conveyed to those for whom the master entrusted it to the steward. In Paul's case, those people were the Gentiles. Given these roles, the steward's essential duty is faithfulness. Preachers, because they are stewards must safeguard the gospel, guarding it from adulteration and distortion, in order to convey it to those whom the master intends to receive it. Whatever else the preacher as steward does with the message entrusted to him, he must be faithful to his Master's intention and command. This is not optional; it is required (4:2).

The Apostle Paul reinforces this idea of faithful stewardship by describing the accountability that accompanies it. Evaluation by others, whether critical or laudatory, is radically relativized. Preachers must not take it too seriously (4:3a). Self-evaluation, whether self-deprecation or self-congratulation, is ruled out (4:3b–4). We are not our own masters. We don't report to ourselves. More to the point, we cannot rely on our own assessments. The only appropriate judge of the faithfulness of our stewardship is the Lord, and even he does not pronounce his praise prematurely (4:5). He waits until the end when everything will be revealed and the purposes of our hearts will be disclosed. Happily, by God's grace, the assessment Paul anticipates is that "each one will receive his commendation from God." Note that the word used is commendation, not condemnation. This verdict indicates that faithfulness, however difficult to achieve, is possible. Stewards must prove themselves faithful and will be judged and rewarded by that criterion.

The biblical case for the necessity of faithfulness is not merely this text, with its rock-solid logic. Another passage which takes up the image of stewardship and expands it is Colossians 1:24–2:5. In 1:25 Paul again uses words for "servant" and "stewardship" underscoring that the stewardship is *from* God and *for* "you," that is, for the church. The stewarded resource is again described as the mystery once hidden but now revealed to his saints. What is noteworthy in this context is not merely that Paul makes known "the riches of the glory of this mystery, which is Christ in you, the hope of glory" (1:27), and that his preaching entails both warning and teaching, and that it is aimed at "everyone" and seeks to "present everyone mature in Christ" (1:28). What is remarkable is not only that Paul credits the inner work of God in this process that yields externally visible power in preaching (1:28). What is remarkable is that Paul wants everyone in Colossae to know of his great struggle in fulfilling this assignment (2:1). He even goes so far as to say that he fills up what is lacking in the sufferings of Christ for the sake of the church (1:24). Why does he say this? I think it is because for Paul the message of which he is a steward can only be faithfully transmitted by one who takes up the cross of Christ in order to manifest resurrection power.[2] Those who had not seen Paul and his sufferings had to be told about those sufferings so they could get the picture that goes with the sound, the video, as it were, that must accompany the audio. Faithfulness in preaching is more than bare accuracy to biblical ideas, for the message as he describes it here is "Christ *in you*" (1:27). For his listeners to embrace the true message in a way that presented them mature in Christ, they had to *see* the message of the cross as well as *hear* it. Faithful stewardship of necessity requires something of the messenger. Indeed, when Paul heard of the transforming work of the gospel among the Thessalonians, he did not hesitate to remind them why the gospel came to them with power. "You know what kind of men we proved to be among you for your sake. And you became imitators of us and of the Lord, for you received the word in much affliction, with the joy of the Holy Spirit, so that you became an example to all the believers in Macedonia and in Achaia" (1 Thess 1:5b–7). No wonder Paul could thank God "that when you received the word of God, which you heard from us, you accepted it not as the word of men but as what it really is, the word of God, which is at work in you believers" (1 Thess 2:13). That is faithfulness, namely, when what we preach can accurately be said to enable our listeners to hear God's voice and for his living word to go to work in those who believe just as it has been visibly at work in those who preach it.

One could also make the case for faithfulness from the New Testament's most prominent word for the preacher, namely a herald.[3] In the ancient world the herald's assignment was to convey a message from the authorities to the populace by going to a place and crying out, proclaiming the message given him for the people by the ruler. As in the case of the steward, the *sine qua non* of the herald is faithfulness: saying what the authorities want the people to know with the authority of those who sent him.[4] Another expression, "entrusted with

---

2. This is also the logic of 2 Corinthians 4:7–18.

3. See Duane Litfin, "Swallowing Our Pride," in *Preach the Word: Essays on Expository Preaching in Honor of R. Kent Hughes*, eds. Leland Ryken and Todd Wilson (Wheaton: Crossway, 2007), 118.

4. The image of the ambassador in 2 Corinthians 5:20 emphasizes both the authority of the messenger and God's agency in speaking through the messenger.

the gospel" (1 Thess 2:4), captures the import of both images, the steward and the herald, from the preacher's standpoint. Yes, the gospel is a gift of God's grace *to us*; but for those of us called to preach, it is not merely *for us*. It is good news entrusted to us *for others*. That is why in Romans 1:14 Paul could say he is a debtor to both Greeks and barbarians. God has entrusted a treasure to him for them, and until he delivers it to them intact he is literally in their debt; he owes it to them.

The biblical case comes into even sharper focus when we consider one negative example of many we could cite. In the Old Testament the Word of God was entrusted to prophets and some priests. God himself, speaking through faithful prophets, is especially scathing in his denunciation of those who should have faithfully stewarded his words but failed to do so. Jeremiah 23 painfully describes some prophets and priests as "ungodly" and "evil" (23:11), as "unsavoury" (23:13) and "horrible" (23:14) among other things. Because they "walk in lies" (23:14) and "speak visions of their own minds, not from the mouth of the Lord" (23:16) and "despise the word of the LORD" (23:17), not only do they lead God's people astray, doing them no profit at all (23:13, 14, 32), they themselves are on a slippery path headed for disaster and under the wrath of God (23:12, 19–20). These so-called prophets were not truly sent by God, though they claimed to be. Their source of material was their own lying dreams (23:32) and words plagiarized from other prophets (23:30). What makes their disastrous folly especially painful is that the faithfulness they could have manifested but did not was not impossible to achieve. Hear the promises of God embedded in his rebukes: "For who among them has stood in the council of the LORD to see and to hear his word, or who has paid attention to his word and listened?" (23:18); "But if they had stood in my council, then they would have proclaimed my words to my people, and they would have turned them from their evil way, and from the evil of their deeds" (23:22). Those who wait on the Lord, listening to his word, can not only proclaim his word but will also see him use it to achieve its God-given purposes.

The Lord Jesus himself crowns the biblical case for faithfulness. If he, the Second Person of the Trinity, could say, "For I have not spoken on my own authority, but the Father who sent me has himself given me a commandment – what to say and what to speak" (John 12:49), who are we to say less or other than God has commanded us?

What faithfulness entails

Faithfulness in preaching means that the sermons we preach should accurately convey the message of the text we are expounding. What the Holy Spirit put into the Bible we are to draw from the Bible. Later I shall describe how we word that message so that it is clear and relevant. Here I concentrate on getting the message itself right. This entails more than might first meet the eye and necessitates postponing audience analysis and contextualization to the preaching situation until we have grasped what our passage is communicating. For the purposes of this essay, I am assuming that the preacher has selected a preaching portion or text that is a unit of thought, usually one or more paragraphs that convey a single dominant idea supported by other thoughts that qualify, expand, apply, or otherwise develop it.

Sermons are to be faithful in at least six ways:

First, a faithful sermon aiming to expound a biblical text is faithful to that passage's *content*, what it is saying. That is, the sermon is about what the passage is mainly about and it says concerning that subject what that text says about it. Such a sermon does not preach what comes to the preacher's mind when he or she reads this text, but what was demonstrably in the biblical author's mind when he wrote it. True, sometimes the Holy Spirit put more in the author's words than the human author fully understood, but we are not at liberty to go beyond what is written (1 Cor 4:6).

Second, a faithful sermon is faithful to the *meaning* of the text. That is, the preacher does not just list the ideas found in the passage, repeating them in some sort of list or running commentary, but understands how the grammar and syntax of the passage, interpreted by means of a sound hermeneutic, form meaning. The text cannot mean now what it never meant, so this is where a grasp of the way language worked for the original hearers is helpful. The Bible is not uniform in the ways it conveys meaning. It was written in various genres including narrative, poetry, epistles, apocalyptic and historical records. Preachers need to understand how each genre conveys meaning in order to discern the meaning of the preaching portion.[5]

Third, a faithful sermon is faithful to its contexts. It notices the preaching portion's immediate *literary* context, its *canonical* context, its *theological* context and the *social/historical* context into which it was written. By placing the passage in its place in salvation history, the preacher can discern its unique contribution to the drama of redemption. When all these contexts are allowed

---

5. See Chris Wright's *How to Preach and Teach the Old Testament for All Its Worth* for help.

to inform exegesis, the preacher is less likely to try to make the text address a subject or situation it was never designed to address. Instead, every passage will be allowed to say what it wants to say in the way it was designed to say it. When we claim that a sermon must be faithful theologically and canonically, we are also saying that it must relate to Jesus in ways the text itself sanctions. Christ is the subject and focal point of the whole Bible but not, in my judgement, the subject of every pericope. Each passage must be allowed to say what it is saying, which will always make some contribution to the drama of redemption, but not necessarily speak directly of the Lord Jesus.[6]

Fourth, a faithful sermon is faithful to the *purpose* of the text, its *intent*. What is this passage doing with what it is saying? Why did the Holy Spirit include these words in the canon? What is the response this text seems designed to elicit from those who read it or hear it expounded? This textual intention must be something that *could be* contextualized later in the sermon to any hearer in any location and of any era after Christ's ascension. If the purpose the preacher discerns fails this test of potential universality, it is probably not faithful to the text. Biblical texts do not say something in Chicago that would be rubbish or heresy in Caracas. Moreover, the purpose of most texts is not to give us a list of items to do, but to transform us at the level of world view beliefs, to change us by challenging our underlying – perhaps even unexamined – assumptions about reality. When preachers notice these in the text and its contexts, and shape the purpose of their sermons to do what the text is doing at that level, they facilitate transformation. Furthermore, faithfulness to a text's purpose recalls that most biblical passages were addressed to the people of God *corporately*. To be sure, faithful sermons are addressed to individuals, for only individuals can have ears to hear, but at the same time they are addressed to groups of individuals, to churches, and God's purposes are purposes for his people *as a people*.

Fifth, the faithful sermon is faithful rhetorically. Rhetoric, simply defined, is purposeful speech. Speech achieves its purposes in various ways. Ideally, the faithful sermon will reflect not only the purpose of the text but also the way the text itself seeks to accomplish that purpose, that is, the way it persuades and transforms its listeners. This is important because the ways we naturally attempt to preach often disregard how the text itself elicits the response it seeks.

---

6. Chris Wright's fine commentaries, including those on Deuteronomy, Jeremiah, Ezekiel and Lamentations, model this well. His three volumes, titled respectively, *Knowing God the Father / Knowing Jesus / Knowing the Holy Spirit through the Old Testament* also help preachers see how to draw valid theological inferences from Scripture.

We may notice and agree with the text's purpose, but fail to seek to replicate (or at least reflect) how it achieves its purposes. When we do notice devices such as repetition, rhetorical questions, or Old Testament citations, and make use of them in shaping our exposition, we are cooperating with the text, letting it do what the Holy Spirit designed it to do in the ways he built into the text. Moreover, as part of its rhetoric, every text of Scripture has a tone that must be noticed if the sermon that expounds that text is to be faithful to it. The tone of Galatians 1 would ruin an exposition of Psalm 23.

Sixth, and finally, a faithful sermon is faithful spiritually. It is preached in submission to God, trusting the Holy Spirit to work through his word, believing that he is alive and active and still speaks through what he has spoken. It is preached prayerfully in faith. It is preached in the realistic knowledge that not all sown seed falls on good soil, but even the good seed that does land on good soil only grows because God gives the growth.

To sum up, the faithful sermon hears and sees in God's word what he actually put there and submits to the content, intent, tone, and rhetoric of the text. Respecting those realities, the faithful sermon is preached by someone who hears God's words in the text and whose own life shows evidence of God's work.

How faithfulness is achieved

The foregoing six facets of faithfulness could seem to be a prescription for failure. How could anyone achieve all of these simultaneously every time he or she opens a text of Scripture? To do so, we must start with the last facet of faithfulness.

First of all, faithfulness is achieved by bathing the whole process of sermon preparation and delivery in prayer. I think this is what God intended when he rebuked the false prophets for not standing in the Lord's council in Jeremiah 23:18, 22. Faithful preachers wait on the Lord to hear and see his word. When we do that, we won't be tempted to go elsewhere than the Bible for sermons. God himself loves his church and wants our sermons to be faithful. He will give us what he wants our listeners to hear. This also means scrupulously avoiding the kind of hard-hearted disobedience that turns him against us. Micah 3:4, 7 reinforces the message of Jeremiah 23. Those who pursue evil will experience the ultimate nightmare for someone who is supposed to speak for God: "Then they will cry to the LORD, but he will not answer them; he will hide his face from them at that time, because they have made their deeds evil . . . the seers shall be disgraced, and the diviners put to shame; they shall all cover their lips, for there is no answer from God."

Faithful preaching is rooted in a posture of submissive teachableness. The Lord Jesus models this supremely as one of the predictive Servant Songs of Isaiah reveals, offering, I think, Jesus's testimony. "The LORD God has given me the tongue of those who are taught, that I may know how to sustain with a word him who is weary. Morning by morning he awakens; he awakens my ear to hear as those who are taught. The LORD God has opened my ear, and I was not rebellious; I turned not backward" (Isa 50:4–5). The secret of faithfulness, the way to get a tongue that can teach, is to have an ear that is eager to hear. Preachers need to open their ears before they open their mouths.

Second, faithfulness is achieved by careful reading and humble, detailed study of the biblical text in its context. This should not have to be said, but it does have to be said. Crucial details of a text, its relationships and dominant idea seldom jump off the page on the first reading. Faulty assumptions about what a text is saying yield only to accurate summaries of what it is actually saying when the preacher takes the time to observe how the words of the text work together and what they are doing in the wider context. This takes time. It cannot be rushed. Start early. This counsel requires no mastery of the original languages, valuable as that is; no stockpile of quality commentaries, as wonderful a resource as they are when used judiciously. It only requires wise realism and humility. Submit to the text; start early.

Third, faithfulness is achieved by continuing to read and study the whole Bible. As the Westminster Confession of Faith wisely says,

> The infallible rule of interpretation of Scripture is the Scripture itself; and therefore when there is a question about the true and full sense of any Scripture (which is not manifold, but one), it must be searched and known by other places that speak more clearly. (2 Pet 1:20, 21; Acts 15:15, 16)

This is not to say we should quote all the verses we read that relate to our text! Far from it. It is to say that the better we know the whole Bible, the more likely we are to interpret any part of it accurately.

There are other important means to faithfulness.[7] These basics will have to suffice.

---

7. Many have found helpful the practice of interrogating the text, described in my book *Let the Earth Hear His Voice* (Phillipsburg: P & R, 2015), 110–121.

Clear

The biblical case for clarity

This case can be made more briefly. When the Apostle Paul asks for prayer for his preaching he asks his friends in Colossae to pray "that I may make it clear, which is how I ought to speak" (Col 4:4). Biblical preachers *ought* to speak clearly. Paul's standard for his letters was the same as for his preaching: "For we are not writing to you anything other than what you read and understand and I hope you will fully understand" (2 Cor 1:13). Paul's penchant for clarity, rooted in the necessity of understanding, is consistent with Jesus's parable of the sower as Matthew 13 records it. Five times in his account of the telling and explanation of the parable, Jesus underscores the importance of *understanding* (13:13, 14, 15, 18, 23). There the problem is mainly one of spiritual blindness that prevents understanding. Only the Holy Spirit can open blind eyes, but he does that by the preaching of his word (2 Cor 4:6; Jas 1:18; 1 Pet 1:22–25). The preacher's task is to state the truth of Scripture so plainly that spiritual blindness, not confusing preaching, is the explanation for a listener failing to see "the light of the gospel of the glory of Christ" when we preach God's word (2 Cor 4:1–5).

How clarity is achieved

Clarity is achieved when preachers use only intelligible words (1 Cor 14:9). Clarity is achieved when preachers make the truth vivid, placarding the gospel (Gal 3:1). Preachers achieve clarity when they use illustrations that take into account the human limitations of their listeners (Rom 6:19–23). Other strategies can claim less biblical warrant but are useful nonetheless in most of our settings. Choose words carefully. Arrange them in sentences that are simple and direct. Use repetition and transitions because in oral discourse people can't look back up the page to catch something they missed the first time. Since all thought is sequential, pay attention to the order of your thoughts, and therefore the structure of your sermon, so that the thoughts flow from or build towards the primary claim of the sermon and every part is anchored in your text. Write out the sermon in full to discover gaps in your thinking and expression. Edit the end product vigorously to eliminate self-generated distractions. "Practise what you preach" in both senses of the words. Do so until you are relatively free from a manuscript or notes and can speak directly to your listeners and are not preoccupied with trying to remember what you are going to say next.

Remember that clarity is in the ear of the hearer, so recruit some friends to give you feedback concerning the clarity of your sermons.

Relevant

The biblical case for relevance

The Bible itself says that all Scripture *is* relevant and is so in specific ways that are profitable. "All Scripture is breathed out by God and profitable for teaching, for reproof, for correction, and for training in righteousness, that the man of God may be complete, equipped for every good work" (2 Tim 3:16–17). Profitability assumes relevance. The preacher's task as an expositor of Scripture is simply to open the Bible to listeners so that it achieves the benefits it was designed by the Holy Spirit to accomplish. God's word sanctifies (John 17:17). Our job is to let it do its sanctifying work. How do we cooperate with the Holy Spirit in this work? We preach sermons that are faithful and clear. They must also be relevant.

How we achieve relevance

First, align the sermon's aim with the response the text calls for. Faithfulness requires this, but it is also the primary way of achieving relevance. If the text is a rebuke, let it rebuke your listeners to the extent they are guilty of the sin that the passage rebukes.[8] Then let it correct what is at fault. If the text is primarily teaching or doctrine, don't rush to insist upon some action in response, just make the truth plain and show how it is part of equipping your listeners for every good work. When you call for the response the text calls for, your sermon will not only be relevant, it will be authoritatively relevant; you will be insisting upon what God requires as Paul told Titus to do in Titus 3:8. When you do this, let the text itself supply the incentives for obedience. Underscore its stated or implied indicatives before moving to its imperatives. That is, make sure what you call for is the obedience *of faith* (Rom 1:5; 16:26).

Second, preach to the people who are there, not to those who are not. Your job is not to offer a critique of the world for being the world but to help your listeners adorn the gospel (Titus 2:10). The better you know your listeners

---

8. See Greg R. Scharf, "The Pulpit Rebuke: What Is It? When Is It Appropriate? What Makes It Effective?" *Journal of the Evangelical Homiletics Society* 15, no. 1 (2015): 60–78, and *Midwestern Journal of Theology* 14 (2015): 63–87.

with their worries, temptations, joys, and sorrows, the more likely you will be able to speak to them. Spend time with them. Listen to them outside of the pulpit so you can speak to them when you are in it. They are not all alike, so tailor your multiple applications to the range of spiritual and social locations they represent. Work hard to understand how to make valid ethical inferences from the passage you preach.[9]

Third, walk in the Spirit, praying continually that the Lord will highlight how your text speaks to your listeners. Your responsibility is to transpose your text's claim from its initial purpose when given to its first hearers into its claim on your contemporary listeners. There is so much you *could* say that you will need God's help to open your eyes to see what this text *does* say to your listeners. Every faithful preacher will eventually have a listener ask, "How did you know I needed this message today?" Then we will say, "I didn't but God did. I asked him to show me what is genuinely in this text for those he knew would be here today and he answered my prayer." May that be your experience because your sermons are faithful, clear and relevant.

---

9. Chris Wright's many writings on Old Testament ethics are exceedingly valuable in this regard. *Old Testament Ethics for the People of God* (Leicester: IVP, 2004) reaffirms and updates insights from *Eye for an Eye* (1983) and *Walking in the Ways of the Lord* (1995).

Afterword:
Of the Making of Books

Pieter Kwant

Pieter Kwant *is the director of Langham Literature. He has worked for several Christian publishers, including Piquant Editions, which he founded. His fierce commitment to Christian scholars and writers in the Majority World has dramatically increased the work of Langham Literature in book distribution, has led to the publication of six major regional one-volume Bible commentaries, and the start of several imprints including HippoBooks, the Langham Global Library, and Langham Monographs.*

Before ever meeting Chris I knew him, and before meeting him he had taught me much, as he led me out of a theological straightjacket that was crushing all life out of me. Such is the power of books we start reading as "anonymous letters" to expectant readers. In those days I loved books more than I loved the authors who wrote them or the readers who read them, but after page 100 in *Living as the People of God*[1] all that started to change. . . .

At that time I found myself in South Africa. I was helped out of hippiedom through wise, far-sighted and self-giving elders. But in the very Reformed "1689 Baptist" theological atmosphere, I remember struggling with the "third use of the law" and the moral, civil, and ceremonial categories of law and getting increasingly frustrated with what to do with the Old Testament and its law in particular. How was I to live now in the 20th century? The theonomist tome by Greg Bahnsen[2] finally landed me in the pit. It was your book, Chris – *Living as the People of God* – with your famous "triangle" that took me out by helping me to see Jesus more clearly. I saw that all is fulfilled and purposed in him. Suddenly I could see the many connections between the Old Testament and the New. The more I read, the more it made me think, and the more it made sense.

---

1. Christopher J. H. Wright, *Living as the People of God: The Relevance of Old Testament Ethics* (Leicester: IVP, 1983). Now page 196 in *Old Testament Ethics for the People of God* (Leicester: IVP, 2004).

2. Greg L. Bahnsen, *Theonomy in Christian Ethics*, 2nd ed. (Phillipsburg: P & R, 1984).

Being a man of hope, I could make immediate sense of the eschatological dimension, and it allowed me to make connections that hitherto I had not been able to make. The covenant refrain I had always been so fond of, and which can be found right through the Scriptures, came into far better focus for me: "You shall be my people and I will be your God." I realized that it was not only about me, but about being part of the people of God and, more importantly, part of the bodily raised, redeemed people of God. Here then, at last, God gave me a deep sense of belonging. A belonging that feels like a tree shooting its roots down through my church family, through Jesus – especially his cross – through Abraham, Noah and Adam into the very soil of creation, receiving all its nutrients from that creation and from reading and meditating on the Old Testament and gaining at last a footing. But there was more. Not only reaching down, but up, as I realized that God was lifting my arms in faith and hope like leaved branches towards the new creation. You showed me in that wonderful book the connectedness of the biblical story: it is one story! And blow me down, what a story, with Jesus clearly at the centre of the biblical world and the world around us, and with God on a mission.

There was much more.

Your paradigmatic approach signalled the end of my personal frustration with the rationalistic Reformed categories. At last I had found a biblical way of making daily choices. Using this approach I could dive into the biblical story to play and swim in its waters, using the *sitz im leben* of the text to work out its principles and build them into our lives and situations. It was then that "context" became important and I started very tentatively to do some "double listening." But I had a long way to go, and as you know I am still going . . .

Your economic, theological and social angles enabled me to see the world in a completely new biblical light. What a joy it has been to find this applies to all of life. And that thinking has been percolating and more recently culminated in all these contextual commentaries with their articles . . . but I am running ahead of myself.

Looking at the book cover, I saw you were in India then and I was in South Africa.

When I became the managing director of Paternoster Press, I approached Howard Marshall to become chairman of our advisory board, and he appointed you to that board. You have no idea how odd it was when I first met you. You were a book to me up to that time, and a very good book! But not a person. It was such a pleasant and great surprise to meet you at last. As I write this I wonder if our meeting with Jesus is going to be a bit like that – we read about him all the time, through the Spirit we "see him," but my gut is that we all will be very surprised and delighted when we see him face to face.

We met, became friends, and as we worked together I came to realize that you live the Christian life very much the way you write: relaxed, wise, and confident in God in a common-clay sort of way that appealed greatly to me. As it turned out we published many theological books at Paternoster in the following years. My love for books became more and more a love for authors. I felt much like a "midwife" helping authors to give birth to their ideas and dreams. It's not easy to give birth to ideas and concepts and turn them into books that can be read, but with people like yourself and Howard next to me to encourage me and to fill in what I clearly lacked in formal education, it all became a dream fulfilled by God himself.

During that time – still with my roots in creation and my head in the new creation – I realized my own limits, and my vocation became more defined: to give voice to those who have something true and useful to write and, as Langham expanded, to giving voice to the voiceless. That meant that I was not going to write, not going to change the world, not going to be a theologian, not going to be a full-time preacher, not going to study theology. And that is why I am writing the afterword in this volume. I realized that fulfilling the vocation God had called me to, helps others to study theology, write, change the world, be theologians, and be full-time preachers. . . . The body of Christ is such a marvellous reality with a place and a use for each of us. (Getting very excited and thankful as I write this.)

After my Paternoster days had come to an end we met again, in your lounge to be interviewed for a position with Evangelical Literature Trust (ELT). I was an hour late. But despite that I found myself working with ELT and you became my boss, continuing at Langham to this day.

There are many things I appreciate about working at Langham, but one thing that stands out is the collegiality that we enjoy. You allowed me to fly, to exercise faith (a certain recklessness and abandon as you no doubt see it at times), to get on with things, to surf the waves of Langham's vision and mission. You never let power or hierarchy get in the way but allowed God to do his thing in all our lives, including mine, and I am forever grateful to you for this.

You taught me about the mission of God and stood cheering as I threw myself heart and soul into that mission and we embarked on changing Langham Literature's emphasis "from the West to the Rest" to "from the Rest to the Rest to the West." Giving voice to the voiceless became my mission. Being a cross-cultural midwife proved a real challenge, but sitting around the editorial table in the Africa Bible Commentary meetings, hearing my African brothers and sisters contextualizing the Bible to Africa, seeing their struggles in doing that and being able and allowed to come alongside, was a rare joy and privilege. I at times felt so excited during those meetings that I thought I would explode for all the new things that I was learning. Next we plunged into the South Asia Bible Commentary, very close to your heart, then the Slavic Commentary, with the Latin American, and the Arabic Commentaries on the horizon. It was a huge commitment and I sometimes felt the waves were just too high, but thankfully you never panicked and were in full support as I surfed them with your help and the grace of God.

These commentaries have taught me to listen to the contexts, listen on behalf of the intended readers, listen to the writers, listen to the world. Working on these projects has made me realize how very useful the presence of Langham is when we come alongside, to partner, to fill in, just like we all were "filled in" by those before and around us. Filled and "filled in" by the one and only Holy Spirit, using us all. So biblical connectedness became personal connectedness and, in some cases, public connectedness.

As your literary agent I have the joy of encouraging you, in return, to write and you have given birth to many books as the bibliography of your works testifies. Your *Sweeter than Honey*[3] was an especially sweet reminder of that first book that introduced you to me.

Very recently I have started a study of the book of Revelation and wondered how to tackle all the opinions and different views on this unique book. Your typological, eschatological and paradigmatic approach, together with all the angles – the theological, the economic and the social – is once more guiding me by providing a sterling framework.

It is ironic that the book of Revelation declares itself to be revealing, yet leaves many readers in despair, feeling they face only an ever-more-complicated sealing. Is it that we need more graceful imagination and fervent worship of the living God before the light starts dawning?

In the light of *The Mission of God*, the "key" to understanding Revelation is God and his mission revealed in Jesus Christ. Any attempt to understand his revelation without beginning and ending with Christ, at the very centre of our thoughts and exegesis, is clearly wrong and wanting. In his book on Revelation, Richard Bauckham makes that clear when he writes, "the theology

---

3. Christopher J. H. Wright, *Sweeter than Honey: Preaching the Old Testament* (Carlisle: Langham Preaching Resources, 2014).

of Revelation is highly theocentric. This along with its distinctive doctrine of God, is its greatest contribution to New Testament Theology. Our study of it must begin with God and will both constantly and finally return to God."[4]

Not a puzzle book then, nor an almanac,[5] but a letter, a prophecy, an apocalypse, an apocalyptic prophecy, and clearly not a literal account of things to come but rather a multi-layered 3D artwork that combines all the genres of the Bible as effortlessly as it does the complete biblical story from beginning to end to new beginning. We are supposed to *see* something and to *hear*, reading it aloud in worship, and to *keep* it or *obey* it (Rev 1:1, 3). And it is indeed the climax of all prophecy! We would expect that of God, an eye-popping closing chapter that has kept the church thinking, praying, loving and hoping through twenty-one centuries; a down-to-earth, fully revealed message addressed to seven real-life churches who, as history testifies,[6] did see, hear and keep the testimony of Jesus Christ – and so should we.

I am quite aware that works of art can be turned into puzzles, as I often witness in art-gallery shops! But why have so many theologians found it necessary to cut up a wonderful painting, losing a few pieces and introducing some foreign ones from other puzzles, before trying to put it all together again? No, as I read Revelation, I now immediately feel its incredible connection to the Old Testament. Just about every verse resounds with it.[7] But not only the Old, we see the New Testament too, in full colour: Matthew, Mark, Luke, John, and the epistles. We see the author, John, rooted in the old creation and Old Testament revelation and he sees what is happening in heaven now, and sees into the new creation. But above all we see Jesus high and lifted up in heaven at the throne, riding out, coming back . . . and as we read we worship and pray. Truly this book graphically describes "Your will be done on earth as it is in heaven," as we move from heaven to earth and back to heaven and back to earth, and back . . .

---

4. Richard Bauckham, *The Theology of the Book of Revelation* (Cambridge: Cambridge University Press, 1993), 23.

5. C. van der Waal, *Hal Lindsey and Biblical Prophecy* (St Catharines, Canada: Paideia, 1978).

6. C. van der Waal, *Het Pascha van Onze Verlossing: De Schrift Verklaring in de Paaspreek van Melito van Sardes als Weerspiegeling van de Confrontatie Tussen Kerk en Synagoge in de Tweede Eeuw* (Johannesburg: De Jong, Franeker, Wever, 1979).

7. C. van der Waal, *Openbaring van Jezus Christus* (Groningen, De Vuurbaak, 1971). From page 174 on he gives his own translation and includes all the OT and NT references relating to Revelation, verse by verse. True monk's work! Literally multiple hundreds of references. All worked out in his magnificent commentary, which is unfortunately not available in English. Greg Beal in his commentary on Revelation in the GNTC also shows this deep connectedness, but his work is far less comprehensive.

It is not difficult to see the cosmic aspirations of this wonderful book. We see on the one hand the full revelation of the holy Trinity and on the other we see the revealing of the unholy trinity – the dragon, the beast and the false prophet. The battle moves from heaven to earth and between heaven and earth. As Christians we come to understand why we have to suffer like Jesus. And like Jesus the church comes out triumphant in a new creation reality. It is true that the church in all the ages has found this book a great comfort and challenge, as theologians tried to contextualize it to their specific needs – for the fall of Jerusalem, the Roman Empire, the rise of Islam, the rise of the papacy.[8]

It seems to me that the devil is indeed in the detail when reading the book of Revelation. But the centrality of Jesus is paramount and beyond discussion, as is his connection to his people. And it seems to me, more and more, that the only way Revelation gives up its secrets to the church is as we worship Jesus in Spirit and Truth – as indeed we see again and again, in the heavenly liturgies presented in the book. And as we read this book of Revelation again and again, we see ever more connections with the rest of the biblical story our eyes being opened to the realities we see all around us in this world, captive to the forces of the unholy trinity.

So I happily study on, and keep making books, giving thanks to God, and not yet having exhausted what your book started teaching me all those years ago!

Thank you again for writing it.

And, happy birthday!

---

8. Lois K. F. Dow, "Commentaries on Revelation" in *On the Writing of New Testament Commentaries: Festschrift for Grant R. Osborne on the Occasion of his 70th Birthday*, eds. Stanley E. Porter, and Eckhard J. Schnabel (Leiden: Brill, 2012). http://booksandjournals.brillonline.com/content/9789004232921, 2012.

Bibliography: Works by Christopher J. H. Wright

Dissertation

"Family, Land and Property in Ancient Israel: Some Aspects of Old Testament Social Ethics." PhD diss., University of Cambridge, 1976.

Books

What Does the Lord Require: Reflections on the Old Testament Contribution to Christian Ethics. Nottingham: Shaftesbury Project, 1978.

Human Rights: A Study in Biblical Themes. Nottingham: Grove Books, 1979.

An Eye for an Eye: The Place of Old Testament Ethics Today. Downers Grove: InterVarsity Press, 1983. (Published in the UK as *Living as the People of God.*)

Living as the People of God: The Relevance of Old Testament Ethics. Leicester: IVP, 1983. (Published in the USA as *An Eye for an Eye.*)

Proverbs – Isaiah 39. London: Scripture Union, 1983.

User's Guide to the Bible. Tring: Lion, 1984.

God's People in God's Land: Family, Land, and Property in the Old Testament. Grand Rapids: Eerdmans; Exeter: Paternoster, 1990.

The People of God and the State: An Old Testament Perspective. Nottingham: Grove Books, 1990.

Understanding Old Testament Law Today. Jigsaw Series, Group Bible Studies. Swindon: Bible Society, 1990.

What's So Unique about Jesus? Oxford: Monarch, 1990.

Knowing Jesus through the Old Testament: Rediscovering the Roots of Our Faith. Basingstoke: Marshall Pickering, 1992. (2nd ed. Carlisle: Langham Preaching Resources; Downers Grove: InterVarsity Press, 2014.)

Tested by Fire: Daniel 1–6 – Solid Faith in Today's World. London: Scripture Union, 1993.

Walking in the Ways of the Lord: The Ethical Authority of the Old Testament. Downers Grove: InterVarsity Press, 1995.

Deuteronomy. Understanding the Bible Commentary Series. Grand Rapids: Baker, 1994.

Deuteronomy. Vol. 4. New International Biblical Commentary. Peabody, MA: Hendrickson; Carlisle: Paternoster, 1996.

Ambassadors to the World: Declaring God's Love. Leicester: IVP, 1998.

The Message of Ezekiel: A New Heart and a New Spirit. The Bible Speaks Today Series. Leicester: IVP; Downers Grove: InterVarsity Press, 2001.

The Uniqueness of Jesus. Thinking Clearly Series. Oxford: Monarch, 2001.

Old Testament Ethics for the People of God. Downers Grove: InterVarsity Press, 2004.

Truth with a Mission: Reading Scripture Missiologically. Cambridge: Grove Books, 2005.

Life through God's Word: Psalm 119. Keswick: Keswick Ministries; Milton Keynes: Authentic, 2006.

Knowing the Holy Spirit through the Old Testament. Oxford: Monarch; Downers Grove: InterVarsity Press, 2006.

The Mission of God: Unlocking the Bible's Grand Narrative. Downers Grove: InterVarsity Press; Leicester: OVP, 2006.

Knowing God the Father through the Old Testament. Oxford: Monarch; Downers Grove: InterVarsity Press, 2007.

Salvation Belongs to Our God: Celebrating the Bible's Central Story. Downers Grove: InterVarsity Press, 2007; Carlisle; Langham Global Library, 2013.

The God I Don't Understand: Reflections on Tough Questions of Faith. Grand Rapids: Zondervan, 2008.

The Mission of God's People: A Biblical Theology of the Church's Mission. Grand Rapids: Zondervan, 2010.

How to Handle Money: A Short Guide to Financial Accountability. Didasko Files. Peabody, MA: Hendrickson, 2013.

Sweeter than Honey: Preaching the Old Testament. Carlisle: Langham Preaching Resources, 2014. (Published in the USA as *How to Preach and Teach the Old Testament for All Its Worth*.)

The Message of Jeremiah: Against Wind and Tide. The Bible Speaks Today Series. Downers Grove: InterVarsity Press, 2014. (Also published as *The Message of Jeremiah: Grace in the End*. Nottingham: IVP, 2014.)

The Message of Lamentations: Honest to God. Downers Grove: InterVarsity Press; Nottingham: IVP, 2015.

Becoming Like Jesus. Carlisle: Langham Creative Projects, 2016. (Published in the USA as *Cultivating the Fruit of the Spirit*.)

How to Preach and Teach the Old Testament for All Its Worth. Grand Rapids: Zondervan, 2016. (Originally published as *Sweeter than Honey* by Langham Preaching Resources.)

Let the Gospels Preach the Gospel: Sermons around the Cross. Langham Preaching Resources, 2017. (Published in the USA as *To the Cross: Proclaiming the Gospel from the Upper Room to Calvary*. Downers Grove: InterVarsity Press, 2017.)

Cultivating the Fruit of the Spirit: Growing in Christlikeness. Downers Grove: InterVarsity Press, 2017. (Published in the UK as *Becoming Like Jesus.*)

Hearing the Message of Daniel: Sustaining Faith in Today's World. Grand Rapids: Zondervan, 2017.

To the Cross: Proclaiming the Gospel from the Upper Room to Calvary. Downers Grove: InterVarsity Press, 2017. (Published in the UK as *Let the Gospels Preach the Gospel.*)

Knowing God: The Trilogy – Knowing Jesus, God the Father and the Holy Spirit through the Old Testament. Carlisle: Langham Creative Projects, 2017.

Edited and Co-authored Books

With Chris Sugden. *One Gospel – Many Clothes: Anglicans and the Decade of Evangelism.* Oxford: EFAC, Regnum, 1990.

With Jonathan Lamb. *Understanding and Using the Bible.* International Study Guide Series. London: SPCK, 2009.

John Stott: A Portrait by his Friends. Nottingham: IVP, 2011. (Published in the USA as *Portraits of a Radical Disciple: Recollections of John Stott's Life and Ministry.*)

Portraits of a Radical Disciple: Recollections of John Stott's Life and Ministry. Downers Grove: InterVarsity Press, 2011. (Published in the UK as *John Stott: A Portrait by his Friends.*)

The Cape Town Commitment: A Confession of Faith and a Call to Action. Didasko Files. Lausanne Movement. Peabody, MA: Hendrickson, 2011.

John Stott: Pastor, Leader and Friend: A Man Who Embodied the Spirit of Lausanne. Didasko Files. Lausanne Movement. Peabody, MA: Hendrickson, 2012.

Christian Mission in the Modern World. Downers Grove: InterVarsity Press, 2016. (Updated and expanded edition of the book by John Stott.)

With John Stott. *The Grace of Giving: Money and the Gospel.* Lausanne Library; Peabody, MA: Hendrickson, 2016.

With David Shepherd. *Ezra and Nehemiah.* Two Horizons Old Testament Commentary. Grand Rapids: Eerdmans. Forthcoming.

Chapters in Edited Volumes

"Inter-Faith Dialogue and the Uniqueness of Christ." In *Restoring the Vision: Anglican Evangelicals Speak Out,* edited by M. Tinker. Eastbourne: Monarch, 1990.

"The Authority of Scripture in an Age of Relativism: Old Testament Perspectives." In *The Gospel in the Modern World: A Tribute to John Stott,* edited by Martyn Eden and David F. Wells, 331–348. Leicester: IVP; Downers Grove: InterVarsity Press, 1991.

"The Uniqueness of Christ: An Old Testament Perspective." In *A.D. 2000 and Beyond: A Mission Agenda: A Festschrift for John Stott's 70th Birthday,* edited by Vinay Samuel and Chris Sugden, 112–124. Oxford: Regnum, 1991.

"No Neutrality in the Struggle against Corruption and Dishonesty: An Old Testament Perspective." In *Mission as Witness and Justice: An Indian Perspective,* edited by Bruce Nicholls and Christopher Raj, 157–170. New Delhi: TRACI, 1991.

With John E. Goldingay. "'Yahweh Our God Yahweh One': The Old Testament and Religious Pluralism." In One *God, One Lord, in a World of Religious Pluralism,* edited by Andrew D. Clarke and Bruce W. Winter, 34–52. Cambridge: Tyndale House, 1991.

"New Testament Interpretation of Old Testament Prophecy concerning Israel." In *Jerusalem Past and Present in the Purposes of God.* Edited by Peter Walker. Cambridge: Tyndale, 1992.

"The Old Testament and Christian Mission." In *Mission and Missions: Essays in Honour of I. Ben Wati,* edited by Jey J. Kanagaraj, 12–27. Pune, India: Union Biblical Seminary, 1998.

"Old Testament Theology of Mission." In *Evangelical Dictionary of World Missions,* edited by A. Scott Moreau, 706–709. Grand Rapids: Baker; Carlisle: Paternoster, 2000.

"Christ and the Mosaic of Pluralisms." In *Global Missiology for the 21st Century: The Iguassu Dialogue,* edited by William D. Taylor, 71–99. Grand Rapids: Baker, 2001.

"The Church as God's Agent in Mission." In *Death or Glory: The Church's Mission in Scotland's Changing Society. Studies Honouring the Contribution of Dr Geoffrey Grogan to the Church,* edited by David Searle, 108–120. Tain, Scotland: Mentor, 2001.

"The Bible and Human Religions." In *The Indian Church in Context: Her Emergence, Growth and Mission,* edited by Mark T. B. Laing, 3–38. Delhi: CMS/ISPCK, 2002.

"The Old Testament – Antiques Roadshow or Tomorrow's World?" In *Thinking Aloud: Keswick Lectures,* edited by Alison Hull, 51–83. Carlisle: Authentic, 2002.

"Truth with a Mission: Reading Scripture Missiologically." In *Fanning the Flame: Bible, Cross and Mission,* edited by Paul Gardener, Chris Wright and Chris Green, 221–239. Grand Rapids: Zondervan, 2003.

"Mission as a Matrix for Hermeneutics and Biblical Theology." In *Out of Egypt: Biblical Theology and Biblical Interpretation.* Vol. 5. Scripture and Hermeneutics Series. Edited by Craig Bartholomew et al., 102–143. Milton Keynes: Paternoster; Grand Rapids: Zondervan, 2004.

"Future Trends in Mission." In *The Futures of Evangelicalism: Issues and Prospects,* edited by Craig Bartholomew, Robin Parry and Andrew West, 149–163. Leicester: IVP; Grand Rapids: Kregel, 2004.

"Covenant: God's Mission through God's People." In *The God of Covenant: Biblical, Theological and Contemporary Perspectives,* edited by Jamie A. Grant and Alistair I. Wilson, 54–78. Leicester: Apollos, 2005.

"Truth with a Mission: Reading Scripture Missiologically." In *Biblical Theology and Missiological Education in Asia: Essays in Honour of the Rev. Dr. Brian C. Wintle*, edited by Siga Arles, Ashish Chrispal and Paul Mohan Raj, 68–87. Bangalore: Centre for Contemporary Christianity, 2005.

"Atonement in the Old Testament." In *The Atonement Debate*, edited by Derek Tidball, David Hilborn and Justin Thacker, 69–82. Grand Rapids: Zondervan, 2008.

"Prophet to the Nations: Missional Reflections on the Book of Jeremiah." In *A God of Faithfulness: Essays in Honour of J. Gordon McConville on His 60th Birthday*, edited by Jamie A. Grant, Alison Lo and Gordon J. Wenham, 112–129. New York: T & T Clark, 2011.

"Mission and Old Testament Interpretation." In *Hearing the Old Testament: Listening for God's Address*, edited by Craig G. Bartholomew and David J. H. Beldman, 180–203. Grand Rapids: Eerdmans, 2012.

"The Care of Creation, the Gospel and Our Mission." In *Creation Care in Christian Mission*. Regnum Edinburgh Centenary Series 29. Edited by Kapya Kaoma, 183–197. Oxford: Regnum, 2015.

"Theological Education, Bible and Mission: A Lausanne Perspective." In *Reflecting on and Equipping for Christian Mission*. Regnum Edinburgh Centenary Series 27. Edited by Stephen Bevans et. al., 141–153. Oxford: Regnum, 2015.

With Michael W. Goheen. "Mission and Theological Interpretation." In *A Manifesto for Theological Interpretation*, edited by Craig G. Bartholomew and Heath A. Thomas, 171–196. Grand Rapids: Baker, 2016.

"Reading the Old Testament Missionally." In *Reading the Bible Missionally*, edited by Michael W. Goheen, 107–123. Grand Rapids: Eerdmans, 2016.

Articles

The Anchor Bible Dictionary. s.v. "Family," "Jubilee, year of," "Sabbatical year."

New International Dictionary of Old Testament Theology and Exegesis. s.v. "*eres*," "*nhl*," "Ethics."

"The Israelite Household and the Decalogue: The Social Background and Significance of Some Commandments." *Tyndale Bulletin* 30 (1979): 101–124.

"Inter-Faith Dialogue." *Anvil* 1 (1984): 231–258.

"The Christian and Other Religions: The Biblical Evidence." *Themelios* 9, no. 2 (1984): 4–15.

"The Ethical Relevance of Israel as a Society." *Journal of Christian Social Ethics*, 1984.

"The Use of the Bible in Social Ethics: Paradigms, Types and Eschatology." *Transformation* 1, no. 1 (1984): 11–20.

"What Happened Every Seven Years in Israel? Old Testament Sabbatical Institutions for Land, Debt and Slaves." *Evangelical Quarterly* 56 (1984): 129–138, 193–201.

"The People of God and the State in the Old Testament." *Themelios* 16, no. 1 (1990): 4–10.

"Ethical Decisions in the Old Testament." *European Journal of Theology* 1, no. 2 (1992): 123.

"The Ethical Authority of the Old Testament: A Survey of Approaches." *Tyndale Bulletin* 43, no. 1 (1992): 101–120.

"God or Mammon: Biblical Perspectives on Economies in Conflict." *Mission Studies* 12, no. 2 (1995): 145–156.

"So Send I You: A Study Guide to Mission by Roger Bowen: A Response to the Review of this Book by Melvin Tinker," published in *Churchman* 111, no. 2 (p. 171). *Churchman* 111, no. 4 (1997): 327–336.

"Interpreting the Bible among the World Religions." *Themelios* 25, no. 3 (2000): 35–54.

"Truth with a Mission: Towards a Missiological Hermeneutic of the Bible." *Missiologic.* All Nations Christian College Occasional Papers on Mission 2 (2001).

"Truth with a Mission: Reading Scripture Missiologically." *Princeton Theological Review* 9, no. 1 (2003): 16–24.

"Implications of Conversion in the Old Testament and the New." *International Bulletin of Missionary Research* 28, no. 1 (2004): 14–19.

With D. A. Carson, Michael A. G. Haykin and Ted Cabal. "Being Missions-Minded: the SBJT Forum." *The Southern Baptist Journal of Theology* 9, no. 4 (2005): 86–95.

"'The Mission of God': An Introduction and Orientation to the Book." *Anvil* 24, no. 4 (2007): 245–248.

"A Response to Ross, McCoy, Dakin and Jensen on 'The Mission of God.'" *Anvil* 24, no. 4 (2007): 289–294.

"An Upside-Down World." *Christianity Today* 51, no. 1 (2007).

"Following Jesus in the Globalized Marketplace." *Evangelical Review of Theology* 31, no. 4 (2007): 320–330.

With John Azumah and Kwabena Asamoah-Gyadu (Lausanne Theology Working Group). "A Statement on Prosperity Teaching." *Christianity Today* 53, no. 12 (2009).

"According to the Scriptures: The Whole Gospel in Biblical Revelation." *Evangelical Review of Theology* 33, no. 1 (2009): 4–18.

"Whole Gospel, Whole Church, Whole World." *Christianity Today* 53, no. 10 (2009).

"The Whole Church: A Brief Biblical Survey." *Evangelical Review of Theology* 34, no. 1 (2010): 14–28.

"The World in the Bible." *Evangelical Review of Theology* 34, no. 3 (2010): 207–219.

"The Righteous Rich in the Old Testament." *Evangelical Review of Theology* 35, no. 3 (2011): 255–264.

"Truth with a Mission: Reading All Scripture Missiologically." *Southern Baptist Journal of Theology* 15, no. 2 (2011): 4–15.

"Learning to Love Leviticus." *Christianity Today* 57, no. 6 (2013): 26.

"Rooted and Engaged." *Evangelical Review of Theology* 38, no. 4 (2014): 324–338.

"Humility, Integrity, and Simplicity." *International Bulletin of Missionary Research* 39, no. 4 (2015): 214–218.

"Lamentations: A Book for Today." *International Bulletin of Missionary Research* 39, no. 2 (2015): 59–64.

Langham Literature and its imprints are a ministry of Langham Partnership.

Langham Partnership is a global fellowship working in pursuit of the vision God entrusted to its founder John Stott –

> *to facilitate the growth of the church in maturity and Christ-likeness through raising the standards of biblical preaching and teaching.*

Our vision is to see churches in the majority world equipped for mission and growing to maturity in Christ through the ministry of pastors and leaders who believe, teach and live by the Word of God.

Our mission is to strengthen the ministry of the Word of God through:

- nurturing national movements for biblical preaching
- fostering the creation and distribution of evangelical literature
- enhancing evangelical theological education

especially in countries where churches are under-resourced.

Our ministry

Langham Preaching partners with national leaders to nurture indigenous biblical preaching movements for pastors and lay preachers all around the world. With the support of a team of trainers from many countries, a multi-level programme of seminars provides practical training, and is followed by a programme for training local facilitators. Local preachers' groups and national and regional networks ensure continuity and ongoing development, seeking to build vigorous movements committed to Bible exposition.

Langham Literature provides majority world preachers, scholars and seminary libraries with evangelical books and electronic resources through publishing and distribution, grants and discounts. The programme also fosters the creation of indigenous evangelical books in many languages, through writer's grants, strengthening local evangelical publishing houses, and investment in major regional literature projects, such as one volume Bible commentaries like *The Africa Bible Commentary* and *The South Asia Bible Commentary*.

Langham Scholars provides financial support for evangelical doctoral students from the majority world so that, when they return home, they may train pastors and other Christian leaders with sound, biblical and theological teaching. This programme equips those who equip others. Langham Scholars also works in partnership with majority world seminaries in strengthening evangelical theological education. A growing number of Langham Scholars study in high quality doctoral programmes in the majority world itself. As well as teaching the next generation of pastors, graduated Langham Scholars exercise significant influence through their writing and leadership.

To learn more about Langham Partnership and the work we do visit **langham.org**

Lightning Source UK Ltd.
Milton Keynes UK
UKOW06f0835041017

310379UK00006B/116/P

9 781783 682973